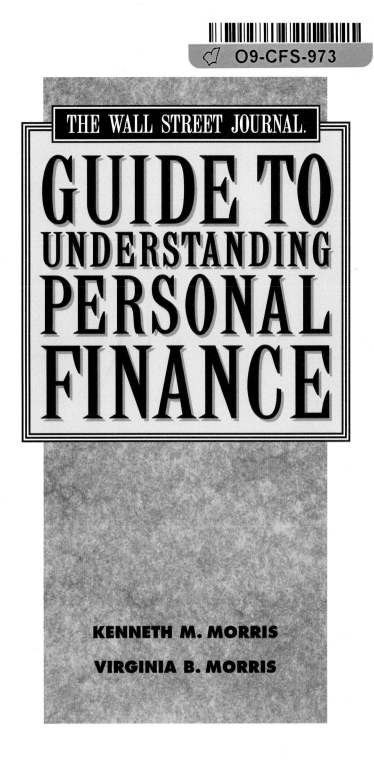

# THE WALL STREET JOURNAL.

# GUIDE TO UNDERSTANDING PERSONAL FINANCE

**KENNETH M. MORRIS**

**VIRGINIA B. MORRIS**

LIGHTBULB

PRESS

**LIGHTBULB PRESS**
Project Team

**Design Director** Dave Wilder
**Editors** Renée Ryerson, Avi Grossman-Spivack
**Production** Carolyn Edelstein, Chris Hiebert, Sally Minker, Thomas F. Trojan, Kwee Wang
**Illustration** Kelly Alder, Daniel Pelavin, Scott Sawyer
**Photography** Steve Underwood, Marissa Shedd, UPI/Corbis-Bettmann (page 31), Susan Wides
**Sales and Marketing** Germaine Ma, Karen Meldrom, Karen Cantor

**SPECIAL THANKS**
**Dow Jones & Co.** Dan Austin, Tom Herman, Doug Sease, Rhonda Aigen, Joan Wolf-Woolley, Lottie Lindberg and Elizabeth Yeh at The Wall Street Journal Library

*DOWJONES*

LIGHTBULB

PRESS

*I*n the first and second editions of *The Wall Street Journal Guide to Understanding Personal Finance*, we explained the principles of making sound banking, credit, and mortgage decisions, as well as the basics of investing, financial planning, and taxes. Our goal was to be comprehensive without being exhaustive, informative without being overwhelming. Our focus was on what you should know, what you can expect to pay—and earn—and the pitfalls you should be aware of as you make financial decisions.

Those goals haven't altered, and neither has our approach. Since 1997, however, there have been significant changes in the world of personal finance, giving people more choices but requiring more decision making. In terms of the financial services they offer, the boundaries between banks, brokerage firms, and insurance companies have disappeared. Online banking and investing have grown by leaps and bounds. Tax-free Roth IRAs and higher contribution limits for deductible traditional IRAs provide greater flexibility in retirement planning. Larger estates can be left to beneficiaries tax-free. To take advantage of these changes, people have to know what they are and how to take advantage of them. That was one of our goals in bringing the *Guide* up to date.

This revised edition blends clear and concise information with visually appealing design—a style that's the trademark of Lightbulb Press. We owe enormous gratitude to The Wall Street Journal for its ideas, its enthusiastic support, its editorial reviews, and the wealth of material drawn from its daily columns, financial tables, and feature articles.

We hope you enjoy the *Guide* and find it helpful and informative in exploring the often perplexing and ever-changing world of personal finance.

Kenneth M. Morris                    Virginia B. Morris

THE WALL STREET JOURNAL.

# GUIDE TO UNDERSTANDING PERSONAL FINANCE

## BANKING

## CREDIT

## HOME FINANCE

# CONTENTS

## FINANCIAL PLANNING

## INVESTING

## TAXES

# Banking

When you choose a bank, you should consider convenience, cost and level of service.

When you think about handling your personal finances, among the things that may come to mind are paying your bills, saving money to pay for the things you want and maybe arranging for a mortgage to pay for a home or a loan to buy a new car. In each case, there's probably a bank involved in your plans.

Banks offer a wide range of checking, savings and investment accounts. They're also one of the first places to look when you need to borrow money. And they increasingly provide access to national and even global financial networks that let you get cash, have your pay check direct deposited or transfer money to pay bills or make investments electronically.

As a rule, banks charge fees for their checking-account services and pay interest on savings accounts.

## BANKING PLUS

If your banking needs are like most people's, you're looking for a checking account to handle your day-to-day finances and perhaps a savings account. Many banks also offer added conveniences:

### Direct deposit
You can have your paycheck or Social Security check deposited directly into your checking or savings accounts.

### Bank cards
Banks offer bank cards so you can use automated teller machines (ATMs).

### Credit cards
Credit cards linked to your bank account include a line of credit that you can use in an emergency.

### Overdraft privileges
You can be sure that all the checks you write will be paid if you have overdraft protection on your account.

### Automatic transfers
You can make regular monthly investments or pay your bills by using electronic transfers.

### Online banking
Many banks offer online banking on the bank's Internet website, where you can check account information, transfer money, and even pay your bills. And since 1998, there have been virtual banks that exist only on the Internet.

Though most banks offer similar products, there may be important differences—so be sure to read the fine print in any agreement. For example, some banks do not pay interest on small savings accounts of less than $100 to $250. Others impose large service charges or monthly fees, or limit your withdrawals from certain accounts.

You'll probably want to pay particular attention to ATM charges if you use cash machines frequently. Some banks charge a fee ($1 to $2) for every use, and almost all charge whenever you use a machine at a different bank. But others have a more generous policy, allowing you to use any ATM that's part of a regional network.

Many grocery, convenience, and other retail stores, as well as movie theaters and casinos also, have ATM machines available when you need cash, but the fee is almost always higher than at a bank.

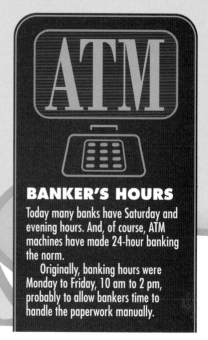

### BANKER'S HOURS
Today many banks have Saturday and evening hours. And, of course, ATM machines have made 24-hour banking the norm.

Originally, banking hours were Monday to Friday, 10 am to 2 pm, probably to allow bankers time to handle the paperwork manually.

## WHAT YOU NEED TO APPLY

Banks make it easy to open basic accounts like checking and savings, if you can provide what they require.

You'll need:

### Money to deposit

To open an account, you need to deposit money in cash, check or money order. Many banks set minimum amounts.

### Identification

Banks require you to have some form of identification. Documents such as a driver's license or passport are best, but you can also use business letters or financial statements sent to your current address.

### Social Security number

You need a Social Security number in order to open a bank account.

### Signature

The bank will ask you to sign a signature card, which they use to identify your handwriting when you cash a check or require other bank services.

### BEYOND PAYING BILLS

You can handle much of your other financial business through a bank, too, using either the same bank where you have your basic checking account or a number of different ones.

Most banks offer certificates of deposit (CDs) plus a wide range of investment choices including mutual funds, annuities and access to brokerage accounts. Some also offer financial planning advice.

### FREEDOM FOR BANKS

The **Glass-Steagall Act** of 1933 was repealed in 1999, breaking down the final barriers that had prevented banks from selling insurance and securities, including stocks and bonds—and insurance companies and brokerage firms from offering banking services. From the consumer's perspective, it means being able to handle all of your financial business with a single institution if you prefer.

The Act was passed originally to eliminate potential conflicts of interest between commercial and investment banks. Their differing financial goals were thought to have contributed to the 1929 stock market crash and the Great Depression that followed.

## UNDER THE MATTRESS

About 15% of all U.S. households are without bank accounts, either because there is no bank close enough to where they live or because the fees to keep an account are higher than they can afford. Several states, including Minnesota, New Jersey and New York, require banks to offer basic accounts with minimum fees. Some state protections cover everyone, but others cover only those younger than 18 or older than 65.

## LIKE MONEY IN THE BANK

Most people think of banks as the safest place to keep their money. One reason is the Federal Deposit Insurance Corporation (FDIC), which was established by the government in the wake of the banking disasters and the depression that followed the stock market crash of 1929. The FDIC guarantees deposits in member banks and thrift institutions, such as savings and loan associations, for up to $100,000 per depositor per bank. If the bank fails, the government will make good on your money up to the established limits. You can actually qualify for more than $100,000 coverage at a single bank, however, provided your assets are in different types of accounts: $100,000 in an account in your name, $100,000 in your individual retirement account (IRA), and another $100,000 as a share of jointly held accounts, for example.

However, money you invest through a bank that's not actually kept in bank accounts—such as investments in mutual funds, annuities or life insurance—is not covered by FDIC insurance.

The first public bank in the world opened in Barcelona, Spain, in 1401. The first savings bank in the U.S. did not open until 415 years later—in 1816. It was the Provident Institute for Savings in Boston.

# Banking Opportunities

You've got some real choices when you're ready to open your bank accounts.

Most of the differences between banking at a traditional commercial bank, a savings bank or a savings and loan (S&L) disappeared with deregulation, which allowed all kinds of banks to provide check-writing services. In fact, the differences that do remain—like whether a bank is under state or federal regulation—matter very little to the average person.

In addition, you aren't limited to banks if you're looking for banking services such as a checking account or a mortgage loan. There are many financial institutions, sometimes called non-bank banks, that may provide what you need. You might want to consider using one of them instead of, or in addition to, a bank.

Many people find, though, that it's handy to have a relationship with a local bank even if they do most of their business elsewhere. If you need a signature guarantee, for example, or a bank check, the nearby bank can provide it conveniently.

> There are currently more than 9,000 banks in the U.S., down from more than 14,000 in 1985, primarily because of consolidations.

## BANK FEES

Knowing what it will cost to do business there may help you identify which bank to use, or even encourage you to shift your accounts to a bank where you can get a better deal.

In addition to per-check charges, you'll want to find out about other fees a bank imposes before you decide to open an account. In recent years, many fees have increased, sometimes dramatically, and a range of others have been added. In fact, some banks have experimented with charging you a fee to talk to a teller.

But fees are not uniformly high at one bank and low at another, so it pays to find out what the differences are. You'll probably want to pay closer attention to the particular services you expect to use. Start by asking about minimum monthly balance requirements and fees on plain checking and interest-bearing checking accounts. Then look at:

- **ATM fees**
- **Debit card fees**
- **Check printing fees**
- **Stop payment fees**
- **Money order and bank check fees**
- **Balance inquiry fees**
- **Bounced check fees**
- **Money market checking fees**

## COMPARING BANKING CHOICES

| INSTITUTION | PROS | CONS |
|---|---|---|
| **COMMERCIAL BANKS** | They serve individuals and businesses, usually have multiple, well-located branches and offer the full range of banking services. Deposits are FDIC-insured up to $100,000 per type of depositor's account. | Fees for checking and other services are generally highest, and service is often impersonal. |
| **SAVINGS BANKS AND SAVINGS AND LOANS (S&Ls)** | Their fees may be lower than at commercial banks. Personal service may be better, especially at the smaller banks. They may be open evenings and Saturdays. Most are FDIC-insured. | They can require you to notify them before withdrawing from checking. Most have only a few branches, so using an ATM card may be less convenient. |
| **CREDIT UNIONS** | Their fees and loan rates are usually lowest because they are non-profit. Earnings are paid out to members at year's end. | About 1% aren't federally insured. Most have only a few branches, so using an ATM card may be less convenient. |
| **MUTUAL FUNDS, BROKERAGE FIRMS AND INSURANCE SUBSIDIARIES** | They offer limited banking services, usually low-cost or free checking linked to interest-paying money market funds. Some brokerage firms provide loans against investment balances. | They tend to require larger minimum balances. They are not FDIC-insured, but may have private insurance. |
| **VIRTUAL BANKS** | They are FDIC-insured, offer real-time processing and account status, viewable transaction history, online wire transfers, all types of savings and checking accounts, and customer service hotlines. | Because the bank has no physical branches, there are always ATM usage fees, and if you don't have direct deposit, you'll have to mail your checks to the bank's home office. |

## THE BOTTOM LINE

Shopping around can save you money on what it costs to bank—sometimes lots of money. For example, if you wrote 25 checks and used the ATM 15 times a month with an account that charged a $7 monthly fee and 30 cents a transaction, it would cost you $19 a month or $228 a year. If you can get free checking by keeping a minimum balance in your checking savings account you'll save the charges plus earn a small amount in interest. Or, the bank might count money in a higher-interest certificate of deposit or other investment account. But if it means keeping $3,000 or more in low-interest savings, you might want to weigh the alternatives. Here are some questions you can ask yourself:

- Do I write enough checks or use an ATM often enough to worry about the charges?

- Will I be saving more on fees than my money could earn if I invested elsewhere?

- Is there another bank that requires a smaller balance but provides the same level of service and convenience?

# Checking

**Checks are the hub of the banking system. You may be paid by check, and you probably pay your bills with checks.**

Originally, checks were hand-written notes telling your banker how much money to pay out of your account, and to whom. Today's standardized, computerized, magnetically imprinted forms are so common, we can't imagine a penciled note having the same effect—though technically it could.

The average American writes about 250 checks a year against a checking account, also called a **demand deposit** or **transaction** account. Demand means that your money is available when you want it. Transaction means that you can tell the bank to give your money to someone else.

## READING A CHECK

**There are three kinds of information on the front of a check—some preprinted, some written in, and some added when the check is processed.**

**Pay to the order of** makes a check negotiable, or transferable, which means that the person it's made out to can demand the amount the check is written for. No other wording requires your bank to pay out the money.

The **name of the person** or **company** who can demand the amount of money from your bank. To get money yourself, you can make the check out to yourself. Making a check out to "Cash" is risky because the bank may honor it—even if the check is stolen.

Your **name** and **address** may be included for convenience, since many stores that take checks require that information. They have no bearing on the legal standing of the check.

LARRY J. EDELMAN

PAY TO THE ORDER OF _The Universal Card_

_Four hundred_

FOR

The **amount to be paid** written both in numbers and in words. If the two don't agree, the words usually take precedence—though the bank may return the check. If you correct an error on the check, initial the correction. That may satisfy the bank's questions. If the check is altered by somebody else—like making a $10 check a $110 by inserting a "1"—and the check is cashed, the bank must refund your money—provided that you did nothing negligent (like signing a blank check) and that you notify the bank within a year.

The **checking routing number** is used when the check is processed. It identifies your bank, the collection arrangement for its checks, and the Federal Reserve Bank for your area.

Your **bank account number** and the **check routing number** are printed in magnetic characters that bank scanners use when processing your check.

## MICR CODES

The strange computer digits you see on checks are called **MICR codes (Magnetic Image Character Recognition)**. The digits actually have iron in their ink so that a scanner can read them magnetically. The numbers have this unusual shape because each image must be a certain height and width to hold enough iron in the ink to be readable.

**TRUNCATION**

American banks have routinely returned your cancelled checks to you. More than half of all banks now use truncation (also called check safe-keeping), which means your checks stop either at the bank where they are deposited or at your bank. The checks themselves are photocopied and then destroyed. Banks like the process because it saves money.

The **date** your bank debited your account, or your check clears. The number of days between when you write a check and when it clears is called a float.

The **date and bank** where the check was deposited are important proof against claims a check was late—or that it never arrived.

**Endorsement**, or signature, is required—and by federal law must appear within the top inch and a half, on the left end. To be sure that checks you deposit are credited to your account, write "For deposit only," and the account number above your signature—if you can fit all that in the space you're allowed. You also have the option of using a stamp with the relevant information.

**THE BACK OF THE CHECK** Processing information on the back of the check provides a record of its travels. When the check is paid, it is cancelled. Cancelled checks are proofs of payment.

The **check number** makes your record-keeping and the bank's processing easier.

The **date** is important because a time limit—usually six months—can be imposed on how long a check is fresh, or valid. The bank can refuse to pay stale, or old, checks. If you postdate a check by writing in some future date, it may be paid sooner than you intended because the electronic scanning equipment can't read the date.

Your **check number** and the **amount of the transaction** are MICR-printed when your check is processed so that bank computers can read them. Now the bottom of the check contains all of the information necessary to debit your account and record the transaction.

Your **signature** authorizes the transaction. It can be legible or illegible—as long as it corresponds with the signature card you signed when you opened the account. If someone else signs your name, it's forgery. If the bank honors a forgery, you are usually not responsible and can demand that the bank credit your account.

The first recorded use of a check dates back to 1374, but checks were rare before 1700. They became really common only after World War II. Today, about 63 billion checks are processed in the U.S. every year, and the number keeps growing.

# How Checking Works

Knowing how checks are paid and when deposits are credited can help you manage your money better.

When you deposit a check in your account, it's sent to the bank of the person who wrote it. The bank **debits**, or takes money out of, that person's account and transfers it electronically to your bank.

If you both use the same bank, the amount is credited to your account the next day. If another local bank is involved, the process takes a day or two. And if the two banks are far apart, the transfer usually goes through the Federal Reserve System.

## HOW CHECKS ARE PAID

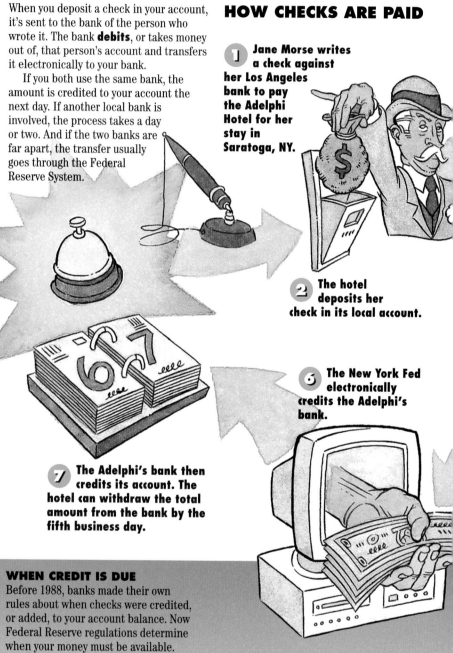

**1** Jane Morse writes a check against her Los Angeles bank to pay the Adelphi Hotel for her stay in Saratoga, NY.

**2** The hotel deposits her check in its local account.

**6** The New York Fed electronically credits the Adelphi's bank.

**7** The Adelphi's bank then credits its account. The hotel can withdraw the total amount from the bank by the fifth business day.

## WHEN CREDIT IS DUE

Before 1988, banks made their own rules about when checks were credited, or added, to your account balance. Now Federal Reserve regulations determine when your money must be available.

Banks can require that you deposit checks with a teller to make the money available promptly. That means deposits in ATMs are usually credited more slowly, especially when you use a machine that isn't owned by your bank.

Your bank can charge you a fee for paying checks that you write against uncollected funds—deposits that haven't been credited yet. Correctly estimating your **float**, the time lag between when you write a check and when your bank clears it, lets you figure out when your checks will clear.

For example, if your paycheck is deposited directly into your checking account on the 15th of the month, checks you mailed to an out-of-town address on the 13th probably won't clear before there is money to cover them.

## BOUNCING CHECKS

If there's not enough money in your account to cover a check you write, your bank can refuse to **honor**, or pay, it. The person who cashed it gets the bad check back, and may have to pay a fee. You're also charged a fee—sometimes as much as $30. If several checks bounce on one day—as they might if you've made an error—the charges can be staggering. It can hurt your credit rating as well.

The best way to avoid rubber checks is to apply for **overdraft protection**, a special line of credit that covers checks you write when there isn't enough money in your account. The bank automatically transfers money to your account to cover the check—and it charges you interest on the amount transferred. In the long run, though, overdraft protection can save you money and aggravation.

**3** Morse's check is routed to the New York Federal Reserve Bank, which forwards it to the San Francisco Federal Reserve Bank, which forwards it to her bank in L.A.

**4** Morse's bank verifies her check and takes the money out of her account, but keeps her check to return to her. Then it tells the San Francisco Fed to credit the amount to the New York Fed.

**5** The San Francisco Fed electronically transfers money to the New York Fed.

## STOP PAYMENT

If you write a check and then decide you don't want to pay, or if you lose the check, you can—for an extra fee—put a **stop payment order** on it. An oral order—either in person or on the telephone—is good for 14 days. A written order lasts for six months. The bank must honor your order if it's *timely*, which generally means before the check is paid. If the bank pays the check anyway, you can demand your money back, but you'll probably have to show written proof that you ordered the payment stopped.

## WHEN YOU CAN WITHDRAW

If you deposit a $1,000 check in your account, when and how much you can withdraw depends on the type of check and where it's from.*

|  | 1 day later | 2 days later | 5 days later |
|---|---|---|---|
| A federal, state, or local government check | $1,000 | | |
| A bank, certified, or travelers check | $1,000 | | |
| A check from your own bank | $1,000 | | |
| A local check | $100 | $900 | |
| A non-local check | $100 | | $900 |
| Electronic transfers | $1,000 | | |

*Deposits in ATMs may take longer.

# Checking Variety

With so many types of checking accounts available, you can target the one that's best for you.

Banks offer a range of checking accounts to appeal to different customers. Some are bare bones, basic accounts for people who write only a few checks a month. Others may offer interest on your account balance, or links to brokerage accounts.

When you're choosing an account, you may also want to think about whether it will be in your name alone or **joint**, which means having two names on the account, each with access to the money in it. Married couples often have joint accounts, allowing either of them to write checks against the balance. But you can have a joint account with anyone you wish, whether a family member or not.

| Type of Account | How They Work | Fees and Balances |
|---|---|---|
| **REGULAR CHECKING** | You can write as many checks as you want, but you earn no interest on your account. | Banks impose a fee for each check, or monthly charges, or both. Typical charges are $2.50 to $15 a month and 30¢ a check. If you keep a certain minimum balance in your checking or savings account, you may get free checking. |
| **INTEREST CHECKING ACCOUNTS** | You can write as many checks as you want and you earn monthly interest based on your bank's rates. | If you don't keep the required minimum balance, usually around $3,000, the fees are sometimes higher than those on regular checking accounts. |
| **MONEY MARKET DEPOSIT ACCOUNTS** | You earn a changing rate of interest to reflect market conditions. When rates go up, they pay well. Banks may offer high initial rates to attract business. | You need a large minimum balance, and fees are high if you keep less than the minimum required. Some accounts limit you to three checks per month and restrict money transfers. |
| **MONEY MARKET FUNDS** | Available through mutual fund companies, these accounts pay market-rate interest and rarely charge fees for checks. There is usually no limit on the number of checks you can write. | The funds may require a minimum balance. Checks must be for a minimum of between $250 and $500. You may have to wait 14 days to write checks against deposits. |
| **ASSET MANAGEMENT ACCOUNTS** | Brokerage houses or banks that handle your investments may also offer checking accounts. You can write an unlimited number of checks and you get a comprehensive year-end statement, plus the advantage of using one account for all your banking and investing. | You need a relatively high balance, often $5,000 to $25,000, to open an account, and you usually pay an annual fee, plus fees for investment services. |

## MINIMUM BALANCES

A minimum balance is the least amount of money a bank requires you to keep on deposit to qualify for certain benefits like reduced fees or free checking, or to earn the stated rate of interest.

Some banks figure your average minimum balance for the month. That means the total amount of money on deposit during the month must average above the minimum. Other banks charge a fee if your balance drops below the minimum at any time during the month.

Some banks define the minimum as the combined amount in all your accounts (checking, savings, money market, even CDs). Others don't.

Taking advantage of minimum-balance options can save you money on bank fees. But you'll want to compare what you save with what you could earn by investing your money elsewhere. And you want to be careful not to sign up for accounts with required minimums for earning interest or avoiding fees if you're not likely to meet them. These accounts could cost you a lot.

# The Art of Checking

Choosing personalized checks today no longer means deciding between pale blue, pale yellow and pale green—although those old standards are still available. Banks offer checks in multiple patterns, type faces and sizes, and often charge extra for special orders. You can also get checks directly—and often more cheaply—from other sources, like printing companies and non-profit organizations. As long as the checks have the correct information, format and MICR coding, they work the same way as the checks a bank supplies. In fact, they may be printed by the same company.

# Special Checks

There are times when your personal checks are just not good enough.

Though your personal check will fill the bill in most cases, there may be times when you'll have to use a check that comes with a payment guarantee. That's usually the case when a large amount of money is involved—when you buy a home, for example—or when an out-of-town merchant ships you an expensive product. Though you can sometimes use credit cards in these situations, your payments can be cancelled or delayed if you dispute the charges—something the seller wants to avoid.

Several types of special checks are available from banks, sometimes even if you don't have an account with them. You can get other checks or check substitutes from the U.S. Postal Service, or from credit card or travel companies.

## Cashier's Checks

**Cashier's checks, sometimes called bank checks, guarantee that the check is good because it is drawn against the bank's account.**

### HOW THEY WORK

You give the bank money for the amount of the check you want written, along with your name and the name of the recipient. The bank officer makes out the check—which is usually machine-printed so it can't be altered—signs it and hands it to you. You also receive a carbon copy as a record, since the cashed check is not returned to you.

The charge for a bank check is usually less than the charge for a certified check. You can't stop payment once the check reaches its destination.

**WHAT'S THE CHARGE?**
A retailer can't charge your purchase to a credit card if the card number has been used simply as identification—even if your check bounces. That's one reason you might have to use a check that your bank guarantees.

## Certified Checks

**Certified checks are personal checks that your bank guarantees it will honor.**

### HOW THEY WORK

After you write the check, your bank **freezes**, or puts a hold on your account for the amount of the check, and stamps **certified** on the face.

There is a fee for each certified check, but there is no limit on the amount of the check, provided you have enough money in your account to cover it. However, you can't stop payment on certified checks after they reach their destination.

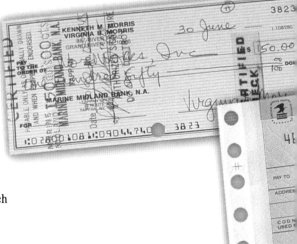

# Traveler's Checks

**Traveler's checks are issued by travel companies, banks and credit card companies to be used in place of cash in places where you might have difficulty using a personal check.**

## HOW THEY WORK

You can buy the checks in various fixed **denominations**, or amounts, in local or overseas currencies. You sign your name when you receive the checks, and again when you cash them. Once you use a check, it is returned to the issuer. You have no official record of using it.

There is usually a 1% fee for buying the checks, unless you get them free for keeping money in a bank account or as a perk of membership in certain groups. They have one drawback and one great advantage. Sometimes you have to pay a fee to cash them, which can double their cost. But if the checks are lost or stolen, you can get them replaced almost immediately by simply calling the issuer.

**American Express traveler's checks first appeared in 1891. Today, traveler's checks have become a $52 billion-a-year industry.**

# Money Orders

**Money orders are useful if you don't have a checking account. They cost about $3 at banks and 80 cents at post offices, making them the least expensive guaranteed checks.**

## HOW THEY WORK

You pay the teller or clerk the amount you want the money order made out for, plus the fee. The amount is printed on the money order. You fill out the requested information, sign it, and send it. (A bank will sell you a money order even if you don't have an account there.)

Money orders are a reasonable alternative to checks if you need them occasionally, but they have limitations. The money order is not returned to you, so you don't know if or when it's been cashed. Also, you can't stop payment once you've sent the money order, and there may be restrictions on the amounts. Post office money orders are capped at $700, though you can send multiple orders, up to a total of $10,000 in one day. Many banks cap money orders at $1,000.

# ATMs: Automatic Tellers

## Automated teller machines have changed banking radically—in most cases for the better.

Instead of having to wait for banking hours to make a deposit or get cash, you can do most basic banking transactions—and even some complicated ones—24 hours a day, seven days a week. All you need is a bank account, an ATM card, a personal identification number (PIN) and a machine that accepts your card.

You can use ATMs to complete as many separate transactions as you want. There are two limits: One is a withdrawal limit per transaction, and the other is a limit on the amount you can withdraw in one day. The average daily limit is $200 to $500.

## A WORLDWIDE NETWORK

Most banks are part of regional and international networks that let you withdraw cash from your accounts at ATMs around the world. If your bank is an international one, you may look first for a branch office. But most domestic banks are part of one or both of the two largest U.S. network systems, Cirrus and Plus. All you have to do is find one of those logos on a bank, airport or retail store machine. You can get cash anywhere the system exists: dollars in Utah, yen in Tokyo, or pounds in London, whether you bank in Atlanta or Timbuctoo.

You'll probably pay a fee for using an ATM outside your regional network. But many people consider it a small price to pay for the convenience. As an added bonus, the exchange rate for the foreign currency you get from an ATM is usually among the best you'll find.

The first ATM appeared in 1978. Today there are more than 227,000 nationwide, and 800,000 worldwide. To be competitive, almost every bank that offers checking accounts offers an ATM card and a machine to use it with.

## WHAT IF SOMETHING GOES WRONG?

The most common ATM problems come from customers—and clerks—who record the wrong amounts on deposit or withdrawal slips. If you spot a problem, contact your bank quickly. The bank must respond within ten days and resolve the problem within 45 days. If you still have a complaint, they must give you a copy of their report to review.

If you discover your ATM card is lost or stolen, report it immediately. You have two business days to report an unauthorized withdrawal listed on your monthly statement to limit your potential liability

to the first $50 withdrawn. Waiting three to 60 days to report the problem extends your liability to $500. Waiting over 60 days can cost you everything in your account.

## FEES FOR EACH USE

Many banks charge for using an ATM, especially for using your card at another bank's machine. And that bank can charge a fee as well. Fees can range from $1 to $2, and are increasing despite customer resentment. ATM fees may be much higher, sometimes up to $5, overseas. Make sure you ask your bank about foreign exchange ATM fees before you travel abroad.

## HOW ATMs WORK

**1** Your ATM card has your name and a 16-digit account number embossed on the front and a magnetic tape, or strip, on the back that identifies your bank and account number.

**2** When you insert your card, the screen asks for your personal identification number (PIN). If you enter the correct one, you can access whichever accounts are tied to your card.

If a PIN is entered incorrectly three times, most machines won't return the card, because they assume an unauthorized person is using it. To get it back, you should notify your own bank. They'll return it or replace it for you.

**3** The machine displays a series of screens that walk you through a number of transactions. For example, you can:

- **Withdraw cash**
- **Deposit checks**
- **Transfer money**
- **Pay your credit card bill**
- **Check your account or credit card balance**

**4** The machine returns your card and a record of what you've done.

Check each receipt against your monthly bank statement and follow up immediately with your bank if you uncover any errors.

ELLER·

Green Bank
09/16    13:08 NY006638

NY NEW YORK,
1200 AVE AMERICAS #1
RECORD NO.        9488-1
WITHDRAWAL    $    121
FROM CHECKING    60.00
AVAILABLE    $
121.00

Thank You

## DEBIT CARDS

Most banks now offer ATM cards that also work as a debit card. When you use the card, the amount of your purchase is **debited** from your checking account and transferred to the retailer's. Almost all retailers will accept debit payment to make a purchase, since it works in their favor. The main disadvantage from your point of view is that you lose the **float period**, the time between your purchase and the time your check clears or your bill is due. Some banks also charge a small fee per use.

Another type of debit card is used specifically to make purchases, in effect replacing checks. (In fact, they are sometimes called check cards.) With these debit cards you do not need a PIN number, so they can be more vulnerable to misuse. There also may be an annual fee for this type of card. Using a debit card, though, is a convenient and cash-free way to shop. Some experts believe that, debit card use may soon outstrip credit card use.

# The Monthly Statement

**Balancing your checkbook every month helps you keep tabs on where your money is going.**

As banking services expand, monthly statements have become important records for managing your daily finances. Besides being a record of the checks you wrote, the statement shows your deposits and withdrawals—both cash and ATM transactions—and may also provide helpful information, such as when your CD will mature or what current loan rates are. Some banks have developed **relationship statements**, which report on all the accounts you have with the bank—checking, savings, CDs and even loans. The advantage is convenience: you have a monthly snapshot of your dealings with the bank all on one document.

Instead of returning your cancelled checks, many banks now send you "images"—electronic reproductions or reduced-size facsimiles of the originals. While some people feel more secure with the originals, the imaged versions are equally acceptable for proof of payment, since electronic documents have become the norm. The IRS, for example, already accepts them.

**Plain** Bank
Statement of Accounts

Test Customer
14329 Beechwood Blvd.
Milwaukee, WI 53214

December 24

Direct inquiries to:
Lakeside Plaza Branch
4900 West Brown Deer Ave
Milwaukee, WI 53202
(414) 123-4567

Closing b
$5

3.

**Summary of Account Balances**

| Account | Number |
| --- | --- |
| Regular checking | 123-456-789-0 |
| NOW checking | 234-567-890-1 |
| Money market | 345-678-901-2 |
| Savings | 456-789-012-3 |
| Certificates of deposit | 567-890-123-4 |
| Line of credit | 678-901-234-5 |

Get more for your money. Consider a deposit to an interest-bearing account and earn current mone
Contact our customer service department today.

Additions

123-456-789-0
45-6789    Subtractions    100.00

**KEEPING TRACK OF CHECKING**

All checkbooks come with ledgers to record the checks you write as well as your deposits and withdrawals. They let you keep a fairly accurate record of your financial transactions. And they help you locate errors by comparing your records against your monthly statement. You can choose from three types of checkbook ledger systems.

**Separate ledger** uses a separate booklet that fits into your checkbook. It lets you keep a running balance alongside the details of each check.

## IF THERE'S AN ERROR

In most cases, bank statements are right. But you should compare your records—such as ATM receipts and deposit slips—since errors do occur. Generally, you have 60 days for questions involving electronic transfers, but only 14 days for other kinds of mistakes. The sooner you notify the bank, the better.

## KEEPING CANCELLED CHECKS

You should keep your cancelled checks as long as you need proof that payment was made. Credit card statements, as well as phone and utility bills, show when the payment was credited to your account. But insurance and mortgage companies usually do not send confirmations. Your cancelled check is your receipt. You should keep checks you write for income taxes until they can no longer be audited, usually three to five years. And you should always keep checks for items that are part of your tax records, such as home improvements.

## GETTING HELP

Most banks will help you cope with problems you're having balancing your checkbook or following up on a check you've written. Sometimes the easiest thing to do is visit your branch and talk to one of the bank representatives. If you take your checkbook and other records, someone there will usually help you sort out the problem. Since banks have computer records of their customers' accounts, finding the point at which you—or your check—went astray should be relatively easy.

You may also be able to find out whether a certain check has cleared your account or been credited to it by calling the bank's customer service number. Beware, though, that in some cases there may be a fee for the information if it's given over the phone—or through an ATM. You may also be able to access this information if you bank online.

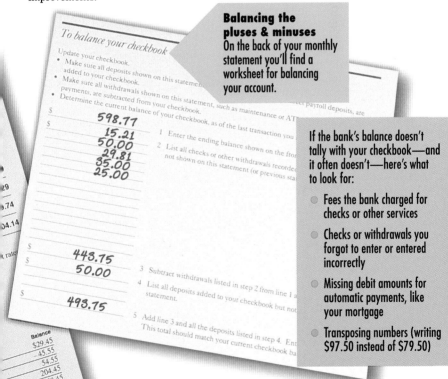

**Balancing the pluses & minuses**
On the back of your monthly statement you'll find a worksheet for balancing your account.

To balance your checkbook

Update your checkbook.
• Make sure all deposits shown on this statement added to your checkbook.
• Make sure all withdrawals shown on this statement, such as maintenance or AT payments, are subtracted from your checkbook.
• Determine the current balance of your checkbook, as of the last transaction you

$ 598.77
15.21
50.00
29.81
35.00
25.00

1 Enter the ending balance shown on the fron

2 List all checks or other withdrawals recorded not shown on this statement (or previous sta

$ 443.75
50.00

3 Subtract withdrawals listed in step 2 from line 1 a

4 List all deposits added to your checkbook but not statement.

$ 493.75

5 Add line 3 and all the deposits listed in step 4. Ent This total should match your current checkbook ba

If the bank's balance doesn't tally with your checkbook—and it often doesn't—here's what to look for:

- Fees the bank charged for checks or other services
- Checks or withdrawals you forgot to enter or entered incorrectly
- Missing debit amounts for automatic payments, like your mortgage
- Transposing numbers (writing $97.50 instead of $79.50)

Balance
$29.45
-45.55
54.55
204.45
858.45

**Check stubs** are attached to checks that are usually packaged in a ring binder. The stub is left in the binder after the check is detached.

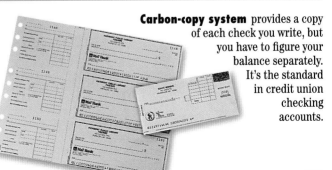

**Carbon-copy system** provides a copy of each check you write, but you have to figure your balance separately. It's the standard in credit union checking accounts.

# CD: Certificate of Deposit

CDs are popular investments because they live up to their promises of safety and income.

When you put money into a bank CD, you expect to get it back at a specific time, plus the interest it's earned. In return for that security, you agree to leave your money on deposit for a specific period of time, typically six months to five years. The minimum deposit is often $500, but there's rarely a **ceiling**, or upper limit. In investment terms, the money you put in is known as your **principal**. The length of the CD is its **term**, and the time it **matures**, or ends, is its **date of maturity**.

## CHOOSING CDs

One of the first things you look for in a CD is the interest rate, since that determines what you earn. Generally, with a longer term, you get a higher rate, to make tying up your money more attractive.

You can buy CDs through almost any bank, and can often handle the entire transaction by mail and telephone. Many people, though, use a local bank for convenience. And unless the rates offered at a distant bank are substantially higher, you may not earn enough extra interest to cover the cost of postage and phone bills. The table here, which appears weekly in The Wall Street Journal, lists the best rates offered around the country on CDs with the most common terms.

## WHAT HAPPENS AT MATURITY

When a CD matures, you decide what you want to do with the principal, but you have to tell the bank in writing what you've decided within the time limit it imposes. If you wait too long or never give instructions, the bank can **roll over**, or reinvest, your CD into another one of the same length at the going rate.

You might ask for a rollover in any case, but if you need the money, or if the new rate will be lower than the interest you've been earning or that you could get on a different investment, you might decide to get out of CDs. In that case, the bank can **sweep**, or move, the money into another of your accounts, wire transfer it to another bank for a fee, or send you a check.

## BUYING FROM A BROKER

You can also buy a CD through a stockbroker or other financial adviser. **Brokerage houses**, firms that buy and sell stocks and other investments, buy bank CDs in large denominations and then break them into parcels and sell them to individual investors. Because you own only part of a CD, you're not committed to holding it to maturity and can sell without penalty

**Compounding method** codes explain which compounding method is used. For example, interest can be compounded daily, monthly, quarterly, or semi-annually.

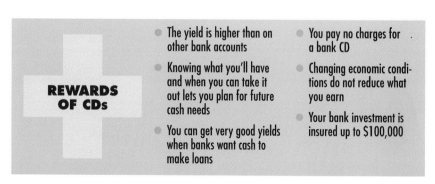

**REWARDS OF CDs**

- The yield is higher than on other bank accounts
- Knowing what you'll have and when you can take it out lets you plan for future cash needs
- You can get very good yields when banks want cash to make loans
- You pay no charges for a bank CD
- Changing economic conditions do not reduce what you earn
- Your bank investment is insured up to $100,000

at any time. You may get a better interest rate, too, since the large underlying CD commands a higher rate. The tradeoff for the flexibility and the earnings often means paying a **commission**, or sales charge, to the broker, something you don't pay for a bank CD.

## YIELD—COMPOUNDING IS KEY

What you actually earn on your CD, in dollars and cents, is the **yield** or the **annual percentage yield (APY)**. The yield depends on whether the interest is **simple** or **compound**, and how it's compounded.

Simple interest is paid only once a year, while compound interest can be paid in a variety of ways, from daily to semi-annually. Here's an example of how interest is compounded when it's paid quarterly:

| | |
|---|---|
| First quarter | **Base amount** + **Interest** |
| Second quarter | = **New base amount** + **Interest** |
| Third quarter | = **New base amount** + **Interest** |
| Fourth quarter | = **New base amount** + **Interest** |
| | = **Value after one year** |

**Yield** is the total amount you earn, as a percentage of what you invest.

**Interest rate** is the percentage of your investment added to your account each time you are paid interest.

**Flexible rates** mean your interest rate could change in either direction. Some flexible-rate CDs have a floor, or limit, on how low the rate can drop. Without a floor, a big drop could reduce the earnings you expect. Sometimes banks offer CDs that let you choose a different (presumably higher) rate once during the term. That carries less risk, since the rate can't go down.

**Floating rates** are interest rates **pegged**, or linked, to another interest rate, like the prime rate or the three-month Treasury Bill rate. When that rate goes up or down, the CD follows suit.

## HIGH YIELD SAVINGS

Minimum balance/opening deposit, generally $500 to $25,000

| Rate | | APY |
|---|---|---|
| 5.86% | mA | 6.02% |
| 5.83% | dA | 6.00% |
| 5.83% | dA | 6.00% |
| 5.75% | mA | 5.90% |
| 5.75% | mA | 5.90% |

| Rate | | APY |
|---|---|---|
| 5.86% | mA | 6.02% |
| 5.75% | siA | 5.90% |
| 5.60% | VA | 5.75% |
| 4.64% | dA | 4.75% |
| 4.65% | qA | 4.73% |

| Rate | | APY |
|---|---|---|
| 6.06% | mA | 6.23% |
| 5.85% | sA | 5.99% |
| 5.62% | VA | 5.75% |
| 5.07% | dA | 5.20% |
| 4.74% | dA | 4.85% |

| Rate | | APY |
|---|---|---|
| 6.20% | mA | 6.38% |
| 6.15% | siA | 6.29% |
| 5.97% | dA | 6.15% |
| 5.88% | dA | 6.06% |

| | Rate | |
|---|---|---|
| **Six Months CDs** | | |
| BankDirect, Dallas TX | 6.30% | dA |
| Bank CaroLine, Greenville SC | 6.30% | dA |
| Advanta Bk Cp, Salt Lake City UT | 6.25% | dA |
| First Internet, Indianapolis IN | 6.25% | mA |
| Florida Bank, Jacksonville FL | 6.26% | qA |
| **One Year CDs** | Rate | |
| Advanta Bk Cp, Salt Lake City UT | 6.77% | d |
| Net.B@nk, Alpharetta GA | 6.64% | d |
| BankDirect, Dallas TX | 6.63% | d |
| Bank CaroLine, Greenville SC | 6.63% | d |
| Advanta Natl, Wilmingtn DE | 6.63% | d |
| **Two Years CDs** | Rate | |
| Advanta Bk Cp, Salt Lake City UT | 7.05% | |
| M&T Bank NA, Oakfield NY | 6.96% | |
| KeyBank USA, Albany NY | 6.95% | |
| TeleBank, Arlington VA | 6.92% | |
| Providian National, Tilton NH | 6.86% | |
| **Five Years CDs** | Rate | |
| KeyBank USA, Albany NY | 7.30% | |
| Providian National, Tilton NH | 7.26% | |
| Providian Bk, Salt Lake Cty UT | 7.26% | |
| Provident Bank, Cincinnati OH | 7.11% | |
| TeleBank, Arlington VA | 7.16% | |

| | |
|---|---|
| cC | 7.50% |
| dA | 7.42% |

## USING CDs

If you have regular costs, like tuition payments, or anticipate a large cost at a specific time, you can time your CDs to come due when you need the money. Banks may be flexible, too, if you ask for a special term. For example, if you are planning to buy a house in seven months, you may be able to get a custom seven-month CD at a better rate than a regular six-month variety.

| RISKS OF CDs | |
|---|---|
| Your money is locked in at a specific rate, even if interest rates go up | The new interest rate may be lower when you reinvest, or roll over, your CD |
| You will probably lose any interest that has accumulated if you take your money out early | If your bank is taken over by another bank, your CD term or rate may change |
| You may earn more with other non-bank options | |

# Savings

Putting money away for a rainy day is the basic idea behind savings accounts.

You can put the money you don't need for everyday expenses into **deposit accounts**, better known as savings accounts. You can move the money in a deposit account into another account at the bank, your checking account for example. You can have it transferred to an investment account, or you can withdraw it. But you can't write a check against it.

Banks generally offer several varieties of savings accounts and pay interest, or a percentage of the amount on deposit, to encourage you to keep your money in the bank. But the appeal of traditional savings accounts has eroded because there are so many other ways for your money to grow faster. That's because the interest rate is low in relation to what you could earn by investing your money in stocks, bonds or mutual funds, or in bank CDs or money market accounts.

The 1991 Truth in Savings Act requires all banks to use the same method to compute yield.

## WAYS TO SAVE

**Passbook accounts**
are the traditional savings accounts. You get a booklet when you open your account showing the amount of your deposit.

Each time you deposit or withdraw, the teller records the amount, adds the interest you've earned and figures the new balance. Your booklet is your record. If you lose it, you'll probably be charged a fee to replace it.

**Statement accounts**
are increasingly common. When you deposit, withdraw or earn interest, the transactions are reported either monthly or quarterly on a statement. If you have more than one account with the bank, they may all be shown on one statement.

**Holiday savings clubs**
require a weekly deposit of a fixed sum of money so you'll accumulate a desired amount in time for holiday spending. You can make the deposit yourself or have the amount transferred from another account. Some holiday clubs pay the same rate as a regular savings account, *but others pay no interest.*

## PLUSES OF SAVINGS ACCOUNTS

- You can get your money any time
- Money in a savings account can reduce—or eliminate—charges on your checking account, so you may save more on fees than you lose because of low interest
- Bank savings are FDIC-insured for up to $100,000 per depositor

## MINUSES OF SAVINGS ACCOUNTS

- Other kinds of accounts, such as CDs and money market funds, pay more—sometimes much more—interest
- Most banks discourage small savings accounts by not paying interest below a minimum balance and/or by charging service fees that can erode the interest you earn, actually costing you money to save

## FIGURING INTEREST

Some savings accounts, including money markets accounts, may pay different rates of interest on different balances or different parts of your total balance. If the rate is **tiered**, you earn the highest rate on your entire balance once you meet the minimum. If it is **blended**, you earn different rates.

**Here's what could happen in an account with a $1,000 minimum and a $12,000 balance.**

**Tiered** means you earn the highest rate the bank offers on the entire $12,000.

**Blended** means you earn one rate on the first $1,000, a better rate on the amount between $1,001 and $9,999, and the highest only on the remaining $2,000.

| | |
|---|---|
| $12,000 | |
| $10,000 | |
| $8,000 | 3.5% |
| $6,000 | |
| $4,000 | 3.5% on entire amount |
| $2,000 | 3.1% |
| $1,000 | |
| $0 | 2.5% |

## NICKELS AND DIMES

The method of figuring compound interest can make a greater difference in the amount you earn than the frequency with which it is added to your account.

Banks use one of two basic methods:

- **Day-of-deposit to day-of-withdrawal** means that all the money in your account earns money every day it's there

- **Average daily balance** means that interest is paid on the average balance in the account for each day in the period

In many cases, the resulting interest is the same. But if you have a choice, experts suggest that the first method will pay you more. Either is better than the **lowest balance** method, or paying interest on the smallest amount of money on deposit in the period for which interest is figured.

It's also a good idea to check when interest is credited before you close an account. You don't want to lose several months of interest by taking the money out just before a quarterly payment, if you can possibly avoid it.

## MONEY MARKET ACCOUNTS

Banks also offer money market deposit accounts, which usually pay a higher rate of interest than regular savings accounts as long as you maintain the required minimum balance. Money market accounts also allow you to write a limited number of checks—frequently three—each month. You can also arrange to have money transferred from your money market into your checking account, either regularly or as you need to.

The chief advantages of a bank money market account over its main competitor, a mutual fund money market account, are that the bank account is insured by the FDIC, while the mutual fund account is not. Plus, there are no management fees for the bank account as there are for the fund account.

However, bank money market accounts tend to pay less interest than mutual funds and impose more regulations on check writing and transfers.

## SAFE-DEPOSIT BOXES

Safe-deposit boxes are designed for keeping important papers and objects such as deeds, jewelry, birth and marriage certificates, plus a list of your valuable possessions. Most banks rent them for anywhere from $15 to several hundred a year, depending on the size of the box. You can spend as much as $3,000 at one New York bank for a safety deposit box the size of a small closet.

However, you can use the box only during regular banking hours. And the box may be sealed if you die, limiting access to valuables for your surviving family—including your spouse—until your will is legally filed.

# Technology: New and Old

## Most of the innovations in modern banking are the result of increasingly sophisticated technology.

Tradition is probably what keeps you and other people writing checks to authorize payments or making trips to the bank to take money from one account and put it into another. If you choose, you can handle much of your day-to-day financial business by telephone or computer without ever leaving home—except for an occasional trip to an ATM.

In fact, your bank—or non-bank—can be in another state or across the country if that's where you find the best service at the most reasonable cost.

### THE COMPETITION KEEPS UP

Brokerage firms and mutual fund companies are using technology the same way that banks are to make moving money quicker, and hands-free. Most of them will accept instructions by telephone or computer to move money from one account to another, buy or sell an investment, or send you a check for all or part of your cash balance. It's their way of providing— usually at the end of the same business day—the same kinds of financial services a bank provides.

Though you usually pay an annual management fee—typically $100 a year—on **cash-management accounts**, or **CMAs**, offered through a brokerage firm, you may find that the service costs at these non-banks are less than your local bank charges.

### INSTANT CASH

If you want to get money to another person quickly, you may be able to use a Western Union Money Transfer or an American Express Moneygram. It's not cheap: usually around $25 to send $250 and about $75 to send $1,000—but the money can be available across the country or around the world in 10 to 15 minutes, fast enough to get somebody out of a financial jam.

### OTHER BENEFITS

There are other advantages to technology that affect the services a bank can provide. Daily compounding of interest—which provides the highest yield—would be almost impossible without a computer. It could still take weeks to get an out-of-state check credited to your account. And if you found yourself without cash on Friday night, you might have to wait until Monday unless you could persuade someone to cash a check for you or give you a loan.

Or, if the person has an ATM card, a PIN and an account in a bank near you, he or she can withdraw as soon as the amount you deposit is credited, provided there's an ATM available. Since these withdrawals come directly out of a bank account, there's no cash advance charge.

---

*Send Envío Send Envío Send*

**MoneyGram**

**To: United States ◆ Canada ◆ International**
A: Esados Unidos ◆ Canadá ◆ Internacional

**Destination:**
Destino: *(Specify city, state and country / Especifique ciudad, estado y país)*

☐ US / US Virgin Islands / Puerto Rico
EEUU / Islas Vírgenes de los EEUU / Puerto Rico
☐ Canada
Canadá
☐ International
Internacional
**Method of Payment**
Método de pago:
☐ Cash
Efectivo
☐ Credit Card
Tarjeta de crédito

**Amount in Words:**
Cantidad en palabras

*Additional information will be captured for transactions of $3,000 or more. See Agent for details.*
*Información adicional será requerida para transacciones mayores de $3,000. Pregúntle por detalles a su Agent*

$

**The person sending:**
La persona que envía

*(First Name / Last Name - Nombre y apellido/s completo/s )*

**Phone Number:** (    )
Su No. de teléfono

**Address:**
Su domicilio

FREE CALL INSTRUCTIONS

**THEIR BANK**

**YOUR BANK**

Direct deposit of paychecks, investment earnings, pensions and Social Security payments speeds up access to your money because it eliminates any delay in checks getting to your bank. The amount is credited electronically to your account on the day of payment and is available either immediately or the next day. Banks are happy to have direct deposits. It cuts down on traffic and keeps money coming in regularly. Some even reduce checking account fees if your paycheck is direct-deposited.

You sign up with your employer, broker or the government by giving them your bank information. They handle the rest. It's also possible to have your check split between two accounts if you want to put money in an investment account as well as a checking account each month.

Problems are rare, but they happen, most frequently when you change banks or your bank changes hands. Dealing with a problem means:

**1** Contacting the source of the check and your bank to have the amount credited

**2** Being sure the problem isn't the result of wrong information, which means it will happen again

**SOCIAL SECURITY**

**Direct deposit** was originated in 1976 by the federal government as a secure way to pay Social Security. More than half of those payments are directly deposited, and people can be signed up automatically when they start to collect. Growing numbers of private and public employees use the option too.

# WIRE TRANSFERS

Wire transfers are another way to move money safely and quickly. For example, if you and your brother were buying property together and he were handling the transaction, you could have money moved from your account to his overnight.

You ask your bank to transfer the money and provide the name and number on the account to which it is going, plus the name and identification number of the bank. Usually, the transaction goes through at the end of the same business day you make the request and is available in the new account during the next day.

You pay a fee for the transfer, usually around $20, a little more than you'd pay to send a check by overnight courier. But in that case, your brother would have to wait several days for the check to clear.

You can also have wire transfer privileges between a money market mutual fund and a bank account, as long as the two are registered in the same name or names. It's usually easy to arrange in advance, at the time you open your mutual fund account. And often there's no fee when the fund initiates the transaction.

# Banking Online

You can turn your home computer or laptop into a 24-hour bank.

Online banking is the next major wave in personal finance. As the Internet continues to grow, more and more existing bricks-and-mortar banks operate online. A growing number of **virtual banks** reside only on the Internet. Increasingly, too, brokerage houses offer banking and investment services online. All three allow you to do all of your banking (and more) from your home computer or laptop. The only thing you can't do—well, not yet—is get cash from your computer.

## WHY BANK ONLINE?

Among the most attractive features of banking online are convenience and real-time account information. That means you can check things as they happen, not after the fact.

Once your account is active, you can check your deposits, pay your bills, and even invest. In fact, you can do anything from opening checking accounts to applying for credit cards to getting mortgage loan quotes, all without visiting a physical bank.

With most banks' online services, you can also view your monthly statement to find out exactly when your checks clear and when they are returned to the bank. And many newer banks offer financial planning education, investment research, home equity and personal loans, and other bank services.

In essence, online banks have become one-stop financial centers, blending the features of a traditional bank with those of a brokerage house.

## HOW TO BANK FROM HOME

If your bank has online services, that means you can bank 24 hours a day, seven days a week.

There are two ways to bank from home through the three different types of banks available to you. One choice is using specialized home-banking software, like Quicken or Microsoft Money. With these programs, you do most of your work offline and then dial into the bank to complete your transactions. The newer method, which most banks are adopting, is an Internet-based system, which allows you to dial in to the bank over the Internet and use its software, or the Internet service provider's software.

## BILL PAYMENT

One convenient and popular feature of online banking is electronic bill payment, which means you don't have to write and mail checks every month. Some banks provide this service for free, but many charge from $4 to $6 a month.

After you create an online list of people and companies to whom you pay bills, here's how the process works:

 Enter your name and password to access the bank's network.

 Open the bill payment screen that displays a check and your current balance.

 Choose the company or person from your existing list to whom you want to write a check, or add a new name.

 Fill in the amount of payment and the date you want it paid.

## COMPARING BANKS

| Type of Bank | Connection |
| --- | --- |
| Bricks-and-mortar bank | Software or Internet access |
| Brokerage bank | Software or Internet access |
| Virtual bank | Internet access |

## WHAT ABOUT SECURITY?

Many people are worried that online banking isn't safe. In fact, online banks are typically equipped with a three-fold security system. It consists of a **firewall**, which is a computer that acts as a gatekeeper between the bank's network and the outside world. The firewall prevents the bank's computers and data from being accessed by an outsider.

Second is a system called **data encryption**, which banks use to scramble information with secret codes when it passes between your computer and the bank. Encryption guarantees that all data you send over the Internet will be unintelligible to anyone who encounters it. The third mode of security is one that you're familiar with: **PINs**, or personal identification numbers, which you use to identify yourself to the bank. Some experts believe that online banks are safer than virtual banks because the data is passing through a private network as opposed to the Internet. But others argue that both are equally secure, and as secure as any physical bank.

**5** Choose whether you want the payment to be made just once, or on a recurring schedule. Click to authorize payment.

**6** Get a confirmation number and your new checkbook balance. Save it for your records.

### VIRTUAL BANKS

If you are interested in a virtual bank, look for these features: reliability of customer service, interest rates, fees, and available options such as bill payment and investment alternatives.

Most virtual banks pay higher interest rates for checking and money market accounts because they have no overhead expenses. However, most do not offer savings accounts.

Because virtual banks have no branches or ATMs, you'll have to pay a surcharge to get cash from an unaffiliated machine. Some of the banks give you a limited rebate each month to offset ATM charges, but the fees can still add up if you make a lot of transactions. Surcharges average between $1 and $2 per transaction, and are rising.

| Services Available | Pros | Cons |
|---|---|---|
| • FDIC-insured<br>• Bill payment<br>• Other bank transactions | Access to regular branches and online services | May charge fees for online use |
| • Linked to investment accounts | One-stop financial services | May require larger minimum balance |
| • FDIC-insured<br>• Bill payment<br>• Other bank transactions | Pays higher interest rates | No branches or ATMs |

# Using Credit

When you borrow money to pay for something or use a card to charge a purchase, you're using credit.

From a consumer's perspective, using credit means being able to pay for things you want or need when you don't have the cash to cover the purchase, or don't want to pay in full all at once. Your part of the bargain is repaying, or paying off, the amount of money you've borrowed, plus a fee for having used it.

Credit cards and loans are the types of credit most people use most often. **Loans**, which let you borrow a lump sum of money, have a longer history. But **credit cards**, which give you revolving access to a fixed sum of money, have become a way of life for a majority of people. Revolving access means that as soon as you repay an amount you've used, you can use it again.

**BUY NOW**

## AVAILABLE CREDIT

Creditors are willing, and often eager, to advance you the **principal**, or the money you use, because they collect a fee, called a finance charge, as you repay. Creditors figure the **finance charge** by adding a percentage of the principal to the amount you owe. The percentage, called the **interest rate**, varies, depending on the type of credit you're using and the amount of competition the creditor has in attracting your business. It's often linked to the interest rates that are current in the economy at large, particularly the **prime rate**, which lenders use as a benchmark rate. In general, though, finance charges on credit cards are figured at a higher—sometimes much higher—rate than those on most loans.

Other factors are sometimes involved in your finance charges, too, including your credit reputation or assumptions a potential creditor makes about you. If a creditor believes there's a risk that you may **default**, or fail to repay, the rate you'll have to pay for credit may be higher than someone who seems to pose less risk.

## CREDIT PARTNERS

Two parties are involved in making credit work, the **consumer**, or user of credit, and the **creditor**, or supplier of credit. And unless you have informal arrangements with family or friends, getting credit usually involves an agreement you make with a financial institution such as a bank or a credit union.

Customarily, the partners agree on the amount of credit available and the conditions under which it will be repaid, as well as the fee the creditor will charge for advancing the money. Since credit is a common phenomenon, those agreements are generally standardized. But that doesn't mean

## TWO FACES OF CREDIT

Credit often gets bad press, typified by the old caution against being neither a borrower nor a lender. You might also recall the not-so-remote spectres of workers owing their lives to the company store or farmers losing their homesteads to the bank.

But credit has also enabled many people to live better by paying for goods or services as part of their regular living expenses rather than having to wait until they could afford to make the purchase. It's more available today to a broader range of people than it customarily was in the past. Many aspects of its use are government-regulated, to protect consumers against some potential abuses. And while it's easy to get overextended, it's not hard to use credit wisely.

In fact, most Americans use credit in one form or another: about 80% of the adult population have credit cards, most people buy homes with a mortgage, and about 60% of college students (or their parents) use loans to help pay tuition.

## PAY LATER

## EVALUATING CREDIT USE

People use credit, or their access to credit, in different ways. And most experts agree that some of those choices work better than others. Here are some of the credit issues you may want to consider:

Credit cards can be a convenient way to simplify bill-paying. If you charge a number of different purchases and write one check to pay them off, at the very least you save money on stamps. You may also be able to take advantage of sales, avoid carrying large sums of cash, or shop conveniently by phone.

On the other hand, if you regularly charge more than you can afford to pay, the finance charges can add substantially to your expenses, and in the worst of circumstances drive you deeply into debt.

Similarly, a car loan or lease can enable you to replace an old car with one less apt to need expensive repairs. But you can also find yourself repaying a loan on a car or other property that's no longer serviceable. Or worse yet, if you overcommit yourself and can't pay, you may lose the property entirely.

that some credit arrangements won't work better for you than others. It's important to understand the details, especially what the credit will cost, and to do some comparison shopping. After all, any creditor you apply to will check to see whether you're a good risk before making money available to you.

**ARTHUR MORRIS** originated the installment loan. His Morris Plan, the first to make credit available to the average citizen, began in 1916 despite common wisdom that lending money to working people was doomed to failure. Today, it's hard to imagine how the American economy could function without credit.

# Credit Cards

## Plastic cards created a revolution in personal finance.

When credit cards were introduced in 1959, people were able to handle their personal finances in a dramatically different way. They didn't have to wait for a paycheck to reach the bank before they could make a purchase. And they didn't have to make a new arrangement every time they needed access to money. By having a one-time credit application approved, they could hand over a plastic card instead of cash or a check, walk away with the goods, and if necessary pay over an extended period of time.

That doesn't mean cards created credit. They just made it easier to use, and available to more people.

## IT'S ALL IN THE CARDS

**Account number**
The first six digits show the company that issued the card. The next four identify region and branch information. The next five are your account number. The final one is attached as a check for extra security protection.

**Customer service number**
You can call the customer service number if you have any problems or need information about your account.

**Holographic image**
One image found on many cards is a special design using a color foil and ultra-violet ink invisible to the naked eye. Merchants can scan the card under an ultra-violet lamp to see if the card is authentic.

**Magnetic strip**
The magnetic strip houses specific information about your account. MasterCard, for example, uses two tracks. Track 1 holds your name, expiration date, card type and data such as your PIN and credit limit. Track 2 holds your account number, start date and other discretionary data.

**Expiration dates**
Cards are usually valid for between 12 and 36 months. In many cases, a new card is issued about 30 days before the expiration date.

## HOW ONE CREDIT CARD WORKS

When you use a VISA card, you initiate a series of steps that insure that the merchant is paid and you are charged.

**1** When you make a purchase, the merchant gets the amount approved, usually by passing your card through an electronic approval machine. When you sign the receipt, you are agreeing to pay the charge.

**2** The merchant deposits the receipt in his or her bank, which credits the merchant's account and sends the transaction electronically to VISA.

## VARIATIONS ON A THEME

The plastic cards in your wallet may all look alike, but they don't all work the same way. Chances are, some of them aren't technically credit cards.

**Credit cards**, including American Express Blue, Discover, MasterCard, and VISA, let you charge purchases up to a preset dollar limit, called your **available credit** or **credit limit**. That amount can range from $500 to $10,000 or more per card. You can pay back the amount of credit you've used in full, or at your own pace, provided you pay the minimum due each month. Once you repay an amount, it's again available for you to use.

**Travel & Entertainment cards**, including American Express, Diners Club and Carte Blanche, let you charge purchases but require you to pay your bill in full each month. If you fall behind, they may charge interest, block use of your card, or both. With these cards, you aren't given a credit limit, though you may sometimes find that no further charges will be approved if you have a large outstanding balance.

**Debit cards** aren't credit cards at all. They're more accurately check replacement cards that allow a retailer to debit your bank account directly for the amount of a purchase (see page 19).

**An American typically carries from one to three credit cards, and owes about $2,000. Together, Americans owe about $600 billion in outstanding credit card balances.**

## BEFORE CREDIT CARDS

Layaway plans, which were once common, let you pay a small amount each week against the purchase price of clothing or a piece of furniture, for example, which the merchant held until you paid off the cost. But if winter came before you finished paying for your coat, you'd still be cold.

Department stores provide **charge cards** that let you make purchases within that particular store and make a single monthly payment. In the past, you generally had to pay in full, or you could no longer use the card. And you couldn't use it across the street, let alone around the world. Today, however, most charge cards work like credit cards, though they're still limited to a single retailer or affiliation of stores.

Many retailers in the U.S. and around the world accept both credit cards and travel and entertainment cards, while some accept only one or the other. In fact, most of the major cards are so widely accepted that they have reduced your need for separate cards for different retailers, and the hassle of multiple bills.

## CREDIT ASSOCIATIONS

VISA and MasterCard are not-for-profit associations that were created to handle the mechanics of credit card transactions. They're owned by member banks, who actually issue the cards and make money on the fees generated when you use them to make purchases. Some banks offer both cards, and some offer one or the other.

---

**SMART CARDS**
A smart card, sometimes known as a chip card, looks like a credit card. But instead of charging with it, you spend the value, or amount of money it holds, by using your card in any terminal that accepts it. When you've spent it all, you can replace the card or add value to it.

---

**3** VISA processes the transaction, crediting the merchant's bank and debiting the card issuer's account.

**4** VISA notifies the card issuer electronically that the transaction has occurred.

**5** The card issuer bills you for the purchase. Many retailers don't mind the fees they pay for accepting credit cards because people tend to spend more using a card than they do when they pay with cash.

# Understanding Card Credit

Your monthly bill is an excellent source of information about your credit card account.

Your bill is a snapshot of your account at the end of each statement period: It shows what you owed to start, what you owe now, and every charge and payment that occurred in between. Combined with your checking account ledger and bank statement, it helps provide a nearly complete record of your monthly expenses.

Though the statement wasn't designed to help you evaluate your spending habits, you can use it for that purpose. If you're trying to find ways to trim expenses or set aside more for investment, you can track money you're spending on discretionary items. Instead of spending all of it, you might consider putting a portion in an investment account.

The version at the right may look different from yours, but all statements contain virtually the same information. And each one figures its charges and fees according to the agreement you made with the company when you signed up to use its card.

**New balance** is the amount you owed on the day the statement was prepared. It includes any finance charges and late fees.

**Credit line** is the amount of credit you can use. It can be anywhere from $500 to $10,000 or more.

**Previous balance** is what you owed on the day your previous statement was prepared. It's used as a basis to figure how much you owed on the day this statement was prepared.

**Minimum payment due** is what you must pay. Typically you owe 2.5% of the new balance or $10, whichever is greater. Whatever you don't pay will be carried forward and subject to finance charges.

## COMPUTING FINANCE CHARGES

The interest you owe depends on the method used to calculate your finance charge: adjusted, average daily or previous balance. For example, suppose you pay an 18% annual finance charge (1.5% per month) on amounts you owe. Your previous balance is $2,000, and you pay $1,000 on the 15th day of a 30-day period:

| METHOD | DESCRIPTION | INTEREST YOU OWE |
|---|---|---|
| ADJUSTED BALANCE | The company subtracts the amount of your payment from the beginning balance and charges you interest on the remainder. This method costs you the least. | $15.00 |
| AVERAGE DAILY BALANCE | The company charges you interest on the average of the amount you owe each day during the period. So the larger the payment you make, the lower the interest you pay. | $22.50 |
| PREVIOUS BALANCE | The company does not subtract any payments you make from your previous balance. You pay interest on the total amount you owe at the beginning of the period. This method costs you the most. | $30.00 |

**Available credit** is the amount of credit you had available on the day the statement was prepared.

**Payment due date** is the last day your payment can be received to avoid additional finance charges or late fees.

**Statement closing or billing date** is the date the statement was prepared. Any charges after this date will appear on the next statement.

**Cash access line** is money you can withdraw from an ATM with your credit card. You need a personal identification number (PIN) to use an ATM.

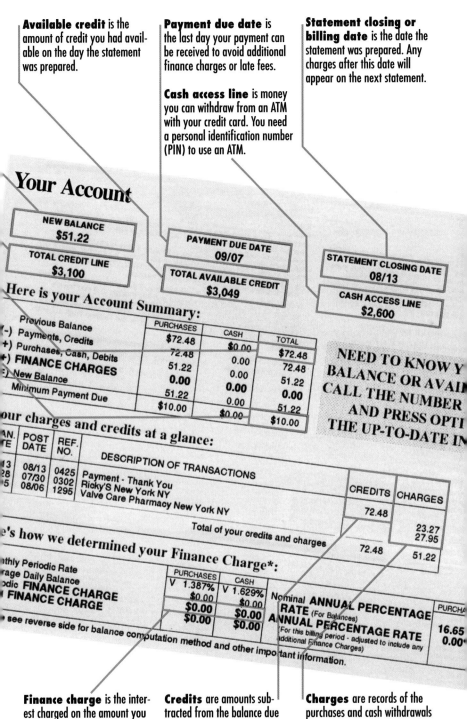

## Your Account

| NEW BALANCE | | |
|---|---|---|
| $51.22 | | |

| TOTAL CREDIT LINE |
|---|
| $3,100 |

| PAYMENT DUE DATE |
|---|
| 09/07 |

| TOTAL AVAILABLE CREDIT |
|---|
| $3,049 |

| STATEMENT CLOSING DATE |
|---|
| 08/13 |

| CASH ACCESS LINE |
|---|
| $2,600 |

### Here is your Account Summary:

| | PURCHASES | CASH | TOTAL |
|---|---|---|---|
| Previous Balance | $72.48 | $0.00 | $72.48 |
| (-) Payments, Credits | 72.48 | 0.00 | 72.48 |
| (+) Purchases, Cash, Debits | 51.22 | 0.00 | 51.22 |
| (+) FINANCE CHARGES | 0.00 | 0.00 | 0.00 |
| (=) New Balance | 51.22 | 0.00 | 51.22 |
| Minimum Payment Due | $10.00 | $0.00 | $10.00 |

NEED TO KNOW Y
BALANCE OR AVAIL
CALL THE NUMBER
AND PRESS OPTI
THE UP-TO-DATE IN

### Your charges and credits at a glance:

| AN. TE | POST DATE | REF. NO. | DESCRIPTION OF TRANSACTIONS | CREDITS | CHARGES |
|---|---|---|---|---|---|
| 13 | 08/13 | 0425 | Payment - Thank You | 72.48 | |
| 28 | 07/30 | 0302 | Ricky'S New York NY | | 23.27 |
| 5 | 08/06 | 1295 | Valve Care Pharmacy New York NY | | 27.95 |
| | | | Total of your credits and charges | 72.48 | 51.22 |

### Here's how we determined your Finance Charge*:

| | PURCHASES | CASH |
|---|---|---|
| Monthly Periodic Rate | V 1.387% | V 1.629% |
| Average Daily Balance | $0.00 | $0.00 |
| Periodic FINANCE CHARGE | $0.00 | $0.00 |
| FINANCE CHARGE | $0.00 | $0.00 |

\* see reverse side for balance computation method and other important information.

Nominal **ANNUAL PERCENTAGE RATE** (For Balances)

**ANNUAL PERCENTAGE RATE** (For this billing period - adjusted to include any additional Finance Charges)

| | PURCHA |
|---|---|
| | 16.65 |
| | 0.00 |

**Finance charge** is the interest charged on the amount you owe. Two cards with the same finance charge won't necessarily charge you the same interest, even if you owe the same amount. That's because what you pay depends on how the company figures the balance on which they charge you interest.

**Credits** are amounts subtracted from the balance due for payment, overpayment, incorrect charges, or returned merchandise. For example, if you dispute a charge, the lender may credit you the amount until the dispute is settled.

**Charges** are records of the purchases and cash withdrawals you made, giving a date and reference number for each. Check these details against your records to be sure that the charges are all yours. There can be mix ups in names and account numbers, as well as times when bills are double-charged.

# What Cards Cost

## Three things affect your card-based credit costs: annual fees, finance charges and grace periods.

You can control your card-based credit costs even if you use credit all the time by choosing a card that's suited to your usage and payment habits. However, if you always have a big outstanding balance and pay only the minimum charges each month, you'll be saddled with huge costs no matter which card you use.

### THE COSTS TO CONSIDER

In shopping for a credit card, you'll want to consider three costs. They may not control your decision about which card to use, but they can help save you money.

**Annual fees** are once-yearly charges for using a particular card. You can often avoid them entirely by choosing a card that guarantees that there'll be no annual fee for as long as you use it.

**Finance charges** are the costs of using credit. Many issuers still charge 18% or more a year (1.5% a month) on your outstanding balances and cash advances, though the justification for those rates dates to a period of high inflation in the early 1980s. However, some banks charge less, sometimes significantly less during an introductory period. If you regularly have an outstanding balance, it can be wise to shop for the lowest rate.

**Grace period**, sometimes called grace days, is the time between when you're billed and when you have to pay. However, some cards with low interest rates charge interest on all purchases from the day they're made, even if you paid your last balance in full. If you always pay on time, you'll probably agree that avoiding interest charges altogether outweighs finding the lowest rate, so be sure to read the small print.

### EXTRA COSTS

In addition to an annual fee, card issuers may charge extra fees for specific situations. For example, if you exceed your credit line, you may have to pay an **over limit fee**, usually about $25, even if your charge has been approved. And if your minimum payment is overdue, there's often a **late payment fee**, also about $25.

You will probably have to pay a **cash advance fee** for withdrawing money from an automated teller machine (ATM) with your credit card, plus interest for the time between the advance and when you pay it off. Or, you can **debit**, or take money directly out of your checking account with an American Express card, for an access fee of 3% of the withdrawal ($3 minimum) if you're enrolled in their Express Cash program.

### MINI CHARGE, MAXI INTEREST

On many cards, even if your balance is as low as $15, you'll have to pay a **minimum finance charge** of 50¢. That's a whopping annual interest rate of 40%.

### SECURED CREDIT CARDS

If you have trouble getting a credit card, as you might if you have no credit history, no regular job, or you've had financial problems in the past, you may be able to arrange for a **secured card** by opening a savings account and keeping a balance equal to your credit line. Then if you don't keep up your payments, the bank can take what you owe from the account. However, if you use the card regularly—and repay what you owe—you may qualify for a regular card and a higher line of credit.

# Card Wars

Card issuers sometimes add extra privileges to attract customers to their gold or platinum premium cards. You may decide these privileges offset the higher annual fees, or that they're not worth the cost.

### COLLISION INSURANCE

There's often no need to buy a collision damage waiver from a car rental agency because many cards automatically cover you.

This is generally considered the best of the add-ons. Some cards have a hotline you can call world-wide for medical or legal help after an accident.

### EXTENDED WARRANTY

You can receive up to a year's warranty beyond the manufacturer's warranty, and may be able to replace lost or stolen goods bought with the card.

### YEAR-END STATEMENTS

With some premium cards, you receive a consolidated statement of all the year's charges, designed to make your record-keeping a little easier.

## AND MAKING IT LIGHTER

Some cards offer low introductory rates, no annual fees or both to attract new customers.

| ISSUER | INTEREST RATE* | ANNUAL FEE | GRACE PERIOD |
|---|---|---|---|
| Capital Bank | 2.9% | $29 | 25 days |
| First Bank | 3.9% | None | 25 days |
| Western Bank | 4.9% | $39 | 25 days |
| Eastern Bank | 4.9% | None | None |
| Central Bank | 5.9% | None | 30 days |

*Introductory rates are only good for a specified period of time, usually five months.

## A CARD AS CURRENCY

Have you ever tried to rent a car without a credit card, or make an airline reservation or order merchandise from a catalog? If you have, you know how difficult—and how lengthy—handling these routine arrangements can be. But with a card handy, you can make almost any transaction as quickly as you can read off your number.

In fact, credit cards have become a nearly universal currency, not only for making purchases but for guaranteeing your promise—whether it's to show up to keep a reservation you've made or return something you've rented. But if you don't follow through, you may find you'll have to pay for it anyway.

### CASH FLOATS OR SINKS

If you make a purchase right after your account closes for the month, you won't have to pay for it until the end of the next payment period, which could mean a 45 day float. However, if you have an outstanding balance on your credit card, you will probably be charged interest from the date of purchase. That increases the price of the item.

### TRAVEL INSURANCE

Using some cards for plane, bus, or ship travel automatically covers you against accidents. However, it doesn't cover trip cancellations.

### SHOPPING/TRAVEL DISCOUNTS

You may get shopping discounts and a guarantee of low prices for hotels, cars and planes when you use the card. But you might do better shopping around.

### AFFINITY CARDS

A credit card that's co-sponsored by a bank and another company or institution—perhaps an oil company, an airline, a college or a charity—offers savvy consumers a smart way to use credit and accomplish something else at the same time, typically saving money on future purchases, adding mileage to frequent flier accounts or making charitable contributions.

If you're interested and are willing to do a little checking, you can probably find a card that does what you want—and does it well. On the other hand, some rebates accumulate slowly and sometimes you're actually paying more in fees or interest charges than the bonus is worth.

# Protecting Your Card Rights

Don't wait until you have a problem with your card to find out your rights. They're spelled out on the back of your statement.

A lot can go wrong when you use a credit card, even if you stay within your limits and pay promptly. It makes sense to keep your receipts, check them against your monthly statement, and notify the card company right away if you spot any errors.

Some card issuers respond promptly to questions, complaints, or reports of stolen cards, while others may give you a more difficult time. Since cards are readily available from a wide range of sources, there is little point in maintaining an account with an unresponsive issuer. In fact, you may be able to transfer any outstanding charges on such an account to a newly opened account.

### GETTING MORE CREDIT

More isn't always better where credit is concerned. Obviously you need a large enough line of credit to be able to charge something you might need—an airline ticket in an emergency, for example. But you can have two types of problems with large lines of credit.

The first, which you can control, is that you might be tempted to spend more than you can repay. The second is that whatever lines of credit you have available count as a liability when potential creditors consider your application for a loan or mortgage, even if you never charge as much as you could.

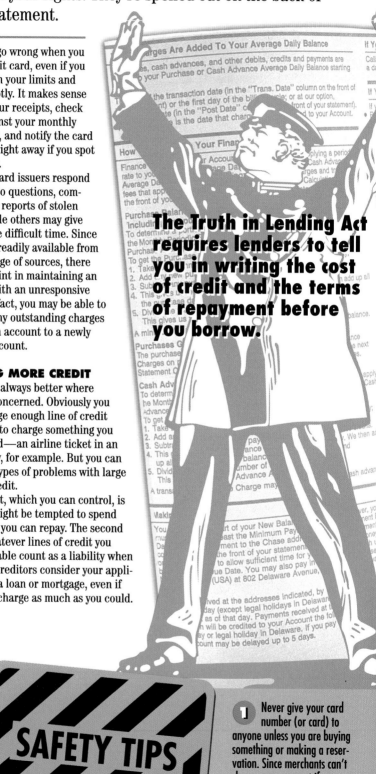

**The Truth in Lending Act requires lenders to tell you in writing the cost of credit and the terms of repayment before you borrow.**

SAFETY TIPS

1. Never give your card number (or card) to anyone unless you are buying something or making a reservation. Since merchants can't charge your account if your check bounces, there's no reason

**The Fair Credit Billing Act sets the procedures for resolving billing errors. In some cases, however, it can take a lot of persistence to get a problem resolved.**

### CANCELLING YOUR CARD

By law, you can cancel your card and avoid paying the annual fee as long as you notify the lender in writing within 40 days of receiving the bill for the fee.

### LOST OR STOLEN CARDS

If you report a missing card immediately by calling the number on the back of the statement, you aren't responsible for any charges. $50 is the most you'll owe even if you don't report losing your card.

Some companies, for a fee, keep all your card numbers on file and will report any problems for you.

### PURCHASES YOU DIDN'T MAKE AND OTHER BILLING ERRORS

You have 60 days to notify the lender in writing about billing errors. This includes wrong amounts of credit extended, wrong goods or services, incorrect payments or credits, computational errors or any other disputed charges.

Card companies have 30 days to respond and 90 days to resolve the problem. They can't stop you from using your card while investigating the problem and can't release a bad credit report on you. And if they don't respond, they can't collect the disputed amount or finance charges.

### DEFECTIVE MERCHANDISE

You can legally refuse to pay for defective merchandise if it cost more than $50 and you were unable to resolve the problem with the merchant. The purchase must be made in your home state or within 100 miles of your mailing address, though companies are flexible on this matter. (The price and mileage restrictions don't apply if the card issuer advertised the product or was involved in the purchase).

12-91 PTG. 5-92

---

to write the number on your check for them. And there's no need to put your phone, name, or address on a credit card receipt. In some states, it's illegal for a retailer to ask you to do this.

**2** Destroy all carbons. Thieves can use your number to charge purchases or even order new cards.

**3** Never make your PIN available to anyone. Don't write it anywhere a thief may have access to it. Many experts also advise you to use a PIN others can't figure out easily. But it has to be one you can remember.

# Loans

You can arrange to borrow and repay the money you need for specific expenses.

When you need money to buy a car, pay a college tuition, fix up your home, or anything else that requires an immediate cash outlay, you are often able to borrow the amount from a lender such as a bank or a credit union. If you know how different types of loans work and the particular features they offer, you will be in a better position to look for the one that will be best suited for you.

In some ways, of course, all loans are alike. You borrow money, called the **principal**, and agree to pay it back over a specific **term**, or length of time, with **interest**. But the conditions of the loan, some of which are listed below, can affect how much you can borrow and how much the loan will cost you.

- Whether you pay in **installments** or return the lump sum
- Whether the interest is **fixed** or **adjustable**
- Whether the loan is **secured** or **unsecured**

# INSTALLMENT
# ADJUSTABLE
# FIXED
# REVOLVING
# SECURED

## INSTALLMENT LOANS

When you take an installment loan, you borrow the money all at once and repay it in set amounts, or installments, on a regular schedule, usually once a month. Installment loans are also called closed-end loans because you must pay them off by a specific date.

**for example**

If you take a five-year $20,000 loan at 10% interest:

| | |
|---|---|
| Monthly payments for 5 years | **$424.96** |
| Total payment | **$25,497.60** |
| Total interest paid | **$5,497.60** |

## SECURED LOANS

Your loan is secured when you put up security or collateral to guarantee it. The lender can sell the collateral if you fail to repay. Car loans and home equity loans are the most common types of secured loans.

## UNSECURED LOANS

An unsecured loan is made solely on your promise to repay. If the lender thinks you are a good risk, nothing but your signature is required. However, the lender may require a co-signer, who promises to repay if you don't. Since unsecured loans pose a bigger risk for lenders, they may have higher interest rates and stricter conditions.

Buying on time, or paying for something while you're using it, was introduced by Isaac Singer in 1856 as a way to sell his sewing machines. At $5 down and $5 a month, the average family could afford a $125 machine—otherwise impossible on a typical $500 annual income.

## LINES OF CREDIT

A personal line of credit is a type of **revolving credit**. It lets you write special checks for the amount you want to borrow, up to a limit set by the lender. The credit doesn't cost you anything until you write a check. Then you begin to pay interest on the amount you borrowed. You must repay at least a minimum amount each month plus interest, but you can repay more, or even the whole loan amount, whenever you want. Whatever you repay becomes available for you to borrow again.

Banks and credit card issuers sometimes offer lines of credit automatically to people they consider good customers. But that doesn't mean you have to use them if you prefer not to.

### for example

If you have a $10,000 line of credit, you have access to that money over and over, as long as you repay what you use:

|   | | |
|---|---|---|
| | $ **10,000** | Line of credit |
| − | $ **6,000** | You borrow |
| = | $ **4,000** | Available credit |
| + | $ **1,000** | You repay |
| = | $ **5,000** | Available credit |

### Advantages
- Only one application
- Instant access to credit

### Disadvantages
- Potentially high interest rates
- Easy to over-borrow

## FIXED RATE

Many installment loans have a fixed rate. The interest rate and the monthly payments stay the same for the term, or length, of the loan.

### Advantages

- Installments stay the same
- Easy to budget payments
- The cost of the loan won't increase
- No surprises

### Disadvantages

- Interest remains the same, even if market rates decrease
- Initially higher than adjustable rate

## ADJUSTABLE RATE

An adjustable-rate loan has a variable interest rate. When the rate changes, usually every six months or once a year, the monthly payment also changes.

### Advantages

- Initial rate lower than fixed rate
- Lower overall costs if rates drop
- Annual increases usually controlled

### Disadvantages

- Vulnerable to rate hikes
- Hard to budget increases
- Not always available

# The Substance of a Loan

When you borrow, you want to know how much, for how long and at what price.

Whether you need a loan only occasionally or borrow on a more regular basis, you'll be concerned with the same basic things:

- **The amount you'll be able to borrow**
- **How long you'll have to repay**
- **What the interest charges will be**

Some loans have built-in limits. For example, if you borrow money to buy a car, the maximum you're eligible for is determined by the price of the car. If you borrow to pay tuition, there is often a per-year or four-year total that you can finance. Home equity loans are generally capped at 80% of your equity (see page 76), and loans in excess of $50,000 may be more difficult to arrange.

Other loans have built-in terms, or time frames. Car loans rarely last for more than five years, in part so that the vehicle hasn't outlived its usefulness before it's paid off. But the only thing that limits interest charges is the competition. If lenders want your business, they offer rates similar to what other lenders are quoting.

### THE LOAN AGREEMENT

When you take a loan, you're committing yourself not only to repay, but to repay on a specific schedule. Those details are spelled out in the loan agreement, or **loan note**, a detailed document the lender provides. When you sign it, you've agreed to its terms and conditions. The fine print may be off-putting, but you should read it carefully. It explains exactly what you're getting—and getting into.

Some lenders have rewritten their loan agreements in recent years to make them more easily understood. And the loan officer you work with should be willing to answer your questions before you sign. You should never hesitate to ask.

## 1. HOW MUCH CAN YOU BORROW?

## 2. HOW MUCH WILL IT COST?

## 3. WHEN DO YOU HAVE TO REPAY?

## 4. WHAT IF YOU DON'T PAY ON TIME?

### IT ALL BEGINS WITH THE APPLICATION

Loan applications may vary, but they all ask for the same basic information:

| | |
|---|---|
| **Employment** | Someone at work may be asked to verify your employment, and you may be asked to provide one or two recent paystubs. |
| **Accounts** | You may be asked for your credit card account numbers and balances, for your banks' and securities firms' names, account numbers and balances, and for recent tax returns. |
| **References** | You may need business and personal associates to supply references. |

# I.O.U.

Contrary to popular belief, an IOU is not a binding promise to repay a loan. American legal interpretation considers it merely an acknowledgement that money is owed.

Usually you request a specific loan amount. The lender can approve it, reject it, or offer you a smaller amount. Sometimes you need to apply to more than one lender to find one who will approve your request. You may have to pay an application fee each time.

The **amount financed**, or the **principal**, is what you borrow. However, you may not actually get the entire amount that is approved. That's because the lender will usually subtract any application fees, credit-check fees, or other costs of the loan from the amount you receive. In addition, the lender may require you to use part of the loan amount to pay off another loan or to purchase insurance to cover the loan if you should die.

The cost of a loan is determined by the interest rate that the lender offers. However, you may be able to find a loan at a better rate if you investigate what various lenders are charging before you apply.

Sometimes lenders are eager to lend, and offer lower rates or waive the fees. While you probably can't time your need to borrow to coincide with those occasions, some borrowers apply for home equity lines of credit when lenders promote them. Then the money is available if it's needed, but there's no charge unless the line is used.

You may also be able to get a **preferred customer rate**, or a small discount on the interest rate, if you maintain a savings or investment account with the lender.

The terms of repayment are part of your loan agreement. In most cases, you pay interest and some of the principal on a regular schedule, usually once a month.

In some cases, including some college loans, you may pay only interest for a specific period and then begin to repay the principal. In others, you pay only interest for the term of the loan and then repay the entire loan in a lump sum. Most lenders allow you to **prepay** a loan at any time. Some charge a prepayment penalty, usually about 2% of the amount borrowed, although many states prohibit this practice.

In many cases, you may have to pay a **late fee** if your payment arrives after the payment due date, and you should expect to be penalized if you send a payment check that bounces.

Failing to live up to the agreement is called **defaulting** on the loan. The lender may have the right to repossess and sell the property you put up as security.

Lenders may also impose a stiff penalty if you default. And, if they hire a collection agency or lawyer, you'll have to pay for those services, too.

Another way lenders can collect if you default is by taking, or **setting off**, the amount owed from any checking or savings account you have with the lender.

Pawnbrokers lend you money in exchange for property you leave with them, though usually only a small portion of its value. If you repay the loan and the interest on time, you get your property back. If you don't, the pawnbroker sells it, although an extension can often be arranged. Pawnbrokers charge higher interest rates than other creditors, but you don't have to apply or wait for approval. And they rarely ask questions.

# The Cost of a Loan

## Two things determine what borrowing will cost you: the finance charge and the length of the loan.

The cheapest loan isn't the one with the lowest payments, or even the one with the lowest interest rate. Instead you have to look at the total cost of borrowing, which depends on the interest rate plus fees, and the term, or length of time it takes you to repay. While you probably can't influence the rate and fees, you may be able to arrange for a shorter term.

## WHAT YOU LEARN FROM ADS

### THE ANNUAL PERCENTAGE RATE
Lenders are required to tell you what a loan will actually cost per year, expressed as an annual percentage rate (APR).

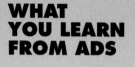

**8.25%** APR·

COMMON SENS
EQUITY LOANS

FREE CHECKING. FREE CHECKS. F
FREE CLOSING COSTS ON MOS

Get our very low fixed rate, tax deductions for your
pay closing costs on Equity Loans c
emier® customers. When you sign
lso get Free Visa Gold, Free Inter
re.

COMMON SENS
FROM A COMM

### ANNUAL PERCENTAGE RATE (APR)
Some lenders charge lower interest but add high fees. Others do the reverse. The APR—annual percentage rate—allows you to compare them on equal terms. It combines the fees with a year of interest charges to give you the true annual interest rate.

For example, suppose you take a $10,000 loan at 10% interest. You also pay an origination fee of $350, leaving you with $9,650 as the actual borrowed amount. Since you are actually getting a smaller loan, but repaying the full $10,000 with interest, the cost is more than 10%. The APR, or actual percentage rate, is closer to 10.35%.

**Periodic interest rate** is the interest the lender will charge on the amount you borrow. If the lender also charges fees, this won't be the true interest rate.

## THE COST OF TAKING LONGER TO REPAY

The term of your loan is crucial when determining cost. Shorter terms mean squeezing larger amounts into fewer payments. But they also mean you'll pay interest for fewer years, which saves you a lot of money.

Consider, for example, the interest for three different terms on a $13,500 car loan at 12.5%.

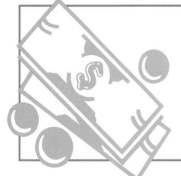

## THE FEES ARE THE THING

Be sure to ask about all fees—they add up very quickly and can substantially increase the cost of your loan.

**Application fee** covers processing expenses.

**Attorney fees** pay the lender's attorney. Fees for your own attorney are extra.

**Credit search fee** covers researching your credit history. **Origination fee** covers administrative costs, and sometimes appraisal fees.

# WHAT YOU LEARN WHEN APPLYING

## TRUTH-IN-LENDING DISCLOSURE

Every lender is required to provide a total cost disclosure, called a truth-in-lending disclosure, before a loan is made. This is the only place where you can see in dollars and cents what the loan will actually cost you.

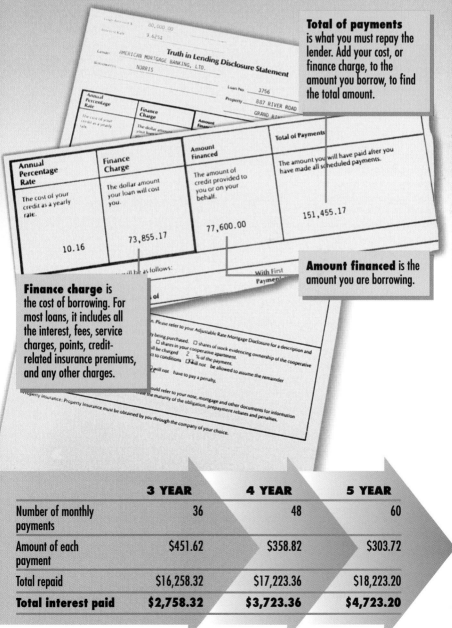

**Total of payments** is what you must repay the lender. Add your cost, or finance charge, to the amount you borrow, to find the total amount.

| Annual Percentage Rate | Finance Charge | Amount Financed | Total of Payments |
|---|---|---|---|
| The cost of your credit as a yearly rate. | The dollar amount your loan will cost you. | The amount of credit provided to you or on your behalf. | The amount you will have paid after you have made all scheduled payments. |
| 10.16 | 73,855.17 | 77,600.00 | 151,455.17 |

**Amount financed** is the amount you are borrowing.

**Finance charge** is the cost of borrowing. For most loans, it includes all the interest, fees, service charges, points, credit-related insurance premiums, and any other charges.

|  | 3 YEAR | 4 YEAR | 5 YEAR |
|---|---|---|---|
| Number of monthly payments | 36 | 48 | 60 |
| Amount of each payment | $451.62 | $358.82 | $303.72 |
| Total repaid | $16,258.32 | $17,223.36 | $18,223.20 |
| **Total interest paid** | **$2,758.32** | **$3,723.36** | **$4,723.20** |

# How Repayment Works

You may write a check for the same amount each time, but the payment always covers a different proportion of principal and interest.

From the first check you write to repay a loan, a certain amount goes to pay the interest, and the rest goes to repay the money you borrowed, or the **principal**.

The chart below shows how a $100,000 mortgage loan is **amortized**, or paid off, over the life of a 30-year loan with a 7% interest rate. Notice how you gradually shift from paying mostly interest in the early years to paying mostly principal in the later years. That's because lenders **front-load** their interest charges to guarantee their profit. In other words, instead of spreading the interest evenly over the life of the loan, they collect most of the interest first.

While most other installment loans have much shorter terms than that of a mortgage, the repayment process is similar.

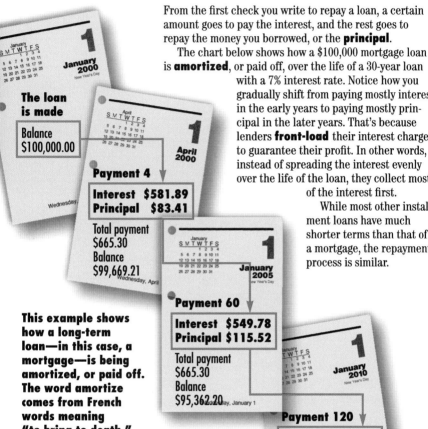

**The loan is made**

Balance
$100,000.00

**Payment 4**

Interest $581.89
Principal $83.41

Total payment
$665.30
Balance
$99,669.21

**Payment 60**

Interest $549.78
Principal $115.52

Total payment
$665.30
Balance
$95,362.20

**This example shows how a long-term loan—in this case, a mortgage—is being amortized, or paid off. The word amortize comes from French words meaning "to bring to death."**

**Payment 120**

Interest $501.53
Principal $163.77

Total payment
$665.30
Balance
$85,812.78

**Payment 180**

Interest $433.14
Principal $232.16

Total payment
$665.30
Balance
$75,311.10

### FINDING A LENDER

Finding a lender isn't like looking for a needle in a haystack, at least not most of the time. There are many potential loan sources, and they're usually willing—and sometimes eager—to do business. But knowing the advantages and disadvantages of different types of lenders can simplify your search and sometimes save you money. The chart to the right provides a quick overview of the most common lenders, the types of loans they make and some information that may help you decide where to look first.

### ASSESSING RISK

What you want is the money you need at the best—meaning the lowest—cost you can find. What lenders want is a profit, which depends on your repaying on schedule. Their willingness to lend depends on whether they consider you a good risk.

Among the things they look at are your income, your job history and your net worth (see page 90).

The catch, of course, is that if you have never borrowed and repaid, you have no credit history for a potential lender to use in evaluating your application. That can make first loans harder to get. One solution may be to build a solid record by using your credit card regularly and paying the bills promptly.

# CREDIT

| LENDERS | Types of loans | Advantages | Limitations |
|---|---|---|---|
| **Commercial Banks** | Home improvement, education, personal, auto, mobile home | ● Widely available locations and funds<br>● Preferred rates for bank customers | ● Require good credit rating<br>● Higher rates than some other sources |
| **Savings & Loans** | Home improvement, education, personal, auto, mobile home | ● Loans often cost less than at commercial banks | ● Require good credit rating<br>● Exist in only some states |
| **Savings Banks** | Home improvement, personal | ● Some loans cost less than at commercial banks | ● Require good credit rating<br>● Exist in only some states |
| **Credit Unions** | Home improvement, education, personal, auto, mobile home | ● Can be easy to arrange for members in good standing<br>● Lowest rates | ● Membership required in organization or group |
| **Sales Financing Companies** | Auto, appliance (major), boat, mobile home | ● Can be easy to arrange<br>● Good terms during special promotions | ● High rates<br>● Since loan is secured, defaulting can mean loss of item and payments already made |
| **Small Loan Companies** (Personal Finance Companies) | Auto, personal | ● Can be easy to arrange<br>● Good credit rating not required | ● High rates<br>● Cosigner often required |
| **Insurance Companies** | General purpose | ● May be able to borrow up to 95% of policy's surrender value | ● Outstanding loan plus interest reduce payment to survivors<br>● Policy ownership is required |
| **Brokerage Firms** | Margin account general purpose loans, using investments as security | ● Can be easy to arrange, with little delay in getting money<br>● Low rates (but subject to change)<br>● Flexible repayment | ● Changing value of investments may require payment of additional security<br>● Margin requirements may change |

January 2020
New Year's Day

**Payment 240**

**Interest $336.18**
**Principal $329.12**

Total payment
$665.30
Balance
$60,803.53

Wednesday, January 1

January 2025
New Year's Day

**Payment 300**

**Interest $198.73**
**Principal $466.57**

Total payment
$665.30
Balance
$38,565.16

Wednesday, January 1

January 2030
New Year's Day

**Final Payment (360)**

**Interest $3.88**
**Principal $661.42**

Total payment
$665.30
Balance
$00.00

Wednesday, January 1

# Loan vs. Lease

## When you choose a car, you also choose how to pay for it.

If you don't have the cash on hand to buy a new car outright—and many people don't—you can consider taking a loan or leasing the car to spread the payments over time. Whether you borrow the money or borrow the car, you'll have to apply for credit and have the application approved.

With a **loan**, a bank or other lender advances you the money to pay for the car, and you repay the principal plus interest in monthly installments, usually over a period of three to five years. The car is your collateral. If you don't keep up your payments, the lender can **repossess**, or take back, the car and keep all the payments you've made.

With a **lease**, you never really buy the car. Instead you make regular monthly payments for the lease period, usually three to five years, which gives you the right to use the car. When the lease ends, you can return the car, buy it back from the leasing company for the price specified in your agreement, or sometimes extend the lease a month at a time.

There's a summary of the basic differences in the chart to the right. You should always read any loan or lease agreement carefully before you sign to be sure you understand the specific details.

### SPECIAL DEALS FROM DEALERS

Car companies periodically offer very low financing rates to promote sales—sometimes as low as 2% or 3%. Provided there are no strings attached—read the agreement carefully—these loans can be very good deals. **Zero percent financing** means you can pay for the car over time without paying any interest, but check carefully for other charges.

## LOAN FEATURES

You can pay off the loan at any time, giving you full ownership, and the right to sell your car.

You can put as many miles on the car as you want.

You are responsible for maintenance, but can get the car serviced wherever you like and keep whatever records you like.

You arrange for insurance. Usually the rates drop as the car gets older.

If the car is stolen or totaled, you settle with the insurance company, but still must pay the full loan amount.

Conventional wisdom says that major repair costs don't occur within the first three years—but you may be saddled with expenses if you keep the car longer.

## THE WIGGLY BOTTOM LINE

Deciding whether to pay cash, take a loan or sign a lease depends on a number of personal as well as economic factors. You can use the following worksheet to make a rough estimate of the costs. The hypothetical example here is based on a car with a sticker price of $18,000, a three-year lease or loan, a local sales tax of 7%, an 8% return on investment and a 10% loan rate.

### LOAN

|   | | |
|---|---:|---|
|   | $ 2,500 | Down payment |
| + | $ 1,260 | Sales tax |
| + | $ 20,126 | Monthly payment ($559 x 36) |
| = | **$23,886** | **Total cost minus potential resale value** |

## LEASE FEATURES

You must pay the full lease amount, or arrange to end it early at added expense. However, if you trade your leased car for a new one with the same dealer, you may be able to avoid that charge.

There are mileage limits—often 12,000 to 15,000 a year. If you exceed the limits, you pay a mileage charge, usually 15 cents to 20 cents for each additional mile.

You are responsible for maintenance. Dealers may have special plans or may provide some services free as part of the lease. You may be required to use an authorized dealer for service, and you must keep records to show that required service was done on time.

You arrange for insurance, but the leasing company may impose conditions.

If the car is stolen or totaled, you must pay the leasing company its cash value, plus any past due payments or charges.

You turn in the car at the end of three or four years. Repairs after that become the dealer's—or the next owner's—problem.

### JUST PAY CASH?

If you have enough money to buy the car, should you lease or take a loan anyway? That depends. If you pay cash, you'll lose the investment interest on the amount you spend. That could be substantial if interest rates are high, or your investment is paying a good return.

But the interest you'll pay on the loan will drive up the real cost of the car. For example, if you took a three-year loan for $13,500 at 12.5% interest to buy a car, the actual cost would be more than $16,000. The same loan paid back over five years would increase the cost to more than $18,000 (see page 45).

With a lease, you don't own the car, so there's no resale value as there is with a car you buy. And there's never a period when you've paid off what you owe but still have a car to drive. That can make leasing the most expensive option.

### THE APPEAL OF LEASING

Leasing's greatest financial appeal is low initial costs. Usually you pay a leasing fee of $500 or less, depending on the car, one month's payment and one month as a security deposit. If you're turning in a car from a previous lease, you may be able to avoid those charges entirely. And there's no up-front sales tax. You pay some tax with each payment.

The downside is that you'll no doubt end up paying more for the car if you decide to buy it when the lease ends than you would have if you'd paid in cash up front.

### CARS ONLINE

You can now research and buy or lease cars on the Internet. Some sites are comprehensive and offer new, used, and pre-owned cars, as well as car repair and accessories, such as stereo equipment. You can also set up a payment plan with a site's rate calculator and choose among a variety of lease and loan terms.

**LEASE**

| | | |
|---|---|---|
| $ | 400 | Leasing fee |
| + $ | 317 | Prepayment |
| + $ | 11,412 | Monthly payment ($317 x 36) |
| = **$12,129** | | **Total cost** |

**CASH**

| | | |
|---|---|---|
| $ | 18,000 | Purchase price |
| + $ | 1,260 | Sales tax |
| = **$19,269** | | **Total cost minus potential resale value** |

Leases

# Credit Histories

Your credit history—and other people's—are being written and rewritten all the time.

There's a staggering amount of information available about the way you and other people use credit. It's also constantly changing. As new reports are created, updated data is fed into existing reports and details are circulated to new and existing creditors. In fact, collecting and reporting credit histories is a $1 billion industry that maintains records on more than 180 million people and supports about 800 local and regional offices.

## CONSUMER CREDIT INFORMATION

Retailers, credit card companies and most other grantors of credit provide information on payment habits to the credit bureaus—roughly two billion items of information a month.

## WHAT CREDITORS MUST TELL YOU

Anyone who turns you down for credit must do the following:

**1** Send you a written rejection within 30 days of the decision.

**2** State in writing the specific reasons for rejection, or at least tell you that you can learn the reasons if you request them in writing.

**3** List the name and address of any credit bureau that issued a report.

**4** Tell you if information from another source was used, and that you have the right to learn about that information if you request it in writing.

## HOW IT WORKS

Three national credit bureaus—Equifax, Experian and TransUnion—collect and collate credit, insurance and medical information and make it available for a fee to retailers, banks, insurers, potential employers and other organizations who are subscribers and have been approved as recipients. In some cases, information becomes part of a database that's reused, and in others it's reported only once and discarded.

You can ask for a copy of your credit history at any time. You'll have to send a written request with a check or money order if required. Include your Social Security number, present and past addresses, date of birth, and other names you've used.

While credit report information is constantly updated, old details sometimes disappear slowly. Some states impose time limits on how long information can remain on record.

## PUBLIC RECORDS

Public records on any bankruptcies, foreclosures, tax liens and court judgments can be gathered by the credit bureaus.

CLERK'S OFFICE

## YOUR CREDIT HISTORY

The bureaus provide summaries of the information they have collected when it is requested by creditors, employers and others. The recipients use the information to make decisions on granting credit, approving loans, providing insurance or hiring job applicants.

CREDIT REPORT

## JUST THE FACTS

The credit bureaus don't evaluate the data they collect and report. Individual creditors or potential employers decide whether you meet their standards, based on their own criteria and the way in which they interpret your records. For example, you may have to receive a certain credit score, based on a point system they devise.

Some kinds of information are not part of your file, including your income. Payments such as rent, utilities, or medical and dental bills aren't reported either.

Sure to be included are bank card, charge card, and often mortgage payment records. Credit experts say that's why it's important to make at least the minimum payment each month on all your outstanding credit accounts.

## HOW TO ORDER A REPORT

Check with the national bureaus or their local affiliates by telephone to find out how to get the information they have about you and what a report will cost. You can reach Equifax at 800-685-1111, Experian at 800-422-4879, and TransUnion at 800-888-4213, or on the Internet at equifax.com, experian.com, and tuc.com. There's usually a small fee unless you're following up on being refused credit. Then you're entitled to a free copy if you ask within 30 days.

A group of tailors formed the first known credit bureau in London in 1803. Members of The Mutual Communication Society of London exchanged information on bad credit risks. The first U.S. credit bureau was started in Brooklyn, New York, in 1869.

# Reading a Credit Report

Credit reporting companies explain how to decipher the information they send you.

Credit reporting companies are sensitive to the public's concerns about invasions of privacy and to the laws governing credit reporting. While you probably won't feel good about the extent of the information in your credit history, at least you should be able to understand it.

Your **accounts** are listed. Those at the top, if they have dashes before and after the identifying number, may have a negative effect on your credit history.

**Type and terms** describe the account as revolving credit or an installment loan.

**Prepared for**
**Jane Q. Consumer**

## experian

### Personal Credit Report

**Credit information about you**

| Source/Account number (except last few digits) | Date opened/Reported since | Date of status/Last reported | Type/Terms/Monthly payment | Responsibility |
|---|---|---|---|---|
| --1-- **UCS/UNIVERSAL CRD SERVIC** PO BOX 44167 JACKSONVILLE FL 32231 4784709000000... | 1-1991/ 7-1994 | 7-1999/ 7-1999 | Revolving/ NA/ $0 | Joint with John Q. Public |
| 2 **SAKS FIFTH AVENUE** 466709000000... | | | | |
| 3 **UCS/UNIVERSAL CRD SERV** PO BOX 44167 JACKSONVILLE FL 32231 539609000000... | | | | |

**Your use of credit**

The information listed below provides **additional** detail about balance history and your credit limit, high balance or original loan. Experian, so some of your accounts may not appear. Also, som more than once in the same month.

Source/Account number
--1-- **UCS/UNIVERSAL CRD SERVIC**
4784709000000...

Between 10-1997 and 5-1999, your credit limit/high balance was $11,500

## REPORTING ERRORS

While credit reporting bureaus provide a valuable service in a society where credit is a way of life, errors do occur in the vast amount of information they process, creating huge headaches for consumers. But if you check your report, you can take steps toward having any problems resolved.

### COMMON ERRORS ON CREDIT REPORTS

- **Confusing you with someone else with the same name or a similar Social Security number**
- **Including incorrect information**
- **Failing to incorporate comments or changes based on information you or your creditors supply**
- **Failing to remove damaging information after the issue has been resolved**

## WHO IS ASKING?

Your credit report also contains the names of the retailers and other creditors who have requested information about you in the previous 24 months. It may seem unfair that the more requests there are, the greater the possibility that a creditor will turn you down. But it can happen, presumably because a potential creditor might decide you're overextended, or that other creditors have already rejected your application. However, routine requests for updates and other informational requests aren't reported to anyone but you.

**Credit limit** is the largest outstanding balance you can have on the account. **High balance** is the most you've ever owed.

**Recent balance** is the amount due, as of the date of your most recent statement.

**Comments** describe the current status of your account, including the creditor's summary of past due information and any legal steps that may have been taken to collect. For example, this account is 30 days past due.

Any information or explanation you provide should be in this section as well.

Negative information may remain on your report for seven years, or sometimes more.

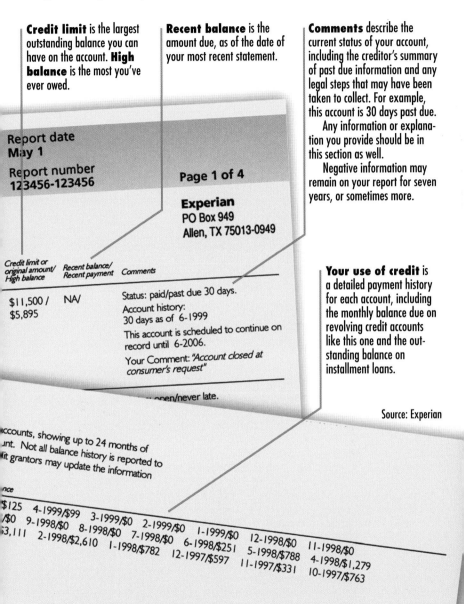

Report date
**May 1**
Report number
**123456-123456**

Page 1 of 4

**Experian**
PO Box 949
Allen, TX 75013-0949

| Credit limit or original amount/ High balance | Recent balance/ Recent payment | Comments |
|---|---|---|
| $11,500 / $5,895 | NA/ | Status: paid/past due 30 days. Account history: 30 days as of 6-1999 This account is scheduled to continue on record until 6-2006. Your Comment: *"Account closed at consumer's request"* |

...open/never late.

...ccounts, showing up to 24 months of ...unt. Not all balance history is reported to ...it grantors may update the information

...nce

| $125 | 4-1999/$99 | 3-1999/$0 | 2-1999/$0 | 1-1999/$0 | 12-1998/$0 | 11-1998/$0 |
| /$0 | 9-1998/$0 | 8-1998/$0 | 7-1998/$0 | 6-1998/$251 | 5-1998/$788 | 4-1998/$1,279 |
| $3,111 | 2-1998/$2,610 | 1-1998/$782 | 12-1997/$597 | 11-1997/$331 | 10-1997/$763 | |

**Your use of credit** is a detailed payment history for each account, including the monthly balance due on revolving credit accounts like this one and the outstanding balance on installment loans.

Source: Experian

## CORRECTING ERRORS

If you find an error in your credit report, you should notify the credit bureau that issued it. Some bureaus provide correction forms with their reports. You must also notify the creditor and request that the information be corrected. The Fair Credit Reporting and Fair Credit Billing Acts say that creditors must respond to your challenge, but do not force them to change a report. For example, you may have refused to pay for a damaged product, but the store can maintain that you simply didn't pay. Check your report again after 90 days. If the mistake is still there, you have the right to make a 100-word consumer comment that must be sent out with future reports.

# Coping with Debt

### If you're awash in red ink and can't pay your bills, you need to act to rebuild your credit.

Job loss, divorce, serious illness or poor financial management can threaten your economic security and your ability to pay your bills. And while you may be able to juggle creditors for a time, sooner or later you're apt to find yourself in dire straits. But if you have problems with debt, you're not alone. There are a number of workable ways to resolve the problem, often known as restructuring debt.

You can ask your **creditors** to rewrite your loans to extend the time you have to pay and to change the payments so that you can afford to make them. The extensions will increase your overall cost, because the creditors will charge you interest over a longer period.

**Non-profit credit counselors** are available in virtually every city. For modest fees, counselors go through your debts, analyze your income and help you work out ways to handle your debts.

**Loan consolidators** are private businesses that lend you money to pay off all your debts. You then owe only one creditor—them.

The good news is that you pay only one check a month, you can repay over a long term and you can make low monthly payments. The bad news is that the interest they charge may be very high, and you may be hit with stiff fees for paying off the loan ahead of schedule.

## PREVENTING DEBT

Credit cards can be lifesavers, most users agree. But many people who find themselves at sea financially are threatened by short-term debt, often credit card debt. According to the Federal Reserve Board, consumers on average owe more than 20% of their income, not counting what they owe in mortgages and home equity loans.

Continuing to charge can help to pull you under if you're in debt, since the interest you pay on your outstanding balances is usually higher than on most loans. Credit counselors often suggest getting rid of your credit cards, which forces you to limit what you spend. Even if you hang onto one card for emergency use, you'll find that it's probably smarter to pay mostly in cash.

## TIME TO REPAY

It takes time to repay accumulated debts, especially if you postpone confronting the problem. The National Foundation for Consumer Credit estimates that three to four years is typical for the people who come to their offices. Some other credit counselors suggest that if it's going to take you five years or more to repay, bankruptcy might be a wiser alternative.

## PAYING THE CONSEQUENCES

**Some of the consequences of failing to repay your debts:**

- You could be assigned a bad credit rating and be unable to borrow again
- Your wages may be garnished: A court may order your employer to pay up to 10% of your salary each pay period to people you owe
- Lenders may sell property you put up as security
- You could be sued and, if you lose, required to pay the legal costs of your creditors as well

## HOW BANKRUPTCY WORKS

Bankruptcy is the solution of last resort—a harsh but legal remedy for staving off financial disaster.

In general, bankruptcy is a three-step process.

**1** You file a petition in federal or state court saying you're **insolvent**, which means you have no assets to pay your debts.

**2** You work out a repayment plan with your creditors and the court.

**3** You **discharge**, or settle, your debts, usually for less than their full amount, so that your creditors receive at least some money.

## HERE ARE SOME ISSUES TO WEIGH WHEN CONSIDERING BANKRUPTCY:

### PROS

- **Provides legal protection from creditors**
- **Staves off financial ruin**
- **Resolves most debts**
- **Prevents loss of your home**
- **Provides chance to start again**
- **Protects you against IRS seizing property for back taxes**

### CONS

- **Loss of privacy**
- **Serious harm to credit history**
- **Some debts remain outstanding**
- **Involvement with courts**
- **Loss of assets**

## TYPES OF BANKRUPTCY

It's always smart to consult a lawyer before filing for bankruptcy, and in some cases it's required. There are two standard ways for individuals to file for bankruptcy, each named for the section of the legal code that governs it.

**Chapter 7, or "straight bankruptcy" (lawyer advisable).** You ask to be released of all your debts after selling all your assets to pay creditors. Some assets, like your home, are exempt from sale. Some debts, like taxes, fines, alimony and student loans must still be paid. You can file for straight bankruptcy only once within a six-year period, and you should work with an attorney to do it.

A lawyer is required if you want to file for **Chapter 13 bankruptcy**. The purpose of Chapter 13 is to allow people to retain their property and to avoid the stigma usually associated with the term bankruptcy.

A court approves a plan to pay out creditors over three to five years using your wages. Payment is not necessarily in full. The plan is supervised by a court-appointed person, called a **trustee**. Some income, like child support, is excluded from the payment plan.

There are people who may call themselves **credit doctors**, and claim they can resurrect your credit. But be very careful, since they are not only expensive but are often involved in fraudulent schemes. One tip-off is someone who offers to fix your credit report for you but doesn't suggest a major change in spending habits.

# The Roof over Your Head

Seeking shelter may be an instinct, but paying for it is a long-term financial commitment.

Owning a home where you're comfortable and happy probably ranks high on your list of financial goals. But if your experience is like most people's, paying for housing and its related costs will cost you more than anything else in your budget.

In the U.S., people spend about **32%** of their incomes on housing and related costs, according to the Bureau of the Census.

## FOR SALE

### BUYING: THE ADVANTAGES

- You build equity in property, which you may be able to sell at a profit
- You can deduct mortgage interest and property taxes on your tax return
- You may be able to exclude capital gains on the sale of your home when you file your tax return
- You are protected against rent increases (though not against property tax or insurance increases)
- You often get more living space for less money
- You can borrow against your equity in the home

## CHANGING PRICES

The cost of buying is reflected in the median price of a home. The median is the point at which half the homes cost less and half cost more. While housing prices rise steadily—as they did in the 1990s—people often think of their homes as the smartest investment they can make. But increases can slow, and experts caution that you shouldn't plan on reaping big profits when you sell. The median home price in the U.S. fluctuates monthly and varies noticeably in different parts of the country.

## STYLES OF OWNERSHIP

|        | You own | Your rights |
|--------|---------|-------------|
| **House** | The building and the land on which it's built | You can rent or sell as you choose |
| **Condo** | Your own private living space (the association owns the building and land) | You can rent or sell as you choose |
| **Co-op** | Shares in a corporation that owns the building and usually the land, which entitle you to live in an apartment | You can choose a buyer, subject to board approval<br><br>Renting may be prohibited |

## BUY OR RENT?

There's no simple way to decide whether it's smarter to rent or buy, assuming you have enough money to have a choice. It's always a combination of financial and personal priorities.

Before you buy—as 67% of Americans do sooner or later—you'll want to balance the costs of owning—the down payment, mortgage interest, property taxes, insurance and upkeep—against the advantages of growing equity, potential tax deductions and the additional space that owning may provide.

You may also want to consider the added responsibility that can come with a home, how long you're likely to live in one place and the earning potential of the down payment if you invested differently.

**67% of all Americans own, rather than rent, their homes, a percentage that has increased slightly during the last few years.**

## FOR RENT

### RENTING: THE ADVANTAGES

- You don't need a large amount of cash for a down payment, and you may be able to invest your money more profitably
- You don't have to find a buyer if you want to move
- You aren't responsible for repairs and maintenance
- Heat and some utilities and services are often included
- Some rents are controlled, which can hold down your living expenses
- You don't risk losing money if housing prices fall when you're ready to sell

## What you pay for

- Real estate taxes based on assessed value of house and land
- All maintenance, repairs, and renovations
- Mortgage and insurance on the property

- Real estate taxes based on assessed value of your individual condo unit
- Monthly maintenance charge for upkeep and real estate taxes on overall condo property
- Mortgage and insurance on your unit

- Monthly maintenance charge (for real estate taxes, mortgage on the building, fuel, insurance, operating costs) based on number of shares held
- Repairs paid by co-op and passed along to shareholders
- Payment of loan used to finance purchase of shares, the equivalent of a mortgage

## FAMILY HELP

If your parents or grandparents want to help you buy a home, each of them can give you up to $10,000 tax-free to help build your down payment reserves. Gifts larger than that are taxable for the giver.

If you borrow from a family member and don't pay interest on the loan, the lender will usually have to pay tax on imputed interest, or the interest that you would have paid for a loan that size. Check with your lawyer or tax advisor to be sure you handle gifts and loans correctly.

# Can You Buy?

Whether you can afford to buy depends on your income and your debts.

When you're thinking about buying a home, you have to take a hard look at your finances. The first question is whether you have enough cash for a **down payment**, usually 10% to 20% of the purchase price. The next is whether you'll be able to borrow the rest of what you need.

## HOW YOU QUALIFY TO BORROW

Being able to find a mortgage depends on passing two qualifying tests: Do you have enough regular income? How much do you owe on other debts?

## Do you have enough regular income?

**Lenders usually require that you spend no more than 28% of your gross income on your mortgage, taxes and insurance.**

### QUALIFYING TEST 1

Lenders fear that if too much of your income is committed to housing, you face a greater risk of not making your mortgage payments on time.

### for example

| | |
|---|---|
| Total monthly pretax income | $ 7,000 |
| Qualifying percentage | x .28 |
| Monthly amount you can pay for housing | = $ 1,960 |

Some lenders will let you spend a larger percentage of your income on housing if you make a larger down payment. With 20% down, it may be as much as 32%.

## CONTRIBUTING FACTORS

The type of home you can afford to buy is directly influenced by the interest rate you'll be paying on your mortgage. For example, if rates are low and you're paying 6%, you could borrow $200,000 for 30 years and repay $1,199 a month. But if rates were 10%, it would cost almost that much each month—$1,097—to borrow $125,000 for 30 years.

To find out how much you'll be able to borrow at current interest rates, you can use a loan and mortgage handbook or payment table. They're available in most bookstores, at your library and online. They list the monthly mortgage payments for different loan amounts at various rates over a number of different terms.

## WHAT YOU CAN AFFORD

The following table shows the monthly payments you can expect to make on a 30-year, fixed-rate mortgage. (Insurance and property taxes would add to this cost.)

## PAYING THE BILLS

Paying your mortgage isn't the only financial responsibility that's involved with owning your own home. Among the added expenses you may initially overlook—but will almost certainly encounter—are the costs of:

**Insurance.** You'll need enough homeowners insurance to cover the mortgage amount. The insurance company may insist that your coverage equal the home's full replacement value.

**Property taxes.** Local school and property taxes vary enormously from place to place. Check before you buy.

**Commuting.** Communities with convenient transportation usually cost more to live in, but can save you time and money in commuting.

**Schools.** Paying more for a home in an area with good public schools may be cheaper in the long run than paying for private school—especially if you have several children. And houses in strong school districts often sell more easily.

**Maintenance charges.** Condominium and co-op charges for monthly expenses can escalate rapidly, so you should anticipate those costs in your purchase decision.

# How much do you owe on other debts?

**You can still be turned down if your mortgage expenses and other regular debt payments are more than 36% of your total income.**

## QUALIFYING TEST 2

Lenders want to make sure that you can keep up all your regular monthly payments—such as insurance and loan repayments—in addition to the mortgage. So they evaluate all your obligations:

### for example

| | |
|---|---|
| Total monthly pretax income | $ 7,000 |
| Qualifying percentage | x .36 |
| Monthly amount of acceptable debt | = $ 2,520 |

If you have exceptionally large monthly expenses, such as high credit card interest or other outstanding debts, you may be turned down for a mortgage.

## OTHER ROUTES TO OWNERSHIP

If the down payment and income requirements make owning a home seem out of the question, you may want to look for other ways to buy. Some government-backed programs that make qualifying for a mortgage easier are described on page 63. You may also want to check:

- **Rent-to-buy option.** You can sometimes arrange with an individual owner or developer to rent a home that's for sale, with your monthly payments counting toward the purchase price when you are able to buy

- **Gifts.** The Federal Housing Administration (FHA) has introduced a variation on the traditional bridal registry, to encourage a couple's family and friends to put money aside for a down payment on a home bought with an FHA mortgage. It may not be a perfect solution, but it can be a good start toward eventual ownership

- **Auctions.** Home auctions, often designed to move property that hasn't sold or has been taken over by a lender, often mean you can get a good price. If your bid is accepted, you may need to make a substantial down payment on the spot

| Home price | Down payment | Mortgage loan | Monthly payment (including interest) | | |
|---|---|---|---|---|---|
| | | | 6% | 8% | 10% |
| $80,000 | $8,000 | $72,000 | $432 | $528 | $632 |
| $140,000 | $15,000 | $125,000 | $749 | $917 | $1,097 |
| $240,000 | $40,000 | $200,000 | $1,199 | $1,468 | $1,755 |

# Buying a House

When you find the home you want, you enter a paperwork maze.

Finding a new home can be as close a few clicks away, as you search for homes on the Internet using a variety of websites.

You can check classified listings, find out home and neighborhood values, use a site's finance and mortgage calculators, learn about loans, and read articles about buying a home. You can even find local real estate agents and information about child care and schools.

Once you have identified the home you want, you'll find yourself following a long-standing ritual that takes you from initial offer to deposit. You can do all of your research on the Internet, but the forms must be signed on paper, so the clearer you are about what's ahead, the easier your home buying process should be.

## CONDUCTING A SEARCH

Most buyers contact a real estate agency when they're looking for a home, in part because most sellers put their property on the market that way. You may work either with a **broker**, who is licensed to operate a real estate company and collect a fee for arranging a sale, or with a licensed **agent** who works for the broker. (A Realtor is a broker who belongs to

the National Association of Realtors, nar.realtor.com, a trade organization.)

Working with a broker or agent can simplify your search because they know what's available in your price range. They'll show you a range of properties and give you a sense of what different communities are like. Most experts agree that location—specifically a desirable neighborhood—is one of the most important factors in choosing a home. They argue that you can always make individual home improvements, but it's hard to change a community.

## CHOOSING A BROKER

Traditionally brokers and agents represent the seller and are paid a commission based on the selling price of the home, although in fact they spend most of their time advising buyers. Legally, they're required to reveal any existing problems, but their incentive is to get the best possible price for the property.

Some shoppers choose a **buyer's agent** instead, expecting to see more homes, get better information and have an advocate who will press for concessions.

# The Steps to Buying

Buying a home can be a speedy process, or it can involve lengthy negotiations. But while every buyer's experience seems unique, the path to ownership is reassuringly consistent across the country.

## 1. The Offer

When you finally decide to buy, you make a **bid** or price offer. If the bid is accepted, you pay a fee (called a binder, or earnest money) of about $1,000 to secure your offer. If the deal goes through, the binder amount counts toward the purchase price. If it doesn't, you get it back.

## 2. Inspection

You should arrange for a licensed building inspector to examine the property. If there are any serious problems, like cracks in the foundation, water damage, or a leaky roof, you may get a credit, lower your offer or withdraw it altogether.

## USING AN ATTORNEY

Most experts advise you to use an experienced real estate lawyer to review any contract you're considering and to handle the details of buying a home. There's always lots of paperwork involved, much of it in specialized language. You don't want to agree, unknowingly, to conditions that aren't in your favor. While you'll have to pay a fee, it's generally modest in comparison to the money you're spending on the property.

## POTENTIAL OBSTACLES

As you move through the buying process, you may trip over some unexpected obstacles:

- House inspections that reveal serious existing or potential problems
- Limited availability of mortgages or a sharp jump in interest rates
- Changing lending rules, like requiring more money down or greater income
- A lender appraisal that is less than the purchase price so you can't borrow enough money
- Temporary living space during renovations— or the time between leaving your old home and waiting to move into the new one

## 5. The Deposit

Signing the contract requires a cash deposit, often 10% of the purchase price. This amount is held in **escrow**, or reserve, and becomes part of your down payment. You get the deposit back if the deal falls through. (But some co-op sales contracts are non-contingent, which means you could lose the deposit if the deal doesn't go through.)

## 4. The Contract

This is the first legal document you and the seller sign. Contracts are standard, but are modified to reflect the details of your purchase—price, date of sale, items included in the sale (like appliances) and the conditions of the sale, such as **free and clear title**, which means no one else has any legal claim to the property. Contracts often are also contingent on your ability to arrange a mortgage.

## 3. Negotiating

Real estate agents sometimes agree to a reduced commission to close a sale that has gotten stalled over price. The chances of negotiating a reduction are better if the agent works for the broker that listed the property, so the commission won't have to be split.

Owners may also agree to a reduced price or to holding part of the mortgage, especially if they're eager to sell.

# Finding a Mortgage

If you look around, you can often get a good deal on a mortgage.

Finding a mortgage can be the most challenging part of buying a home, though you can often simplify the process by doing some research first.

Traditionally, buyers have found the home they wanted and then applied for a mortgage. But some experts suggest a smarter approach is to investigate your chances of qualifying first, by estimating the amount you have available to spend and what you can afford.

**THE AVERAGE MORTGAGE IS HELD FOR 7 YEARS BEFORE IT'S PAID OFF—USUALLY BECAUSE THE HOUSE IS SOLD.**

You can get a sense of mortgage availability and the current rates by watching the ads in local newspapers or by contacting HSH Associates, a New Jersey-based company that tracks mortgage rates nationwide and will sell you a printout of lenders and rates in your area. You can call 800-873-2837 or contact them on the Internet at www.hsh.com.

You can also telephone Consumer Reports Home Price Service. For a small fee you can get information on property prices and sales figures in your area. The number is 800-775-1212.

## PREQUALIFICATION

You may be able to save time, aggravation and money by investigating **prequalification** for a mortgage. That means a lender tells you not only whether you'll be approved to borrow, but also the size of the loan you could get.

With that information, you can tailor your search and make an offer to buy confident that you'll be able to close the deal. Prequalification may also give you added bargaining power with the seller if you can promise that there'll be no delays in closing the deal.

You may also be able to lock in a mortgage rate when you prequalify, so you know what you'll be spending each month. But you'll want to be sure that if the rates drop between the time of your agreement and the actual date of purchase that the lender will give you the lower rate.

## MORTGAGE STANDARDS

The national standard most lenders follow in deciding whether you qualify for a mortgage—the 28%-36% ratio—is set by Fannie Mae (www.fanniemae.com). Together with the Federal Home Loan Mortgage Corporation, or Freddie Mac, this quasi-public corporation buys mortgages from lenders for resale as investments in what is known as the **secondary market**. Since lenders use the money they get from these sales to make additional loans, most of them adhere strictly to the standards.

## WHO PROVIDES MORTGAGES?

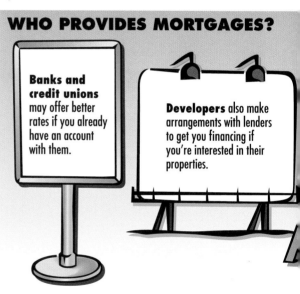

**Banks and credit unions** may offer better rates if you already have an account with them.

**Developers** also make arrangements with lenders to get you financing if you're interested in their properties.

The oldest recorded mortgages were in Egypt during the time of the Pharaohs, and mortgages of various kinds have been used throughout history. They took their modern form of paying principal and interest in the 1500s, but conventional mortgages as we know them today were first offered in the 1930s.

## MORTGAGE HELP

The Community Reinvestment Act (CRA) requires some local banks to lend to home buyers whose income is less than what's usually required to qualify for a mortgage. A number of programs let you borrow even if your down payment is only 3%, or sometimes less, of the purchase price. They include the Community Home Buyer's Program sponsored by Fannie Mae and two programs through Rural Development (www.rurdev.usda.gov).

To locate other mortgage sources in your community, you can contact the U.S. Department of Housing and Urban Development (HUD) at www.hud.gov.

In addition, many states provide mortgages at below-market rates for first-time buyers, provided that your income and the price of the home meet their guidelines. You should be able to find the number to call in the state government section of your telephone book.

It's easy to get frustrated with the red tape when you're trying to track down mortgage lenders, especially if you're investigating government-sponsored programs. But persistence can pay off.

## VA AND FHA MORTGAGES

**VA (Veterans Administration) mortgages** enable qualifying veterans to borrow up to $144,000, and sometimes more, with little or no down payment. For more information, call the VA's local toll-free number listed in your phone book.

**FHA (Federal Housing Administration) mortgages** let you borrow up to the maximum loan limit, which varies state-to-state, if the price plus closing costs are within their guidelines. Your income is not a factor, but in many parts of the country few houses qualify. You can get information from lenders or directly from the FHA (www.fhatoday.com).

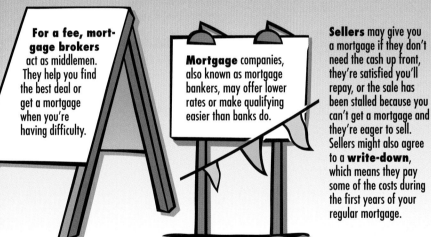

Virtually all financial service companies, including brokerage firms, have entered the mortgage market.

**For a fee, mortgage brokers** act as middlemen. They help you find the best deal or get a mortgage when you're having difficulty.

**Mortgage** companies, also known as mortgage bankers, may offer lower rates or make qualifying easier than banks do.

**Sellers** may give you a mortgage if they don't need the cash up front, they're satisfied you'll repay, or the sale has been stalled because you can't get a mortgage and they're eager to sell. Sellers might also agree to a **write-down**, which means they pay some of the costs during the first years of your regular mortgage.

## NEWER MAY BE SIMPLER

Buying a newly built house is often simpler, since you deal directly with the builder, or a designated agent. Some of the advantages:

- There's usually less paperwork
- Surveys and title searches may be provided
- Interest rates may be lower
- If the builder is eager to sell, you can sometimes negotiate a **buy-down**, which means the builder will pay some of your initial mortgage costs

## ASSUMABLE MORTGAGES

**VA** and **FHA** mortgages can sometimes be **assumed by** (or passed on to) a buyer. This eliminates closing costs and often

preserves a low interest rate. However, the buyer needs enough of a down payment to cover the seller's equity, the percentage of the house the seller owns. And the seller may be liable for the loan if the buyer defaults. More recent loans are rarely assumable, but some older ones may be.

**Electronic mortgage information has revolutionized the mortgage business. The Internet lets you research lenders and their interest rates, get loan advice, and arrange a mortgage online.**

# Dealing with the Lender

**Most lenders require you to complete a mortgage application—a comprehensive financial statement.**

The information you provide on your application determines whether you qualify for a loan and how much you can borrow. The key numbers are:

- **Your regular income**
- **The value of what you own**
- **Your expenses and debts**

The application itself is fairly standard from lender to lender, usually because it meets Fannie Mae's requirements (see page 62).

## WHAT THE LENDER REQUIRES

As part of the application process, you'll need to pay for:

- A **survey**, or official surveyor's drawing, of the property and the buildings on it.

- An **application fee** and an **origination fee** to cover the costs of processing the application. This includes an appraisal of the house by the lender to make sure it's worth the mortgage loan. Plan to spend at least $250 to apply, plus 1% of the mortgage amount.

- If your down payment is less than 20%, the lender may require **private mortgage insurance (PMI)** to guarantee payment if you default on the loan.

## THE COMMITMENT LETTER

If your mortgage is approved, you'll receive a commitment letter spelling out how much you can borrow and how long the offer is good for. It may also state the interest rate, which you can **lock in**, or fix. Otherwise the rate is determined when the final loan documents are prepared.

## WHAT IF A LENDER TURNS YOU DOWN?

If one lender says no, try another one. All lenders use the same basic information, but they may evaluate it differently. Your real estate agent or a mortgage broker can help you find mortgage sources. You can also ask if the seller is willing to reduce the price or lend you a portion of the money required.

**Details of purchase** asks about how much you want to borrow, how much down payment, or cash part of the purchase price, you have, and where the rest of the money will come from. Borrowing a large amount from another source—even from your family—could disqualify you.

**Monthly income** is a key figure for lenders. It can include non-salary income, such as earnings on your investments or money you get from rentals, but you'll have to prove the income is regular. You can also count alimony or related payments to establish your eligibility.

**Job information** focuses on regular employment so you'll probably need verification from your employer. If you're self-employed, you often have to provide more information, including income tax returns, credit reports and profit and loss statements for your business.

**Monthly housing expenses** shows what you are spending now and what you expect to spend at the new house, including taxes, utilities and homeowners insurance.

**Your credit history asks:**

- If you've declared bankruptcy
- If there are any liens, or legal claims, against your salary or property
- If you have outstanding debts

**Net worth** is the total value of what you have, or your assets, minus what you owe, or your liabilities. Assets include cash, bank accounts, investments and property. Liabilities include debts and loans, credit cards, leases, alimony and child support. Mortgage loans usually require the numbers as well as the location of accounts, loans and credit cards.

## WHAT THE APPLICATION ASKS

A mortgage application is the lender's way of evaluating your credit-worthiness and determining whether to take the risk of lending you money. Although it can be an intimidating document, you'll be ahead of the game if you keep good financial records. You'll especially want a complete list of your investments, including money in your retirement plans, for a picture of your net worth.

Many experts suggest you can strengthen your application by having channelled at least part of what you're saving to buy a home into a portfolio of investments—including stocks, bonds and mutual funds. That approach can have the double advantage of boosting your net worth, while helping you to build your down payment amount.

Remember, however, that investment portfolios fluctuate in value. If market prices have dropped when you need money for your down payment, you may risk having less than you need.

# Surviving the Closing

You'll write many checks, sign your name countless times, and sift through mounds of paper—but in the end, you'll walk away with the keys to your new home.

At the **closing**, or **settlement**, you and the seller, the lender, all the attorneys, a representative of the title company, the real estate agent and assorted others meet to sign the papers and pay the costs that legally complete a real estate deal.

To help prepare you for this ritual, the lender will provide a good faith written estimate of the closing or settlement costs you can expect to pay— usually from 5% to 10% of the loan amount. You can also get a helpful government guide called "Settlement Costs" from your lender, or by calling the local HUD office.

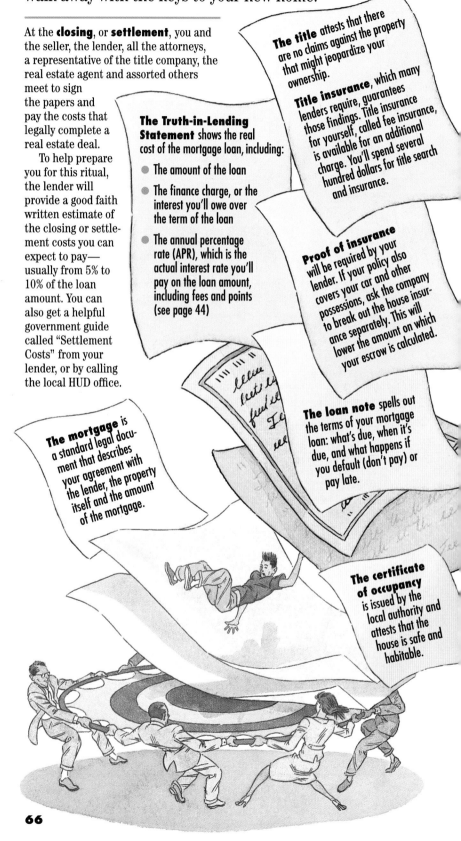

**The title** attests that there are no claims against the property that might jeopardize your ownership.

**Title insurance**, which many lenders require, guarantees those findings. Title insurance for yourself, called fee insurance, is available for an additional charge. You'll spend several hundred dollars for title search and insurance.

**The Truth-in-Lending Statement** shows the real cost of the mortgage loan, including:

● The amount of the loan

● The finance charge, or the interest you'll owe over the term of the loan

● The annual percentage rate (APR), which is the actual interest rate you'll pay on the loan amount, including fees and points (see page 44)

**Proof of insurance** will be required by your lender. If your policy also covers your car and other possessions, ask the company to break out the house insurance separately. This will lower the amount on which your escrow is calculated.

**The loan note** spells out the terms of your mortgage loan: what's due, when it's due, and what happens if you default (don't pay) or pay late.

**The mortgage** is a standard legal document that describes your agreement with the lender, the property itself and the amount of the mortgage.

**The certificate of occupancy** is issued by the local authority and attests that the house is safe and habitable.

## THE CLOSING STATEMENT

Your lender will provide a closing statement that itemizes all the charges you'll have to pay at settlement. In most cases you receive it on the spot.

**Down payment balance** is the amount you still owe the seller in cash.

**Points** are up-front interest charges paid to the lender. A point is 1% of the mortgage amount, and paying two to three points is typical. The amount is either deducted from the mortgage loan, or you may write a separate check, which is preferable for tax purposes. Since points are fully deductible on an original purchase, you'll need to keep a record of the payment.

**Filing fee** and other fees required for recording the transfer of ownership are paid to local authorities.

**Mortgage tax** is paid to the state where the sale occurs. This amount is not tax deductible.

**Attorney's fees** for both your lawyer and the lender's are your expense. To save money, you can use the lender's lawyer or even represent yourself, but this is risky if there are any hitches. Lawyer's fees can be a flat fee or a percentage of the mortgage amount.

**Real estate taxes** are paid to the seller to cover your portion of taxes that have already been paid for the year.

### for example

If you bought a home on April 1, and the seller had paid school taxes in September and town taxes in January, you would pay:

| SCHOOL TAXES | 6 months or 6/12 of total |
|---|---|
| TOWN TAXES | 9 months or 9/12 of total |

**Escrow** is a kind of enforced savings paid into a reserve account with your lender. It covers your real estate taxes and home insurance when they come due. That's good for lenders, who want to protect their interest, but not good for you, since you must prepay these costs ahead of time. And most lenders pay little or no interest on your escrow account.

## HOW ESCROW WORKS

As this simplified chart illustrates, each month you pay $1/12$ of your annual tax and insurance bills along with your basic mortgage payment, plus the extra amount the lender requires be held in reserve. In this case, if the annual total were $3,600, you'd pay about $300 a month.

| Payments | Due date | Annual amount due | Amount paid at closing | Estimated monthly payment |
|---|---|---|---|---|
| County tax | January 1 | $300 | $0 | $25 |
| School tax | September 1 | $1,900 | $632 | $158 |
| Town tax | June 1 | $700 | $406 | $58 |
| Insurance premium | April 1 | $800 | $603 | $67 |

The escrow statement above assumes a closing date of January 1.

### ESCROW OVERCHARGES

The law says that at least one month a year your escrow account should hold no more than 1/6 of your total tax and insurance bills. For example, if that total is $3,600, there must be at least one month when your account has no more than $600. A good month to check is the one after your biggest payment is due.

Call the lender if you think you're paying too much escrow. If you can't resolve your differences, call your state's Attorney General.

### STOP PAYING ESCROW

You may be eligible to stop paying escrow if you've paid off 20% of your mortgage and have never been late with a payment. You may be able to avoid escrow altogether if you put down more than 20% of the purchase price and have an excellent credit history. If you have the discipline to put the money aside, you can generally invest it to produce a better return than you'll get from the lender.

# The Cost of a Mortgage

The cost of a mortgage depends on the amount you borrow, the interest you pay and how long you take to repay.

Since monthly payments spread the cost of a mortgage over a long period of time, it's easy to forget the total expense. For example, if you borrow $100,000 for 30 years at 8.5% interest, your total repayment will be around $277,000, more than two and a half times the original loan.

Minor differences in the interest rate—8.5% vs. 8%—can add up to a lot of money over 30 years. At 8% the total repaid would be $264,240, almost $13,000 less than at the 8.5% rate.

**TERM (LENGTH OF THE LOAN)**
The length of time you want to borrow the money. The longer the term, the lower the monthly payments, but the more you'll pay in the end.

**RATE**
The interest rate may be fixed for the length of the loan or adjusted periodically to reflect prevailing interest rates. Over time, a lower interest rate will have the greatest impact on overall cost.

**Bottom line:** Any of the factors will increase the overall cost, but a higher interest rate and longer term will have the greatest impact.

## LOAN AMOUNT (PRINCIPAL)

The amount you actually borrow after fees and points are deducted. It's the basis for figuring the real interest, or APR (annual percentage rate), on the money you're borrowing.

## + INTEREST

Interest or finance charge is what you pay to borrow the money. The amount, repaid along with part of the principal in regular installments, is determined by the interest rate and the term of the loan.

## + POINTS (PREPAID INTEREST)

Interest that you prepay at the closing. Each point is 1% of the loan amount. For example, on a $90,000 loan with three points, you'd prepay $2,700.

## + FEES

Fees include application fees, loan origination fees, and other initial costs imposed by the lender.

## = THE COST OF YOUR HOME

## CUTTING MORTGAGE EXPENSES

You can reduce your cost several ways.

**1** **Consider a shorter mortgage.**
With a shorter term, you'll pay less interest overall, and your monthly payments will be somewhat larger. A 15-year mortgage, as opposed to a 30-year mortgage for the same amount, can cut your costs by more than 55%. Some banks also offer 20-year mortgages, which reduce the overall interest cost without significantly raising monthly payments.

**2** **Consider amortizing, or paying off, the loan faster.** You can pay your mortgage bi-weekly instead of monthly, or you can make an additional payment each month.

● With **bi-weekly payments** you make 26 regular payments instead of 12 every year. The mortgage is paid off in a little more than half the time, and you pay a little more than half the interest

● You can make an **additional payment** each month, which reduces your principal. With a fixed-rate mortgage, you pay off the loan quicker, but regular monthly payments remain the same. With an ARM, interest is figured on a smaller principal each time the rate is adjusted, so your monthly payments could become lower

Be sure your lender knows that you want the extra payments credited toward the principal. Your mortgage bill should have a line for entering the additional amount, and you can send a separate check. When you pay extra, you can change the amount or stop at any time.

The catch to additional payments: You may come out ahead by investing your extra cash elsewhere. This is especially true in the last years of a fixed-rate loan, when you're paying off mostly principal so you probably can't reduce the interest cost by very much.

### THE EFFECT OF THE TERM ON A $100,000 MORTGAGE

| Term | Monthly amount at different interest rates | | | |
| --- | --- | --- | --- | --- |
| | 7.5% | 8.0% | 8.5% | 9% |
| 15-year | $927 | $956 | $985 | $1,014 |
| 30-year | $699 | $734 | $769 | $805 |

| Term | Total payment | | | |
| --- | --- | --- | --- | --- |
| | 7.5% | 8.0% | 8.5% | 9% |
| 15-year | $166,860 | $172,080 | $177,300 | $182,520 |
| 30-year | $251,690 | $264,240 | $276,840 | $289,800 |

### A POINT WELL TAKEN

Lenders might be willing to raise the rate by a fraction (say ⅛% or ¼%) and lower the number of points—or the reverse—as long as they make the same profit.

The advantages of fewer points are lower closing costs and laying out less money when you're apt to need it most. But if you plan to keep the house longer than five to seven years, paying more points to get a lower interest rate will reduce your long-term cost.

The following chart shows the effect of points and interest on a 30-year, $100,000 mortgage.

| | LOAN A | LOAN B |
| --- | --- | --- |
| Interest rate | 8.75% | 8.5% |
| Number of points | 1 | 2 |
| Cost of points | $1000 | $2000 |
| Year 1 total | $10,441 | $11,227 |
| Year 2 total | $19,881 | $20.454 |
| Year 3 total | $29,321 | $29,681 |
| Year 4 total | $38,762 | $38,908 |
| Year 5 total | $48,202 | $48,135 |
| Year 10 total | $95,405 | $94,270 |
| Year 30 total | $284,215 | $278,811 |

**Years 1–4:** Loan A (higher interest rate but fewer points) costs less.
**Year 5:** Loan B's lower interest rate compensates for the higher initial points, and begins to cost less. The longer you have the mortgage, the cheaper Loan B becomes compared to Loan A.

# Mortgage Rates

Mortgages can have either fixed or adjustable rates, or sometimes a hybrid of the two.

You can often choose the method that's used to figure interest on your mortgage. With a fixed-rate loan, the total interest you'll owe is determined at closing. With an adjustable loan, the rate you pay changes as the cost of borrowing changes.

## Fixed-Rate Mortgages

**Fixed-rate** or **conventional** mortgages have been around since the 1930s. The total interest and monthly payments are set at the closing. You repay the principal and interest in equal, usually monthly, installments over a 15-, 20- or 30-year period. You know right from the start what you'll pay and for how long.

In most cases, though, you can choose to pay your mortgage more quickly, which means you'll owe less interest. Or you can renegotiate the loan to get a lower rate.

### PLUSES

- You always know your housing costs, so you can plan your budget more easily
- Your mortgage won't increase if interest rates go up

### MINUSES

- Initial rates and closing costs are higher than for ARMs
- Your monthly payments may be larger than with ARMs
- You won't benefit if interest rates drop; you'll have to refinance to get the lower rates

## HYBRID MORTGAGES

Choosing between a fixed-rate or an adjustable-rate mortgage isn't an all-or-nothing proposition. In fact, there are hybrids that offer certain advantages of each type while softening some of their drawbacks.

Among the most popular are mortgages that offer an initial fixed rate for a specific period, usually five, seven or ten years, and then are adjusted. The adjustment may be a one-time change, to whatever the current rate is. More typically, it changes regularly over the balance of the loan term, usually once a year.

One appeal of the **multiyear mortgage**, as these hybrids are often called, is that the borrower can get a lower rate on the fixed-term portion of the mortgage than if the rate were set for the entire 30 years. That's because the lender isn't limited by a long-term agreement to a rate that may turn out to be unprofitable.

The lower rate also means it's easier to qualify for a mortgage, since the monthly payment will be lower. That's a real plus, especially if you're a first-time buyer.

For people who plan to move within a few years, especially if it's within the period during which they're paying the fixed rate, there's the added appeal of paying less now and not having to worry about what might happen when the adjustable period begins. In fact, the typical mortgage lasts only about seven years. Then the borrower moves or refinances and pays off the balance.

## TEASER RATES

The introductory rate you pay for the first months of an adjustable-rate mortgage is almost always lower than the actual cost of borrowing the money. What it means for the borrower is not only a few months of relief but also lower closing costs. The effect is to make mortgages more accessible to more people.

What it means for the lender is being able to adjust the rate upward within a few months while staying competitive with other lenders.

## TAKING PRECAUTIONS

Lenders are required to use 7% as the base rate for determining whether you qualify for a mortgage—even if they offer you a lower rate initially. The logic is you're less likely to default if interest rates rise.

# Adjustable-Rate Mortgages

**ARMs** were introduced in the 1980s to help more buyers qualify for mortgages, and to protect lenders by letting them pass along higher interest costs to borrowers.

## HOW ARMs WORK

An ARM has a variable interest rate: The rate changes on a regular schedule—such as once a year—to reflect fluctuations in the cost of borrowing. Unlike fixed-rate mortgages, the total cost can't be figured in advance, and monthly payments may rise or fall over the term of the loan.

Lenders determine the new rate using two measures:

- **The index**, which is often a published figure, like the rate on one-year U.S. Treasury securities or the cost-of-funds indexes. Be sure to check the index. Some fluctuate more—and change more rapidly—than others

- **The margin**, which is hundredths of a percentage point added to the index to determine the new rate

## CAPPED COSTS

All ARMs have **caps**, or limits, on the amount the interest rate can change. An **annual cap** limits the rate change each year (usually to two percentage points), while a **lifetime** cap limits the change over the life of the loan (typically to five or six points).

Be careful: Lifetime caps are often based on the actual cost and not on the introductory rate. For example, with a 6% teaser rate and an 8.5% actual interest cost, your rate could go as high as 14.5% with a six-point lifetime cap.

## PLUSES

- Low initial rates (sometimes called **teaser rates**) reduce your closing costs and early monthly payments

- Your interest rate will drop if interest rates go down

## MINUSES

- It's hard to budget housing costs, since monthly payments can change yearly

- Interest costs may jump after the teaser rate expires

- You may have to pay more interest if rates go up

## NEGATIVE AMORTIZATION

Negative amortization means you still owe money when the mortgage ends, because interest rates have gone higher than your cap.

Put simply, if interest rates rise 5% one year, but your annual cap is 1%, you owe the 4% difference. The additional interest is added to the amount of your loan. Eventually, the term may be extended, creating extra payments to cover the money you owe.

Not all ARMs allow negative amortization. If they do, the most they can accumulate is 125% of the original loan amount. Then some resolution must be arranged, such as a lump sum payment or loan extension.

# Refinancing

When interest rates go down, you may want to refinance your mortgage to get a lower rate.

Though some mortgages do turn out to be the lifetime commitment they seem to be when you're in the middle of a closing, you may choose to **refinance**, or arrange for a new mortgage at a lower rate or for a different term. With the new money you borrow, you pay off the original mortgage.

Because interest rates change constantly, what seems like a good rate at the time you buy may be much higher than typical rates just a few years later. Refinancing can bring your housing expenses more in line with what other people are paying.

Refinancing doesn't come cheaply, though. You often have to pay up-front fees and closing costs again even if your mortgage is only a few years old. That's especially true when you switch lenders.

## WHY REFINANCE?

You may want to refinance your mortgage for several reasons:

- You can get a lower interest rate, which will reduce your monthly payment and often the overall cost of the mortgage
- You may want to consolidate outstanding debt—for example, by combining a first and second mortgage into a single new one
- You may want to reduce the term of your loan. While this may increase your monthly payment, it will dramatically reduce your total cost

**The rule of thumb is that it pays to refinance if you can get an interest rate at least TWO PERCENTAGE POINTS lower than you're currently paying.**

But every situation is different. To figure out whether you can save money by refinancing you need to consider:

- How much lower your monthly payments will be
- What refinancing costs you must pay
- How long you plan to stay put
- How many years remain on your current mortgage

Your best bet is to tell the lender what you paid for the house, what you still owe and how much you're paying each month. Have the lender itemize all the expenses involved in the refinance and estimate your new payments. Then you can figure when you will break even.

For example, if you save $1,600 a year by refinancing, but it costs you $4,800 to do it, you'll have to stay put more than three years to realize any savings.

## OTHER CONSIDERATIONS

If you've been paying your present mortgage for a number of years, deciding whether or not to refinance is a little more complicated. That's because you may have paid off a substantial part of the interest you owe on the loan and have begun to chip away at the principal. When you refinance—which means you're taking a new loan—the bulk of your monthly payment goes once again toward interest.

A potential lender or real estate attorney should be able to help you compare the combined total interest you'd owe if you refinanced with the amount remaining on your existing mortgage.

## WEIGHING YOUR CHOICES

You can arrange refinancing to switch from one fixed-rate loan to one at a lower rate, from an adjustable-rate loan to a fixed-rate (something experts often advise), or from fixed to one of the hybrid adjustables, such as a 10-year fixed/20-year adjustable.

Refinancing moves in predictable patterns. A big drop in rates or the introduction of a new strain of loans provokes a flurry of activity, generally followed by a period of calm. Experts agree, however, that if you're paying between 7% and 8% on a fixed rate mortgage, rates aren't likely to drop low enough to make refinancing worthwhile.

## When Does It Pay to Refinance?

People who refinance their mortgages should be planning to stay in their homes at least long enough to recover the costs. This worksheet can help estimate how long it will take before refinancing begins paying off. (The example shows the estimated payback period for refinancing a $100,000 mortgage if an existing loan at 10.25% is replaced with an 8.5% loan; amounts shown are typical, but will vary by bank and by area.)

| ITEMIZED COSTS OF REFINANCING | | EXAMPLE |
|---|---|---|
| Discount Points | $ | |
| Origination Points (if any) | | $2,000 |
| Application Fee | | 0 |
| Credit Check | | 350 |
| Attorney Review fee (yours) | | 70 |
| Attorney Review fee (lender's) | | 200 |
| Title Search Fee | | 200 |
| Title Insurance Fee | | 50 |
| Appraisal Fee | | 400 |
| Inspections | | 250 |
| Local Fees (taxes, transfers) | | 350 |
| Other Fees | | 1,000 |
| Estimate for other costs | | 0 |
| Prepayment penalty on your existing mortgage (if any) | | 250 |
| Total of all fees on your new mortgage | | 0 |
| Current mortgage's monthly payment[2] | | 5,120 |
| New mortgage's monthly payment[2] | | 896 |
| Difference between the two payments | | 769 |
| Number of months to recoup costs: (Total of all fees, divided by the difference in monthly payments) | | 127 |
| | | 40 months |

[1] Varies by area, from 0% to about 2.5%
[2] Principal and interest only

Source: HSH Associates

## WHAT IF YOU FALL BEHIND IN YOUR MORTGAGE PAYMENTS?

Although lenders can **foreclose**, or repossess, your house if you're 90 days behind in your payments, most will agree to less drastic measures. Some solutions:

- Add the amount you're behind to the end of the mortgage, which extends the term and cost of the loan

- Renegotiate with the lender to reduce each monthly payment. Then pay the difference, plus the amount you're behind, at the end of the mortgage

If you sometimes feel you're a slave to your mortgage, consider the ancient Romans. They *did* become slaves if they defaulted on a mortgage—at least before 326 B.C.

- Temporarily reduce current payments and increase later ones, or make a balloon, or one-time, payment to catch up

- Increase future payments slightly until you've paid up the amount you're behind

### MORTGAGE PENALTIES

If you refinance, you'll come out better if your original mortgage doesn't impose a **prepayment penalty**. That's a charge the lender makes if you pay off your mortgage early for any reason. A number of states forbid such charges, but the rest don't. Most experts advise you to avoid taking a loan with a penalty, if you have the choice.

# Your Home as Investment

Since a lot of your money is probably invested in your home, it's important to keep an eye on its value.

The value of your home, or any property, can be set in several ways.

**Market value** is the price you pay when you buy a home. It's what the market will bear. A house built in a certain style, or in a prestigious neighborhood, will often command a higher price. And a house in a booming area may sell for tens of thousands of dollars more than essentially the same house in a depressed or undesirable location.

**Appraised value** (sometimes called **fair market value**) is what a real estate appraiser says your house is worth. The appraisal is based on the selling prices of similar houses in the area, as well as subjective judgment. So two appraisers may value the same house differently.

The appraised value doesn't dictate the market value. But many appraisers are also real estate agents, so there's usually a strong correlation.

**Assessed value** is assigned by the local tax assessor and is the basis for your real estate taxes. There can be a large difference between assessed and appraised value, depending on how recently the assessment was done and the standards used in your community.

Often a house is reassessed when it is sold or remodeled. If you consider the assessment too high, you can appeal it on **grievance day**. Be prepared to show the assessments of comparable houses and to point out shortcomings the assessor might have overlooked, which could reduce its value.

## CHANGING VALUES

Property values change regularly, sometimes dramatically. If interest rates are high and the economy is sluggish, people don't buy as readily as they do when rates are lower. You might be forced to sell for less than you paid, which reduces the value of your investment.

Neighborhoods change as well, reducing the value of individual properties. Sometimes it's the intrusion of a superhighway or an airport. Or it may result from changing employment patterns, a downturn in the economy or new construction elsewhere.

While you can't prevent change, many experts advise buyers to consider the location of homes they're interested in as carefully as they consider the homes.

## The value of a house changes continually —and so does your equity for as long as you have a mortgage.

250

200

If you purchased your house for $200,000 and you put $100,000 down and have a $100,000 mortgage, your equity is 50%.

150

E Q U I T Y

*50%*

100

50

## WHAT IS EQUITY?

When you make a down payment on a home, the amount of the payment determines your **equity**, or the percentage of the property which you actually own. The more you put down, the greater your equity.

As you pay off the principal on your mortgage, your equity in the house increases. When your mortgage is fully paid, your equity is 100%. The house is yours free and clear, and you get the **deed**, or legal title, to it.

## MAKING IMPROVEMENTS

Improvements can be a real asset when you want to sell. Modern kitchens and bathrooms usually pay for themselves by increasing the market value of your home. So does a fireplace. But you may have a harder time getting back the installation cost of a swimming pool, sauna, or converted garage.

And if improvements make your home overpriced for the neighborhood, it may be harder to sell at a price that reflects what you invested.

Local governments and condo and co-op associations often have strict building and zoning rules that govern additions and renovations. There may be a fee, based on the estimated cost of improvements. And you'll have to get approvals and permits, schedule inspections for electrical and plumbing work and get a certificate of occupancy.

## RENTING YOUR HOME

You may also be able to make money by renting your home. The rent is taxable income, but you may be able to deduct the cost of improvements up to certain limits. You can also rent out a second home, but special tax rules apply to how often you may use it if you want to deduct expenses. You'll want to consult your tax adviser or other expert on the best way to handle rental income.

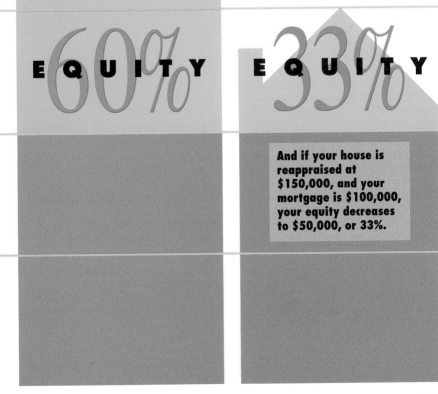

If your house is reappraised at $250,000 and your mortgage is $100,000, your equity increases to $150,000, or 60%.

EQUITY 60%

EQUITY 33%

And if your house is reappraised at $150,000, and your mortgage is $100,000, your equity decreases to $50,000, or 33%.

# Home Equity Borrowing

**If you need to borrow, a home equity loan usually offers the best rates, plus the advantage of tax savings.**

Home equity loans let you borrow using the equity you've built up in your home as **collateral**. You can often borrow more money at a lower interest rate than with other types of loans. And, in many cases, you can deduct the interest you pay on the loan when you file your tax return, reducing the actual cost of borrowing still further. Most of the other interest you pay, on car loans or personal loans, for example, isn't deductible.

You can choose between:

- **Home equity loans, sometimes known as second mortgages**
- **Home equity lines of credit**

## HOME EQUITY LOANS

With a home equity loan, you borrow a lump sum, usually at a variable rate of interest although some fixed-rate loans are available. You pay off the debt in installments, just as you repay your mortgage, with some of each payment going toward the interest you owe and the rest toward the **principal**, or loan amount. At the end of its term, or payment period, the loan is retired.

You may have to pay closing costs on your loan, just as you did for your first, or primary, mortgage. But lenders may offer loans with no up-front expenses as part of a promotional deal. You might also be offered a **teaser rate**, or a period of low interest as an incentive to borrow. If that's the case, the lender has to tell you the actual cost, or **annual percentage rate (APR)**, and when the temporary rate ends.

## HOME EQUITY LINES OF CREDIT

Home equity lines of credit are actually revolving credit arrangements, which you can use in much the same way you use a credit card. Your **credit line**, or limit, is fixed, and you can write a check for any amount up to that limit. Whatever you borrow reduces what's available until you repay. Then you can use it again.

The terms of repayment vary, and are spelled out in your agreement. In some cases you begin to repay principal and interest as soon as you borrow, or **activate the line**. In others, you pay interest only, with a **balloon**, or one-time full payment of principal due at some set date. Or, you may make interest-only payments for a specific period, and then begin to pay principal as well.

Most credit lines have an access period, often five to ten years, during which you can borrow, and a longer payback period. The longer you take to repay, the more expensive it is to borrow.

## WHAT YOU CAN BORROW

As a general rule, you can borrow up to 80% of your equity in your home with a home equity loan. For example, if you owed $75,000 on a home appraised at $250,000, your equity would be $175,000. In most cases, you'd be able to borrow up to $140,000, or 80% of $175,000.

Some home equity lines of credit, especially those offered without closing costs or other up-front expenses are capped at a fixed amount, often $50,000.

While you have the loan, your equity is reduced by the amount you owe. When it's paid off, your equity is restored. However, if your home loses some of its value during the loan period, you still owe the full amount you borrowed.

## BEWARE THE RISK

While home equity borrowing has many advantages, it has one serious drawback: If you **default**, or fall behind on repayment, you could lose your home through **foreclosure**. That means the lender takes over the property and becomes the owner. That's true even if you've made all the payments on your first, or primary, mortgage.

## ATTRACTIONS

- **They are easy to get**
- **The rates are usually lower than on unsecured loans**
- **The interest is tax deductible, though there may be a cap and other restrictions. Check with your tax adviser**

That risk is the chief reason most experts caution against using home equity borrowing—lines of credit in particular—to pay day-to-day expenses. If you're using the money to make improvements in your home, pay tuition bills or meet other major expenses, and include loan repayment as a regular item in your budget, home equity borrowing can be a wise choice. But if you're in the position of not being able to repay, you're exposing yourself to losing everything you've invested in your home—and having no place to live.

## DANGERS

- **They can be very expensive when you consider total cost**
- **You risk losing your home if you default on the payments**
- **Even if the value of your house decreases, the amount of your loan stays the same**

### FINDING A LOAN
Home equity loans are generally easy to find. Banks offer them, and so do credit unions, mortgage bankers, brokerage houses and insurance companies.

You can start by checking rates and terms advertised in the newspaper and making some phone calls to see what's available. But before you commit yourself, you should get a description—in writing—of the rates, the term and the other conditions of the loan.

### SETTING THE RATE
Each lender sets the terms and conditions of loans it makes, though the basic elements are usually similar. If the loan has a variable rate, it must be tied, or pegged, to a specific public index, usually the prime rate, rather than to some internal index that the bank controls.

The lender adds a **margin**, usually hundredths of a percentage point, to the index to determine the new rate each time it's adjusted. It may happen once a year or sometimes more often.

### REVERSE MORTGAGES
For older people with lots of equity but limited income, a **reverse mortgage** may be an appealing alternative to selling their homes or depending on family members to meet their bills. A reverse mortgage allows owners to borrow against the value of their home, either by getting a regular monthly check (either for a fixed term or for as long as they live in the home), a line of credit or some combination.

You can arrange for reverse mortgages through individual lenders, the Home Equity Conversion Mortgage program of the Federal Housing Administration (FHA), or Fannie Mae. The amount you can borrow depends on your home's market value, your age and the cost of the loan. In addition, some lenders impose caps on the amount they will lend.

While interest rates quoted on reverse mortgages can be similar to those for other mortgages, there are additional fees and charges that can make them more expensive than other types of loans. Lenders must provide a "Total Annual Loan Cost" disclosure form that estimates the average annual cost as an interest rate, or percentage of the loan.

Some experts think that as competition among lenders grows, borrowers may be able to arrange better deals. Others have expressed serious reservations about the wisdom of borrowing in this way.

### BUYER BEWARE
You can protect yourself against paying inflated rates on home-equity loans if you check the rates a number of different lenders are quoting before making a deal—especially if you're shopping for a loan when you're financially stressed.

## COMPARING HOME EQUITY LINES OF CREDIT

| Bank | %Rate | % Above Prime | Promotional Rate | Access Period | Repayment Period |
|------|-------|---------------|------------------|---------------|------------------|
| First | 11.25 | 1.75 | (None) | 5 years | 20 years |
| State | 11.00 | 1.50 | Prime, 1st 2 years | 5 years | 20 years |
| Regional | 11.40 | 1.40 | Prime 1st year | 10 years | 30 years |
| TriState | 10.65 | 0.90 | (None) | 10 years | 30 years |
| Western | 11.25 | 1.75 | Intro rate: 9.00% | 10 years | 30 years |
| LBSB | 11.50 | 1.75 | | 10 years | 20 years |

# Insuring Your Home

Insurance protects your investment in your home. It can also protect you if you are sued for damages or injury you cause.

You want to be sure you have the right amount and type of insurance, so you are covered when there's a loss. Homeowner's insurance covers your house and its contents, including your personal possessions and valuable articles, against damage or loss. If you rent, you can get insurance just for the contents. There are also special policies for condos and co-ops.

Most homeowners insurance is sold by agents representing one or more insurers. You can ask for bids from several insurers to find the best prices, but you'll also want to check the insurer's reputation.

## WHAT'S COVERED?

Policies vary in terms of the kinds of **perils** or **hazards** they cover, and how they compensate you for a loss.

A standard, or **named perils**, policy provides limited protection—it lists the specific perils (for example, fire, theft) that are covered. Broader coverage gives you insurance for all types of losses except those excluded from the policy.

You can also get special insurance for valuable articles—jewelry, art work, collectibles—for which you pay a separate premium.

The insurance industry codes Homeowners policies from HO1 to HO8 to reflect the range of coverages. The broader the policy, the higher the premium you'll pay.

## WHAT'S EXCLUDED?

Virtually no basic policy covers losses resulting from war, riots, police actions, nuclear explosion, or "acts of God." You can sometimes get a **rider**, or an endorsement to your policy to cover situations that are normally excluded, such as floods and earthquakes, but you'll pay an extra premium for this coverage.

## LIABILITY COVERAGE

Liability coverage can protect you if you're sued for causing property damage or injury to someone. **Excess liability** increases the amount of coverage and may give you added protection for a wider range of activities, such as your role in community or government organizations.

Benjamin Franklin organized the first fire insurance company in North America in 1752. It's still doing business in Philadelphia.

## WHAT'S A DEDUCTIBLE?

Every policy has a **deductible**, an amount you pay for a loss before the coverage kicks in. Deductibles may vary from a few hundred to a few thousand dollars. You can reduce the cost of your insurance by taking a larger deductible, but you'll have to pay the amount of any loss up to the deductible.

## THE COVERAGE YOU NEED

You should insure your house for at least 80% of its **replacement value**—what it would cost to repair or rebuild the house at today's prices. But it probably makes better sense to insure your house for its full replacement value. Most companies will automatically increase your coverage and raise your premium each year to cover rising costs. It can also pay to get replacement cost coverage for the contents of your home.

## AFTER A LOSS

What you receive after a loss depends on the policy terms (the fine print), which you should read carefully, or discuss with your insurance agent, when you get the policy. Learning how much—or how little—you'll get paid after a loss can be an unpleasant surprise.

Some policies require you to replace the damaged or stolen property, and then reimburse you for the expense. Others give you the money for the agreed-upon value, but don't require the replacement, so you can spend the money as you see fit.

# Selling Your Home

On average, people stay put for five to seven years before selling and moving on. So buying is only half the story: The other half is getting a good deal when you sell.

Your first decision is whether to sell through a broker or sell your home yourself. Using a broker costs money—often 5% to 7% of your selling price in commissions or fees.

However, brokers generally know the local market, help you determine a fair selling price and screen potential buyers. It pays to invite several different ones to suggest an asking price and explain their commission structure. They'll ordinarily do this for free: They want your business.

Selling on your own requires more time. You must be available to show the house, and you'll have to make decisions about everything from setting a price to accepting an offer. You'll also have to judge if potential buyers are serious, and whether they'll be able to get a mortgage.

## WHAT IF NOTHING HAPPENS?

The seller's nightmare is a house that won't sell. If it's the economy—national or local—you can't do much about it.

But you can consider:

- Lowering your asking price
- Changing agents—or using one if you haven't used one already
- Offering to finance all or part of the purchase price yourself

## DOES FIX-UP PAY?

Opinion is divided about whether you should spend money to fix up your home before you put it on the market. Some believe that buyers want to do their own fixing up, so it isn't worth the trouble. Others argue that buyers respond better to places that look good. Minor repairs and cosmetic touch-ups don't hurt, and they don't cost much. Neither does cleanliness.

And if there are major problems— like a leaky roof— that you don't repair, you may have to lower your price in negotiating the final contract.

According to a recent study, using a buyer's agent can reduce your home buying process by more than two weeks.

## SELLERS' HEADACHES

- Getting the price you want
- Deciding how much fix-up to do before selling
- Selling in a slow market
- Lowering the price or having to provide financing yourself
- Paying extra costs for needed repairs identified during inspections
- Avoiding unacceptable contract terms, like long delays or zoning approvals
- Discovering unexpected liens against your property, like unpaid contractor bills or court costs

## GETTING A FAIR PRICE

Realistically, a fair price is whatever you can get. To judge if your price is fair, check local sales records of **comparables**— similar homes that have sold in your community recently. Charts available in real estate agents' offices tell you the asking price, time on the market and selling price of other houses.

Don't be misled by the **asking price** for houses in your area. It's what they actually sell for that counts.

You may also be able to get information on prices in your neighborhood from Consumer Reports Home Price Service (see page 62), Home Price Check or Home Price Live. They all have 800 numbers.

## NEGOTIATING A CONTRACT

When you get a good offer, you'll need a real estate lawyer to be sure the terms of the contract don't tie your hands if the buyer delays or drops out.

The sale usually depends on the buyer's being able to get a mortgage and a free and clear title to the property. But any unusual contingencies—like dependence on inheritance or insurance money—should have a time limit. The contract should also spell out who pays specific closing costs, since these practices vary.

## THE CLOSING

Though there's a lot of paperwork, selling all comes down to paying off what you owe and settling with the buyer. Here's what you can expect to pay:

- The balance of your mortgage, plus fees
- The real estate agent—usually 5% to 7% of the selling price
- Pro-rated real estate taxes
- Transfer taxes
- Your lawyer
- Other costs specified in the contract

If you're providing some of the financing, you'll also get a copy of the loan agreement that the buyer signs. Be sure to record it with the local government to secure your claim if the buyer defaults. Otherwise the primary mortgage lender could reclaim the property, leaving you unpaid.

**Bridge loans—sometimes called swing loans or turnarounds—let you buy a new house if the sale of your old one hasn't been completed. You borrow the amount you need, pay only interest while you have the loan, and repay the lump sum when your sale closes. A signed contract can make a bridge loan easier to get.**

# Figuring Your Profit or Loss

## You can make or lose money when you sell your home.

If you sell real estate for more than your **cost basis**, or the original purchase price plus the cost of improvements, you have a **capital gain**.

If that property is your primary home, you get a tax break on any capital gain you may realize when you sell. That's because, if you meet certain conditions, you can exclude up to $250,000 of that gain if you're single. If you're married, you can exclude up to $500,000. You don't even have to report any gain that's less than the limit when you file your tax return for the year. The excluded amount goes straight to your bottom line.

The conditions are that you owned and lived in the home for at least two of the five years before you sold, and haven't sold or exchanged a different home within the past two years. There is an exception if you're disabled.

If you sell for less than you paid, you have a **loss**, but it's a personal, not a capital, loss. That means you can't use the loss to reduce taxes you may owe on other capital gains or on regular income.

### WHEN TAX IS DUE

There are cases when you do owe capital gains tax on your profit from selling your home. That happens when

- Your gain is larger than the amount you can exclude
- You haven't live in the home for two of the past five years

- You've sold another home in the last two years
- You rented part of your home or took a deduction for using part of it as a home office or place of business

Then you report the amount on Schedule D, using instructions from IRS Publication 523, "Selling Your Home." It might be smart to get a copy of the publication in any case, since it has worksheets to help you figure your gain and the amount you can exclude.

Any tax you do owe on property you've owned more than a year is considered a long-term capital gain and is figured at the capital gains rate, which is lower than your regular rate. If you've owned the property less than a year, tax on your gain is figured at your regular rate.

### FIGURING COST BASIS

The higher the cost basis of your home, the lower your capital gain will be when you sell, making it easier to qualify for the exclusion. Among the things that increase cost basis, which are added to the amount you paid to buy your home initially, are certain settlement fees or closing costs, the cost of any permanent improvements or additions you made to the property, the cost of repairing any damages, and any amounts you spent to sell it including fix-up costs.

On the other hand, your basis can also be decreased. That can happen if you get

## FIGURING YOUR PROFIT (OR LOSS)

To figure the profit or loss on a sale, you subtract the cost basis of your home and the selling costs from the selling price: The result is called the adjusted selling price.

| | | |
|---|---|---|
| **Selling price** | | **$392,000** |
| Original purchase price | $54,450 | **– $54,450** |
| Improvements | | |
| Replaced the roof | $3,400 | |
| Remodeled the bathroom | $4,000 | |
| Converted the attic | $3,900 | |
| Added kitchen cabinets | $1,700 | **– $13,000** |
| Costs of selling | | |
| Title insurance and transfer taxes | $1,500 | |
| Legal fees | $450 | |
| Real estate commission (5%) | $19,600 | **– $21,550** |
| **Adjusted selling price** | | **= $303,000** |

certain subsidies or credits, receive an insurance payment to cover losses, or took a depreciation for using part of your home as an office. Check Publication 17 or talk to your tax adviser for the full list.

In any case, you should keep detailed records to prove what you spent to buy your home and make any additions or improvements. You'll need them to figure out any increase in basis at the time you sell. And once the transaction is complete, the IRS suggests you hold onto the supporting documents for at least three years.

## A WORD TO THE WISE

If you're a first-time homebuyer, you might want to get a copy of IRS Publication 530, "Tax Information for First-Time Homeowners." It can make it easier to benefit from all the tax advantages that come with owning your own home.

Remember that a home doesn't have to be a single-family house. It can be a cooperative apartment, a condominium, a mobile home, or even a houseboat if that's where you live.

---

**SCHEDULE D**
**(Form 1040)** (U)
Department of the Treasury
Internal Revenue Service
Name(s) shown on Form 1040

**Capital Gains and Losses**

▶ Attach to Form 1040. ▶ See Instructions for Schedule D (Form 1040).
▶ Use Schedule D-1 for more space to list transactions for lines 1 and 8.

OMB No. 1545-0074

Attachment Sequence No. **12**

Your social security number
1 2 3 4 5 6 7 8 9

**Part I** Short-Term Capital Gains and Losses—Assets Held One Year or Less

| (a) Description of property (Example: 100 sh. XYZ Co.) | (b) Date acquired (Mo., day, yr.) | (c) Date sold (Mo., day, yr.) | (d) Sales price (see page D-5) | (e) Cost or other basis (see page D-5) | (f) GAIN or (LOSS) Subtract (e) from (d) |
|---|---|---|---|---|---|
| 1 | | | | | |

> Sometimes, people whose goal is a larger home than they can initially afford count on using the gain from selling one home to buy the next one. People who are ready to retire may also plan on a gain as a source of future income. But experts caution that while real estate has often been a profitable investment, there's no guarantee that you'll make money by investing in a home.

from Forms 4684,
estates, and trusts

| 4 | |
| 5 | |

6 Short-term capital loss carryover. Enter the amount, if any, from line 8 of your 1998 Capital Loss Carryover Worksheet

| 6 | ( ) |

7 Net short-term capital gain or (loss). Combine lines 1 through 6 in column (f)

| 7 | |

**Part II** Long-Term Capital Gains and Losses—Assets Held More Than One Year

| (a) Description of property (Example: 100 sh. XYZ Co.) | (b) Date acquired (Mo., day, yr.) | (c) Date sold (Mo., day, yr.) | (d) Sales price (see page D-5) | (e) Cost or other basis (see page D-5) | (f) GAIN or (LOSS) Subtract (e) from (d) | (g) 28% RATE GAIN or (LOSS) (see instr. below) |
|---|---|---|---|---|---|---|
| 8 Home @ 123 Main | 3/28/80 | 7/16/99 | 392 000 — | 89 000 — | 303 000 — | |
| Section 121 Exclusion | | | | | (250 000) | |

from

| 9 | |

nts. | 10 | 392 000 |

ain from Forms 2439 and 6252; and
3781, and 8824

| 11 | |

s, S corporations, estates, and trusts

| 12 | |
| 13 | |

oth columns (f) and (g) the amount, if
Carryover Worksheet

| 14 | ( ) ( ) |

he lines 8 through 14 in colur

gains and losses" (as define

ons.  Cat. N

---

## COST BASIS

The original purchase price and cost of improvements together are called the cost basis.

Selling Price
- Original purchase price
- Cost of improvements
- Cost of selling

= PROFIT (OR LOSS)

## GHOSTS OF THE PAST

If you sold a home before May 7, 1997, and postponed tax on the gain because you used the money to buy another home, different rules may apply. You should read chapter 3 in Publication 523, and you may want to consult your tax advisor.

# Financial Planning

When you plan, you identify financial goals and develop strategies to meet them.

When you do financial planning, you're looking toward the future, specifically at building the kind of security you'd like to have and being able to afford the lifestyle you want. But to plan successfully, you also have to evaluate the present, including the financial choices you're making now. Otherwise it's too easy to find yourself making random decisions that won't move you toward your goals effectively, or that may even interfere with your ability to achieve them.

It's never too soon, or too late, to begin. Financial planning is important, whether you've just started working or are thinking seriously about retirement. And it should be a continuing process, so that you can evaluate your progress, revise your goals and update your strategies.

Without planning, you run certain financial risks. You may not have enough in reserve to meet expenses you're expecting, like the down payment on a home or the price of a college education. You may have to revise your retirement plans. Or you might leave your family without enough to live comfortably if something happens to you.

## PLANNING STRATEGIES

In financial planning terms, creating a strategy means defining the steps you'll take to have the money you need to pay for the things you want.

To begin, you need a clear sense of what your goals are, and what they will cost. You will have to evaluate the performance of the assets you already have. And you must find ways to increase the amount you're investing and select how you will invest it.

## A DEFENSIVE BACKUP

Planning is also important because it helps you anticipate and handle the obstacles that come between you and your goals:

**BEAT INFLATION**

If your investments grow faster than the inflation rate, you'll be in a much better position to afford the things that are important to you.

**MINIMIZE TAXES**

You can take advantage of tax-deferred investments to postpone taxes and make tax-exempt investments to avoid them. Trusts may also reduce the taxes your heirs will owe down the road.

**PLAN FOR THE UNEXPECTED**

With a cash reserve fund plus adequate health and life insurance as hedges against unexpected expenses and illnesses, you're less vulnerable to potential hardship.

## DEFINING YOUR GOALS

Planning is important because it helps you identify a range of goals that you're working to achieve:

**Short-term goals**
You can invest for things you hope to have in a couple of years, like a new car or a new home.

**Mid-term goals**
You may have expenses to meet several years in the future, like tuition payments or a vacation home.

**Long-term goals**
You probably have hopes for a comfortable retirement, the opportunity to go places and do things you've always wanted, or a chance to provide security for your heirs.

A financial plan is a game plan that evaluates your current assets and debts, identifies the things you want (or need) to provide for and lays out a strategy to pay for them. Developing the plan is one thing. Sticking to it is another.

**SIX OUT OF TEN AMERICANS** rate a steady source of retirement income as their primary financial goal.

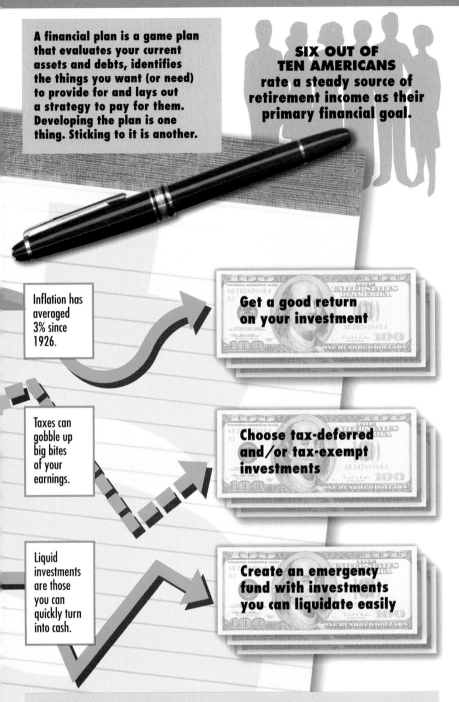

Inflation has averaged 3% since 1926.

**Get a good return on your investment**

Taxes can gobble up big bites of your earnings.

**Choose tax-deferred and/or tax-exempt investments**

Liquid investments are those you can quickly turn into cash.

**Create an emergency fund with investments you can liquidate easily**

## SEEKING ADVICE

Many people take advantage of professional advice in drawing up a financial plan and putting it into action. You can work with an adviser from the beginning, consult a number of different experts or choose someone to execute the decisions you make on your own. The biggest danger isn't making a mistake by choosing the wrong approach. It's in doing nothing about investing.

In fact, many experts suggest that a major advantage of working regularly with an adviser is the added incentive it can provide to get started and stay focused. Help is increasingly available, too, as all types of financial institutions compete to provide the services their customers are looking for.

Among the people you can turn to for help with financial planning are:

- **Bank representatives**
- **Certified Public Accountants**
- **Financial planners**
- **Insurance agents**
- **Stockbrokers**

# Making a Financial Plan

A financial plan is a working document that can be as flexible or as focused as you want it to be.

Whether you work with an adviser to create a plan, use computer-based software, tap into a financial planning site on the Internet or devise one on your own, you'll need to use some basic financial documents to establish where you're starting from. Advisers, for example, usually ask to see recent income tax forms, a summary of your investments, information on your retirement plan and your life insurance policies.

Some advisers develop a detailed written plan, also called a personal financial analysis. The document summarizes the information you've provided, includes an overview of various financial planning strategies and recommends specific investments or other steps you should take to achieve your objectives.

If you prefer, you can request a simpler approach, and receive a letter summarizing the goals you're working toward, the approach to investing you want to take and the type of investments the adviser recommends.

1. Your Current Financial Situation
2. Financial Goals
3. Making a Financial Plan
4. Paying for College
5. Planning for Retirement
6. Social Security
7. Wills and Trusts
8. Estate Planning

## OWNERSHIP: ONE OF THE KEYS TO PLANNING

The kind of ownership you select for property and other assets determines what you can do with them, how vulnerable they are to creditors and what happens to them after you die. Laws are complicated and vary from state to state, so you should get professional advice.

| Type | Features |
|------|----------|
| Individual (or sole) | ● You own the asset outright |
| Joint tenants with rights of survivorship | ● You share the asset equally with one or more joint owners <br> ● At your death, the assets automatically transfer to joint owner(s) <br> ● You generally can't sell property without consent of joint owner(s) |
| Tenants in common | ● Each owner holds a part, or share, of the whole <br> ● Individual shares can be sold, given away or left as owner wishes |
| Tenants by entirety | ● You must be married <br> ● Mutual consent is needed to divide or sell the property <br> ● At death the property goes to the surviving owner |
| Community property | ● In the nine states with community property laws, most property acquired after marriage is owned equally by both partners <br> ● Once property becomes community property, it remains such even if you move out of the state |

# Choosing an Adviser

If you're looking for a financial adviser, you'll want to set up some criteria to help you evaluate the people you may work with. Among the questions you can ask to help you make a choice:

## How much experience have you had working with clients that share my situation and goals?

Experts suggest that ten years of experience isn't too much to expect, especially if you're new to investing.

## What's your background and expertise?

You'll want to work with an adviser who has a strong reputation in the field, either as an individual or as an employee of a respected company.

## What kinds of investments do you sell most often?

Some advisers emphasize one or two types of investments while others suggest a broader range of stocks, bonds and mutual funds.

## How are you paid?

Some advisers are paid commissions on the products they sell, some receive flat or hourly fees for their service, and some are paid a combination of fees and commissions.

## Will you explain how the investments you recommend will help me achieve my goals?

You'll want an adviser who's willing and able to explain how investments work and why they're suited to your needs.

## How will I know if my investments are producing the results I want?

Advisers should provide regular reports on the status of your accounts and be willing to explain how well your investments are performing and what adjustments to consider.

## THE RISK ISSUE

Financial planning almost always involves making investments. One issue you'll have to resolve is the kind of investing risk you're comfortable taking. The choice ranges from very little to a great deal, with a broad middle ground between the extremes.

Conservative investing usually means putting money where there's little risk to principal. Typical choices are certificates of deposit (CDs) and U.S. Treasury bills, bonds and notes. Putting money in savings accounts and money market funds isn't generally considered investing, since your principal grows little, if at all.

Aggressive investing usually means taking the risk of losing your investment in exchange for the possibility of making a large profit. Typical investments are stock in new or troubled companies, high-risk bonds and derivative products like futures and options.

Most experts suggest you work for balance among the various risk categories. That might mean, for example, some conservative investments, a few aggressive ones and most of your money in stocks, bonds and mutual funds. One of their concerns is that if you invest too conservatively, you won't have enough money down the road to afford your goals even if you've been diligent in following your plan. Another is that by taking too many chances, especially as you get older, you risk losing too much of your capital.

## BEATING INFLATION

Conquering the effects of **inflation**, or the gradual increase in what things cost, is one reason financial planning is so important. Because prices rise, money doesn't buy as much this year as it did last. Ten years from now, it will buy even fewer of the things you need.

The **inflation rate**, which has averaged about 3% a year since 1926, measures how quickly prices increase. At that rate, for example, a shirt that costs $20 this year would cost almost $40 in twenty years or so. And there'd be comparable increases in other prices.

That means to maintain the same standard of living, you need an equivalent increase in income every year. One way you may achieve that is by investing money so it earns more than inflation, even after you've paid the taxes on your earnings. What you have left of your earnings after taxes and inflation is called your **real rate of return**.

Identifying the kinds of investments you expect to perform well, and choosing the specific ones you'll make, are two of the things you're doing when you make a financial plan.

Many experts advise you to schedule a face-to-face meeting with any potential advisers. They should ask about your goals, assets and objectives. And they should be interested in you as a client. Otherwise, continue your search.

# Managing Your Cash Flow

Cash flow is how you're spending your money. With planning, you can adjust your expenses to cover immediate needs and still invest for long-term goals.

Your finances are in constant motion. Even as money comes in from employment, investments and other sources, it goes out for regular living expenses like food and shelter, and for periodic bills like taxes and insurance. This in-and-out movement is called your **cash flow**.

## HOUSEHOLD BUDGETS

A budget is a plan that helps you set spending goals and monitor how well you're meeting them. Using last year's expenses as a base, you allocate how much you will spend this year for housing, food, transportation and so forth—including the large bills like insurance that you pay quarterly or annually.

If your expenses are too high or you want to invest more, you can review what you're spending to see where you can cut back. The simpler and more realistic your budget, the more you're likely to stick to it.

## REGULAR EXPENSES

| | |
|---|---|
| **Weekly** | Food, transportation, household supplies, childcare |
| **Monthly** | Housing, utilities, phone, loan repayments |
| **Quarterly/ annually** | Insurance, taxes |
| **Other** | Medical and dental expenses, repairs, entertainment |

## REGULAR INVESTING

If you're serious about financial planning, experts say **you should invest between 5% and 10% of your gross income regularly**—preferably each time you get paid. If you reinvest your dividends, interest and other investment income instead of spending it, you'll build your net worth more quickly.

## FINDING MONEY TO INVEST

If you'd like to invest more of your household budget, but aren't sure how to get started, consider these suggestions:

## IT DOESN'T TAKE MUCH

If you invest $166 a month in an IRA, you'll have contributed all but $8 of the $2,000 limit by the end of the year.

## FUNDS IN RESERVE

Irregular income, unexpected repair bills, medical expenses, or loss of your job can pose special cash flow problems. It pays to have a safety net—customarily two to six months take-home pay set aside in cash reserves—to meet sudden expenses. Most experts agree that it's smart to choose safe short-term investments for your cash reserve. But they also point out that some investments—such as U.S. Treasury bills or CDs—almost always provide better returns than savings accounts. You can often wait until their maturity dates to pay off unexpected bills, and you can always cash them ahead of schedule though you may lose some interest.

## USING THE CASH FLOAT

Between the time you buy something and the time you actually pay for it you're getting the advantage of a **cash float**. If you charge something, you wait for the bill before paying. When you write a check, it takes time to clear your account (see page 12). Understanding cash float lets you plan deposits to your checking account to cover your payments.

For example, suppose you buy a television with your credit card on July 10 and get the bill on August 5. The due date is August 25. You write a check on August 20, which doesn't clear your bank until August 27. You've had a cash float of almost seven weeks. (But be careful—some credit cards charge you interest from the day of purchase. See page 34.)

If you pay cash or use a **debit card**—which deducts the amount of your purchase from your checking account instantly—you have no cash float.

1. Have a percentage of your salary deducted from your paycheck and invested in an employer-sponsored retirement plan.

2. Write a regular investment check when you pay your bills each month.

3. Invest any money you get from gifts, bonuses or extra jobs.

4. Reinvest all the money you make on your existing investments, automatically if you can.

5. Pay off your credit card balance. Then put an amount equal to what you were paying in interest into an investment account.

# Your Net Worth

Your net worth statement is a snapshot of where you stand financially at a given point in time.

## WHAT YOU OWN

**Cash reserve assets** are cash, or the equivalent of cash, that you can use on short notice to cover an emergency or make an investment. They include the money in your checking, savings and money market accounts, CDs, Treasury bills and the cash value of your life insurance policy.

**Investment assets**, like stocks, bonds and mutual funds, produce income and growth. Retirement plans and annuities are considered long-term investments.

**Personal assets** are your possessions. Some—like antiques, stamp collections, and art—may **appreciate**, or increase in value, making them investments as well. Others—like cars, boats, and electronic equipment—**depreciate**, or decrease in value over time.

**Real estate** is a special asset because you can use it yourself, rent it, or perhaps sell it for a profit.

## Assets

| CURRENT ESTIMATED VALUE | for example |
| --- | --- |
| Cash in banks & money market accounts | $20,000 |
| Amounts owed to you | 0 |
| Stocks/bonds | $14,000 |
| Mutual funds | $15,000 |
| Life insurance (cash surrender value) | $8,000 |
| IRA & Keogh accounts | $40,000 |
| Pension & 401(k) (vested interest) | $135,000 |
| Real estate: | |
| Home | $200,000 |
| Other | 0 |
| Business interests | 0 |
| Personal property* | $30,000 |
| **TOTAL ASSETS** | **$462,000** |

\* Includes furnishings, jewelry, collections, cars, security deposit or rent, etc.

### THE STARTING POINT

As part of deciding how to pursue your financial goals, you should take a look at where you stand right now. You do that by adding your **assets**—such as cash, investments and pension plans—in one column and your **liabilities**—or debts—in the other. Then subtract your liabilities from your assets to find your **net worth**.

Net worth doesn't measure cash flow, but there's a clear relationship between how you spend your money and what your financial picture looks like. If your assets outweigh your liabilities, you have a positive net worth. If your liabilities are larger, you have a negative net worth. Most experts would say your first goal should be getting into the black.

Knowing how your assets are divided is especially helpful for financial planning. For example, if you have more money in cash than invested in stocks and stock mutual funds, your first priority may be to emphasize growth. And if you have nothing set aside for retirement, you may want to find a way to start.

**FAIR MARKET VALUE**
When you're calculating what your assets are worth, the number to use is their fair market value. That's the price a willing, rational and knowledgeable buyer would pay for things you are willing to sell.

## WHAT YOU OWE CURRENTLY AND LONG-TERM

## Liabilities

| AMOUNT | for example |
|---|---|
| Mortgages | $160,000 |
| Bank loans | 0 |
| Car loans | $7,000 |
| Lines of credit | $3,000 |
| Charge accounts | $1,800 |
| Margin loans | 0 |
| Alimony | 0 |
| Taxes owed: | |
| Income | $21,000 |
| Real estate | $3,200 |
| Other | 0 |
| Other liabilities | |
| College loan | $7,000 |
| Insurance | $3,500 |
| Business loan | 0 |
| **TOTAL LIABILITIES** | **$206,500** |

**Short-term debts** are your current bills: credit card charges, installment and personal loans, income and real estate taxes, and insurance. Your present credit card balances are generally included, even if you regularly pay your entire bill each month.

**Long-term debts** are mortgages and other loans that you repay in installments over several years.

**OTHER PERSPECTIVES**
When potential lenders assess your application—basically a net worth statement—to decide whether you qualify for a loan, they look at what you already owe. But they may also calculate what you might owe if you charged as much as

## ASSETS MINUS LIABILITIES

**USING NET WORTH STATEMENTS**
Figuring your net worth is not only a critical first step in financial planning. It will also come in handy in many financial situations. For example:

- Mortgage lenders require a statement of your assets and liabilities as part of the application
- College financial aid is based on your net worth, so you'll have to report your assets and liabilities when your children apply
- Loan and line-of-credit applications usually require net worth statements
- Certain high-risk investments may require that you have a minimum net worth—say $1 million or more

you could on all your credit cards and drew on all your potential lines of credit.

What most lenders like to see is a net worth statement that shows substantial investments, including money in retirement plans. Investments mean that you have resources to tap in an emergency, including assets that could be sold to pay your debts.

# The Cost of a College Education

## Going to college is a goal many people share. But paying for it can be an extraordinary expense.

One of the biggest expenses you may face is college tuition. Whether your child goes to a private or public college, the price tag for education can be very hefty.

Since these costs keep going up—increases in college tuition consistently exceed the rate of inflation—planning ahead is essential.

## How Much Will You Have to Save?

Four-year college costs, including tuition, room and board, books and transportation, and the monthly investments required to finance them. Table assumes 6% annual increase in college costs and 8% annual after-tax investment return, and no additional investments or earnings on balance invested once the child starts college.

| YEARS UNTIL CHILD STARTS COLLEGE | PROJECTED COST OF 4-YEAR PROGRAM | | MONTHLY INVESTMENT FOR 4-YEAR COST | |
|---|---|---|---|---|
| | PUBLIC | PRIVATE | PUBLIC | PRIVATE |
| 1 | $47,330 | $101,977 | $3,776 | $8,137 |
| 3 | 52,182 | 112,428 | 1,279 | 2,755 |
| 6 | 57,531 | 123,951 | 778 | 1,676 |
| 9 | 63,429 | 136,657 | 562 | 1,211 |
| 12 | 69,931 | 150,665 | 441 | 951 |
| 15 | 93,710 | 201,902 | 269 | 580 |
| 18 | 108,479 | 233,724 | 224 | 484 |

Source: T. Rowe Price Associates, Inc., 1999.

## THE GROWING COST OF EDUCATION

Tuition at private colleges and universities has increased anywhere from 5% to 13% every year since 1980. At the current rate, which has slowed but not stopped, annual tuition bills at private colleges will average $39,000 in 2018, when the children born in 2000 start college. Tuition at public institutions has also increased, sometimes dramatically.

While many people equate high-quality education with a high price tag, a number of the country's most prestigious institutions are public. In fact, annual tuition at about half the nation's public colleges and universities is less than $4,000. Whatever your specific costs turn out to be, though, you need an investment strategy to meet them.

## AVERAGE ANNUAL COST FOR PUBLIC EDUCATION: $10,458*
(in-state, 4 years)

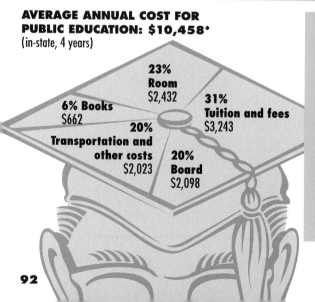

**23% Room** $2,432

**6% Books** $662

**20% Transportation and other costs** $2,023

**31% Tuition and fees** $3,243

**20% Board** $2,098

### TUITION
The charge for instruction, including salaries, facilities, and the general operations of the institution. Public, tax-supported schools cost less than private ones.

### ROOM
Housing in the dorms. Other housing options, like apartments, fraternities, and sororities aren't billed through the college, but the costs are comparable.

## INVESTING FOR A COLLEGE EDUCATION

You might want to investigate some of the specific college-planning options described below. In some cases, there may be salary caps on how much you can earn and still participate. Or you may find you can't use all of the options in the same year. You can get helpful, up-to-date information on the websites of the U.S. Department of Education (www.ed.gov) or The College Board (www.collegeboard.org).

**Education IRAs.** You or another relative or friend can contribute up to $500 of earned income per child per year to an Education IRA set up in the child's name. The earnings in the account are completely tax-free if the money is used to pay qualified higher education expenses, such as tuition, room, and board, anytime before the beneficiary reaches age 30. Putting money in an Education IRA doesn't reduce the amount you're eligible to contribute to your own IRA.

**U.S. savings bonds.** Interest earnings on U.S. savings bonds are completely tax-free if you use the money to pay qualified higher education expenses. However, there is a ceiling on the amount of income your family can be earning at the time you cash in the bonds to qualify for the tax break.

### TAXPAYER RELIEF
In 2000, you may qualify for up to a $1,500 **Hope Scholarship** tax credit each of your child's first two years of college, and for up to an annual $1,000 Lifetime Learning Credit in the student's third and fourth years. You're eligible for full benefits if you're single and earn up to $40,000, or you're married and have a combined income of up to $60,000.

### Tax deductions on student loan
**interest.** The interest you pay on student loans may now be tax-deductible. You can deduct up to $2,000 in 2000, and up to $2,500 in 2001 and thereafter. You are eligible for full benefits if you earn less than $40,000 as a single tax filer, or if you and your spouse together earn less than $60,000 and file jointly.

### SAVING IN YOUR CHILD'S NAME
You can save for college by opening a custodial account in your child's name.

One advantage is that the earnings are taxed at the child's rate once the child reaches age 14. Before then, some of a child's earnings may be taxed at your rate.

But the strategy can backfire if your child applies for financial aid. That's because most financial aid formulas require students to contribute 35% of their savings, while parents are required to supply, at most, 6% of theirs.

### WHAT'S AVAILABLE?
If you don't have as much as you need, schools may offer a package of aid:

**Scholarships or grants**, which do not have to be repaid.

**Loans**, which must be repaid, but usually not until after graduation. Working in certain jobs or locations can reduce the loan or delay repayment.

**Work/study grants**, which colleges offer students. Sometimes their earnings are deducted from tuition and other times the student earns a salary.

### BOARD
Dining hall meals. Most schools offer several different plans, at different costs. Students who don't live in college housing may pay for food individually.

### ACTIVITY FEES
Extra money for clubs, the yearbook, school newspaper, and graduation. Everyone pays a standard fee, though it varies from college to college.

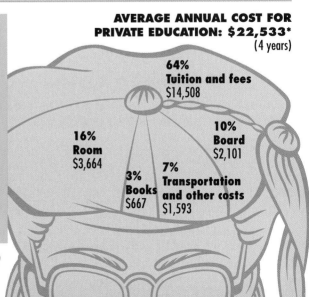

**AVERAGE ANNUAL COST FOR PRIVATE EDUCATION: $22,533\***
(4 years)

**64%**
**Tuition and fees**
$14,508

**16%**
**Room**
$3,664

**10%**
**Board**
$2,101

**3%**
**Books**
$667

**7%**
**Transportation and other costs**
$1,593

\* Source: The College Board, 1999

# Financial Aid

**More than half of all American college students or their families borrow part of the cost of their education.**

When your child is ready for college, will you be ready to pay for it? That's the question you're probably going to face, even if you've been actively investing in a college fund since your son or daughter was small.

Financial aid may provide the extra funding you need. But to get it, you must provide detailed information about your family's finances by filing the Free Application for Federal Student Aid form (www.fafsa.ed.gov). This will determine whether you qualify for federally funded assistance and what you'll be required to contribute.

You may also have to file an application for state-sponsored aid, and some colleges require individual applications in addition to the federal form.

## FACTORS THAT DETERMINE ELIGIBILITY FOR AID:

- Income
- Family assets, including all savings and investments
- Number of other students in the family also paying tuition
- Family expenses, both ordinary and unusual

## THE AMOUNT YOU'RE EXPECTED TO PAY IS FIXED

Your child is eligible for the difference between what a college costs and the amount you're expected to contribute, based on your financial situation.

## FACTORS THAT INFLUENCE WHAT YOU GET:

- Financial resources of the college or university
- Needs of other students
- Special interest in your child

## FOUR YEAR'S WORTH

When a college offers a financial aid package, it's usually for one year at a time. The amount can be—and often is—less after the first year, even if the student does well. Ask the college to make a four-year commitment as long as your child meets academic requirements. You've got nothing to lose. Colleges are sometimes willing to negotiate.

## SPREADING THE PAIN

You might look into the year-round payment options some colleges offer. They let you divide the year's cost into ten or more equal payments, usually for a small fee. Your money can earn enough to offset the charge—and then some.

**COLLEGE B TUITION $19,500**

**Available aid $10,000**

**COLLEGE A TUITION $12,000**

**Available aid $2,500**

**Assume you're responsible for $9,500**

## PREPAID TUITION AND SAVINGS PLANS

Since the cost of a college education continues to grow faster than the rate of inflation, you might want to use one of the innovative approaches that have been introduced to help families plan ahead. You can prepay tuition, a program which was initiated in two states in 1988, or you can put money into a state-sponsored college savings plan.

More than a million people in 21 states are using prepayment plans. Although the programs' details differ, all of the plans let you pay future tuition at today's rates. You prepay that amount either in a one-time lump sum or in monthly installments during the year whose rates you want to lock in. The program promises to pay your child's tuition when he or she enrolls in an eligible school, usually within the state offering the plan.

The programs project that they will be able to meet the future costs by pooling the money from all participants and mak-ing long-term investments whose earnings grow at a faster rate than tuition.

The increasingly popular and diverse savings plans, currently available in 31 states, allow you to put money into a special college savings account on behalf of a designated beneficiary's higher education expenses. What you have to spend when the child enrolls is based on the amount you contribute, the child's age when you begin to participate, and the investments that the plan makes.

Because the plans vary from state to state, you should contact the College Savings Plan Network at 1-877-CSPN-4-U, or at www.collegesavings.org.

Not everyone agrees that using these plans is the best way to cover college expenses. Some financial experts suggest that you may realize a stronger return by putting your money into stocks or mutual funds because you control how the money is invested.

## LINING UP THE MONEY

When you're borrowing to help pay for your child's tuition, it's smart to apply early. If you wait until August, when the first semester's bill is due, you could get caught short. It can take six weeks or more to get action on applications for government-sponsored loan programs, such as PLUS.

## LOAN SOURCES

| | |
|---|---|
| **Stafford Loans** | ● U.S. provides money for direct loans or guarantees loans from other lenders<br>● Total amount of loan can be up to $23,000 over four years<br>● There is a six-month grace period for repayment from the date of graduation<br>● **Unsubsidized** loans are available regardless of family income, but **subsidized** loan awards are based on family income |
| **Perkins Loans** | ● Money is a combination of government and school funding<br>● Total amount of loan can be up to $15,000 over four years<br>● There is a nine-month grace period for repayment from the date of graduation |
| **Parent Loan for Undergraduate Students (PLUS)** | ● Federally funded and guaranteed loans are provided through local banks, credit unions and S&Ls<br>● Interest rates are variable and loan insurance is required<br>● Repayment begins immediately<br>● Total loan amount is equal to cost of college minus financial aid |
| **Home-equity loan** | ● Interest on loan is tax-deductible<br>● Can typically borrow up to 80% of home equity |

## WHERE TO GO FOR MORE INFORMATION

● Information about college costs and financial aid are available in libraries, high school guidance offices, and online
● Financial aid offices publicize their own programs as well as government loan and work/study programs

● The U.S. Department of Education has regional offices—listed in the phone book—and a website (www.ed.gov) for information on state scholarships, grants, and work programs

● High school guidance offices should know about local scholarships, and your employer, service club, or religious organization will know about the ones they sponsor

# Planning for Retirement

**Retirement planning means making sure you'll have enough to live on.**

After several decades when Social Security and **pensions** provided many people with a large chunk of the money they needed to live comfortably after they retired, some things have changed. While you may be entitled to a pension, or income during retirement, you're increasingly likely to be responsible for providing for your own needs.

## EMPLOYER-SPONSORED PLANS

Employers can offer different types of qualified retirement plans, though it's legal to provide none at all. Some plans are funded and controlled by the employer, while others require your active participation. In each case, though, there is a specific account in your name.

Retirement plans differ in the ways they're funded and the promises they make about your benefits.

A **defined-benefit plan** guarantees you a specific dollar amount when you retire. It's based on your salary or length of service, or a combination of the two. Your employer contributes enough to meet that amount and manages the investment.

In a **defined-contribution plan**, you or your employer, or sometimes both of you, contribute money to your retirement account each year. The benefit amount is not guaranteed because it depends on the amount that's contributed, the management of the plan, and changing economic conditions.

**Profit-sharing retirement plans** are funded by a company, often based on annual profits. They make no payment guarantees. The company determines the rate of contributions each year. In lean years, there may be none at all.

When you retire or leave the company, the money is paid out either:

- As a **lump sum**, known as a distribution
- As a **pension annuity**, or regular payments for as long as you live (and in some cases, as long as your husband or wife lives too)

## PENSION POINTERS

Most pensions are not adjusted for inflation, which means that each year the fixed amount you receive will buy less. And some plans known as paired pensions reduce the amount of your pension by the Social Security you get.

That doesn't mean working forever. By taking advantage of a range of tax-deferred retirement savings plans to invest for the future, you can postpone paying taxes on your earnings until you use the money. Tax-deferral means your nest egg can grow faster and ultimately provide more retirement income.

## TIME ON THE JOB

If you're part of a defined benefits plan and change jobs frequently, you'll probably end up with a smaller pension than if you'd stayed put. Four jobs in 40 years rather than 40 years in one job can cut a pension in half.

## THE TRADE-OFF

Because earnings on retirement-plan investments are tax-deferred, you agree, as a condition of participating, that you'll leave the money invested until you reach at least age 59½. If you withdraw it before then, you usually have to pay a 10% penalty in addition to the tax that's due.

There are some exceptions to the early withdrawal penalty, including paying college tuition, buying a first home, and covering certain medical expenses, but retirement plans are designed to provide the cash you'll need after you stop working.

## WHEN IT'S YOURS

If you're part of a retirement plan, what happens if you leave your job? The answer depends on the type of plan it is.

With a defined-benefit plan, you're entitled to the value of your account (contributions plus earnings) provided you're **vested**, or have worked there long enough to qualify for a pension. Vesting rules vary, though being 100% vested after five years or 20% after three years and 100% after seven is typical with non-government employers. Usually, though, you don't get any payout until you retire. And since no contributions are added after you leave the job, the account may not provide much income.

With a defined contribution plan, any contributions you've made are automatically yours, though you may have to be vested to be entitled to employer contributions. You can always roll the money in your account into an IRA or your new employer's plan and continue to build it. That's why the plans are described as **portable**.

## RETIREMENT PLAN DISTRIBUTION BASICS

When you retire or take a new job, you can move the money in your retirement plan into a Rollover Individual Retirement Account (IRA) to preserve its tax-deferred status. Or you can take a lump-sum withdrawal of the entire amount and reinvest it as you choose.

- You can have the money rolled over directly into another qualified retirement plan or IRA where it can continue to grow tax-deferred. You'll owe no tax until you begin withdrawing.

- You can get the money yourself, keep it for up to 60 days (using it anyway you want) and then roll it into another qualified plan so that it continues to grow tax-deferred. However, if you get the money even briefly, your employer must withhold 20% of the total.

- You can get the money yourself, pay the taxes that are due and use it any way you like. If you're younger than 59½ you may owe a 10% penalty.

**But remember:**

- If you're handling a rollover yourself, you must deposit the entire amount (including the 20% that's withheld) or be vulnerable to taxes and penalties. The 20% that's withheld will be refunded after you file your income tax return.

- Most experts urge you to keep retirement rollovers in separate accounts because that's the only way you can roll it back into another employer's plan.

- The one thing you don't want to do is use a distribution for everyday expenses instead of keeping it invested.

# IRAs: What They Are

IRAs are easy to set up—but not always easy to understand.

**IRAs, or Individual Retirement Accounts**, are tax-deferred, personal retirement plans. There are three types: the traditional deductible IRA, the traditional nondeductible IRA and the Roth IRA. (The Education IRA is a college savings plan, not a retirement plan.)

- All **traditional IRAs** are **tax-deferred**. That means you owe no tax on your earnings until you withdraw

- **Roth IRAs** are **tax-free** if you follow the rules for withdrawal. That means you owe no tax at all on your earnings as they accumulate or when you withdraw

## WEIGHING THE CHOICE

If you have a choice of which IRA to open, you'll want to weigh the pros and cons:

| | ROTH | TRADITIONAL IRA | |
| --- | --- | --- | --- |
| | | **Nondeductible** | **Deductible** |
| **PROS** | • Tax-free income<br>• No required withdrawals | • Tax-deferred earnings | • Immediate tax savings on tax-deferred investment<br>• Tax-deferred earnings |
| **CONS** | • Not deductible<br>• Account must be open five years to qualify for tax-free provision | • Not deductible<br>• Tax paid at regular rates at withdrawal<br>• Required withdrawals beginning at 70½ | • Tax paid at regular rates at withdrawal<br>• Required withdrawals beginning at 70½ |

## DO YOU QUALIFY FOR A ROTH IRA?

**Single**

You don't qualify for a Roth

$110,000

Partial Roth

$95,000

You qualify for a Roth

**Adjusted Gross Income**

**Married**

You don't qualify for a Roth

$160,000

Partial Roth

$150,000

You qualify for a Roth

**Adjusted Gross Income**

### THE $2,000 DEAL

The only requirement for opening an IRA is having earned income—money you get for work you do. Your total annual contribution is limited to $2,000, whether you put it all in one account or divide between a traditional IRA and a Roth. Any amount you earn qualifies, and you can contribute as much as you want, up to the cap. But you can't contribute more than you earn. For example, if you earn $1,800, that's how much you can put in. And whether you earn $3,500 or $350,000, the top limit is the same.

### SPOUSAL ACCOUNTS

If your husband or wife doesn't work, but you do, you can contribute up to $2,000 a year to a separate spousal account. The advantage for the nonworking partner is being able to build an individual retirement fund.

## WHICH IRA FOR YOU?

If you qualify for all three types of IRAs, based on your **adjusted gross income** (AGI), you'll have to choose among a traditional deductible IRA, a traditional nondeductible IRA or a Roth IRA.

The traditional deductible IRA has the strictest limits, and the traditional nondeductible has none at all. The Roth, which many experts describe as the best deal for most people, is in between.

In 2000, for example, you can deduct all of your IRA contribution if you're single and your AGI is less than $32,000, a gradually decreasing portion as your income gets closer to $42,000 and nothing if it's above $42,000. You can always deduct the full amount of your contribution if you're not covered by a retirement plan at your job.

You're eligible for a full Roth if you're single and your AGI is less than $95,000. With an AGI between that amount and $110,000, you can put a portion of your contribution into a Roth.

For a married couple, the limits for a deductible IRA are $52,000, phased out at $62,000. Either of you can deduct if you have no retirement plan of your own at work. But if your spouse has a plan, deductibility is reduced gradually if your joint income is over $150,000 and eliminated if it's over $160,000. In the past, you weren't eligible to deduct if you were married to someone covered by a plan, but now each partner qualifies separately. The Roth limits are $150,000, phased out at $160,000.

## IT'S YOUR ACCOUNT

It's easy to open an IRA. All you do is fill out a relatively simple application provided by the bank, mutual fund company, brokerage firm or other financial institution you choose to be **custodian**, sometimes called the trustee, of your account.

Because IRAs are self-directed, meaning that you decide how to invest the money, you're responsible for following the rules that govern the accounts. Basically, that means putting in only the amount you're entitled to each year and making approved investments. You must also report your contribution to the IRS, on your basic return if it's deductible and on Form 8606 if it's not.

You can invest your IRA money almost any way you like, from putting it in sedate savings accounts to buying volatile options on futures. The only things you can't buy are fine art, gems, non-U.S. coins and collectibles. And you can buy and sell investments in your IRA account whenever you please without worrying about paying tax on your gains.

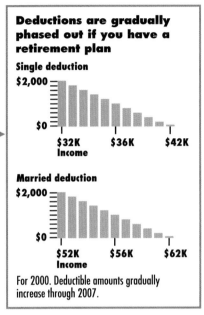

**Deductions are gradually phased out if you have a retirement plan**

**Single deduction**

$2,000

$0

$32K    $36K    $42K
Income

**Married deduction**

$2,000

$0

$52K    $56K    $62K
Income

For 2000. Deductible amounts gradually increase through 2007.

---

You have until April 15—the day taxes are due—to open an IRA account and make the deposit for the previous tax year.

You can contribute $2,000 to your IRA in a lump sum or spread the deposit out over the 15 months. You get the best return on your investment if you put in the whole amount the first day you can, January 2 of the tax year you're making the contribution for. If you're like most people, you're more apt to make the deposit the last possible day. The most practical solution may be weekly or monthly contributions.

**WHEN TO CONTRIBUTE**

**January 2**
Best day to deposit lump sum

**April 15**
Last day to deposit lump sum

**Installment deposit over 15 months before taxes are due**

| F M A M J J A S O N D | F M A |

Jan 1, 2000    Jan 1, 2001    Apr 15, 2001

# Salary Reduction Plans

## 401(k)s and their cousins are blue-ribbon retirement plans.

For simplicity, convenience and tax savings, it's hard to find a better deal than a 401(k), or similar retirement plan.

These plans allow you to defer taxes on part of your salary by contributing to a special retirement account set up by your employer. You don't pay taxes on the contribution amount or earnings until you begin to withdraw money, usually at retirement.

The amount you contribute is not reported on your W-2 to the IRS, reducing your taxable income for the year. For example, if you contributed $4,000 of your $60,000 salary to a 401(k) plan, only $56,000 would be reported as income.

You'll receive periodic statements showing the amounts you have in each investment option and how each one performed. The statement will also report your contributions and any matching contributions made by your employer.

The plans are self-directed, which means you choose the investments, sometimes from a limited group available through your employer's plan and sometimes from a wider assortment offered through the plan's administrator.

You must choose to participate, however. If you don't contribute, you run the risk of being short of retirement income, especially if it's the only retirement plan your employer offers.

### PRETAX CONTRIBUTIONS

You may be able to contribute a percentage of your pretax salary up to a preset dollar limit—$10,500 for 2000. The cap on 403(b)s is 20% of your salary, up to a limit of $10,500. The caps on 401(k)s are increased regularly to keep pace with inflation.

### POST-TAX CONTRIBUTIONS

Some plans allow you to make after-tax contributions as well. You get tax-deferred earnings, but your money is tied up in retirement investments.

### MATCHING CONTRIBUTIONS

Many employers contribute up to 50¢ for every $1 put in by an employee, though the matching contribution may be higher, or lower. With SIMPLE plans, introduced in 1997, your employer must contribute a specific percentage of your salary.

### BORROWING FROM THE PLAN

You can borrow from your plan if your employer allows loans. The loan has to be paid back on a regular basis, usually at market rates. Since you're repaying the money, it's not considered a withdrawal and isn't taxed.

### EARLY WITHDRAWALS

You'll pay tax on withdrawals, plus a 10% penalty, if you are younger than 59½, and you may not be allowed to make contributions for a period of time. The IRS has softened these rules to allow withdrawals in hardship cases—such as paying for medical emergencies, college tuition or a principal residence.

**Savings Plan—401(K) Statement**

Period: 6/1–9/30

| | Company Stock (25%) | Equity (50%) | Balan... |
|---|---|---|---|
| **Account To Date** | | | |
| Employer contributions | $21,312.50 | $42,625.00 | |
| Pre-tax | $0.00 | $0.00 | |
| After-tax | $2,664.00 | $5,328.00 | |
| Company match | $0 | $0.00 | |
| Rollovers | $23,976.50 | $47,953.00 | |
| Totals | | | |
| **Activity This Period** | | | |
| Employee contributions | $1,375.00 | $2,750.00 | |
| Pre-tax | $4,000.00 | $0.00 | |
| After-tax | $343.75 | $687.50 | |
| Company match | $0.00 | $0.00 | |
| Withdrawals | − $500.00 | $0.00 | |
| Loans | 1,000.00 | 0.00 | |
| Transfers in | 0.00 | − 1,000.00 | |
| Transfers out | | | |
| Totals | $6,218.75 | $2,437.50 | |
| **Current Totals** | $30,195.25 | $50,390.50 | |

## IRA OR 401(k)

If you've got the choice between a salary reduction plan and an IRA, what should you do? Many experts would say do both. But if the amount you can contribute is limited, you may want to weigh the options against each other.

401(k) plans have higher contribution limits, offer the possibility of matching contributions and reduce the income tax you owe. However, your investment options are limited to those offered through the plan.

IRAs offer you practically limitless investment opportunities, but you're limited to a $2,000 annual contribution, which may not reduce your taxes. Your IRA contributions aren't matched.

### K[...]

tribu[...]
of your profita[...]
tribution is optional, b[...]
tributions is lower. If you have [...]
you must contribute the same percent[...]
of income for them as you do for yourself.

While Keoghs provide substantial tax savings, they can be complicated to set up. You'll probably need professional advice to do it correctly.

### Annuities

Tax-deferred a[...]
long-term inv[...]

When you inv[...]
term invest[...]
due on y[...]
begin t[...]
of y[...]
tio[...]

| | Fixed (25%) | Totals |
|---|---|---|
| | $21,312.50 | $85,250.00 |
| | $0.00 | $0.00 |
| | $2,664.00 | $10,656.00 |
| | $0.00 | $0.00 |
| | $23,976.50 | $95,906.00 |
| | | |
| | $1,375.00 | $5,500.00 |
| | $0.00 | $4,000.00 |
| | $343.75 | $1,375.00 |
| | $0.00 | $0.00 |
| | $0.00 | - $500.00 |
| | $0.00 | 1,000.00 |
| | 0.00 | - 1,000.00 |
| | 0.00 | $11,375.00 |
| | $1,718.75 | |
| .00 $25,695.25 | | $106,281.00 |

### INVESTMENT OPTIONS

Employers typically provide a number of investment options:

- **Mutual funds**, usually including at least one stock fund, a bond fund, a balanced fund and sometimes a money market or index fund

- **Annuities**

- **Savings bonds**

- **Company stock**

- **Fixed-income accounts**

Most plans let you shift your investment mix from time to time. For example, you may switch from 100% balanced to a mix of 25% company stock, 50% equity, and 25% fixed.

### YOU CAN TAKE IT WITH YOU

If you leave for another job, your 401(k) balance can be transferred to your new employer's plan, if the plan allows it. Or you can roll it over into an IRA or leave it with your old employer.

### THE PLANS AT A GLANCE

There are several varieties of salary reduction plans, which allow you to contribute pretax dollars to a qualified retirement plan. The one you're eligible for depends on the employer you work for. Most plans have similar contribution limits, $10,500 for 2000, though the newest plan, SIMPLE, has a $6,000 cap for 2000.

### 401(k)
- All employees of businesses that sponsor plans
- Matching contributions optional

### 403(b)
- Employees of non-profit, tax-exempt organizations
- Matching contributions optional

### Section 457
- State and municipal workers
- No matching contributions

### Thrift or Savings
- Federal employees and employees of companies offering plans
- Matching contributions optional

### SIMPLE
- Employees of companies with fewer than 100 workers
- Matching contribution required

nuities are another way to build your
estments.

st in an **annuity**, or long-
ment contract, no taxes are
r investment earnings until you
receive income under the terms
contract. There are no contribu-
limits on annuity investing as
here are with IRAs or employer-

sponsored retirement plans. That means you can build a substantial nest egg for your long-term needs. However, putting money into an annuity doesn't reduce your salary or income tax the way 401(k)s and related plans do.

# Building Up

You can invest in a **single premium annuity** with a lump-sum purchase, or build your annuity account by adding money regularly over a period of time. During this **accumulation phase**, while the money is invested and you are not withdrawing, you pay no taxes on earnings in the account.

# Annuity Agreement

**Your annuity contract defines the terms and conditions:**

- **Amount of investment**
- **Earnings at fixed or variable rate**
- **Method of payout**
- **Fees and other investments costs**

### DEFERRED ANNUITIES

**OR**

With a deferred annuity, you get the benefit of tax-deferred compounding for an extended period, at either a fixed or variable rate. When you're ready to begin withdrawals, the way you'll collect is spelled out in the terms of your contract. Usually it's in regular monthly installments, but it may be in a fixed number of lump-sum payments. The part of your payout that comes from earnings is taxed at your regular tax rate.

### IMMEDIATE ANNUITIES

You buy an immediate annuity with a single payment and begin the payout period right away, or within the first year. The amount of each payment is set by the terms of your contract. In the sense that an annuity provides regular income, usually after you retire, these plans resemble employer-sponsored pensions. You can also buy an immediate annuity to provide a lifetime stream of income for another person.

## LOOKING AT THE BOTTOM LINE

Annuities are popular investments, but they also have critics who argue that other investments give you more for your money. It pays to look at both sides:

| Pluses | Minuses |
|---|---|
| ● Tax-deferred compounding | ● Some variable annuity contracts have high fees and other expenses |
| ● No caps on contributions | ● Some annuities impose stiff surrender charges |
| ● Guaranteed income stream with fixed-rate contract | ● Taxes are due at regular income-tax rates, not the capital gains rate |
| ● With variable annuities, there is opportunity for growth of principal that may keep up with or exceed the rate of inflation | ● Income from fixed-rate contract may not keep up with inflation |

## FIXED OR VARIABLE?

Deferred annuities are available in two forms: those that pay a **fixed rate** of interest for the life of the annuity and those that pay a **variable rate**.

When you buy a fixed annuity contract, the insurance company that issues it guarantees payment of a fixed rate of return during the build-up period and a guaranteed income for life if you **annuitize**, which means converting your annuity into a stream of regular income. The company invests your principal and takes responsi-bility for earning enough income to meet its obligations to you.

With a variable annuity, you decide how your money will be allocated among a specific menu of **subaccounts** offered by the issuer. Subaccounts are pooled investments, similar to mutual funds, with varying investment objectives and strategies. Variable annuities give you the chance to direct your own investment and potentially make more than you could with a fixed rate. However, the contract makes no payment promises, so you could also end up earning less if the markets are weak or you choose poorly performing investments.

# Paying Out

You start collecting on your annuity investment during the **payout period**, usually after you retire. If you're age 59½ or older when payments begin, you owe income tax on your earnings. If you're younger than that, you'll usually have to pay an additional 10% of the withdrawal as a penalty.

## MONTHLY PAYMENTS

**OR**

You can get regular monthly payments for as long as you live or for a set period of time, such as ten or 20 years.

## LUMP-SUM PAYMENT

Or you can transfer the money to another annuity. You may lose money if your plan imposes a penalty for early withdrawal.

## IMMEDIATE ANNUITY PAYOUTS

The most common payout options for both deferred and immediate annuities are:

**Single life**, which pays a set sum per month as long as you live. When you die, the payments stop.

**Life or period certain**, which covers your lifetime or a set number of years, whichever is longer. Your heirs get the balance if you die before the term is up.

**Joint and several**, which makes payments for your lifetime and the lifetime of your beneficiary.

## WEIGHING THE ISSUES

Immediate annuities provide the security of a regular income for people who are uncomfortable managing their investments. But they have some potential drawbacks:

- If you choose a single life annuity and die within a few years, the company keeps the balance of your money and your heirs get nothing
- Your annuity income may not keep pace with inflation
- The seller, usually an insurance company, may not fulfill its part of the contract

## CHECKLIST FOR ANNUITY INVESTORS

✓ Consider annuities only if you're investing for the long term. Withdrawals before age 59½ face a 10% penalty tax, plus income tax.

✓ Investigate the reputation of the company offering the annuity to be sure it's sound.

✓ Compare surrender periods. Most annuities have surrender charges in the first seven years. You can avoid annuities with lifetime surrender charges.

✓ Look beyond the initial rate if buying a fixed-rate annuity. Approach unusually high rates with caution.

✓ Look for maximum flexibility on getting your money out. You can avoid annuities that don't offer a lump sum or give you a lower interest rate if you take one.

✓ Research the fees an annuity charges. Experts caution against paying more than 2% annually.

✓ Compare costs. Some annuities cost more than others offering a similar income stream.

# Social Security

## For more than 50 years, Social Security has been a source of retirement income.

Social Security was introduced in 1935 in the aftermath of the Great Depression to provide a safety net of regular income to retired and disabled workers and their families. It's a mandatory plan, requiring most employees and the self-employed to contribute a percentage of their yearly salary to support the program. In return, they, their spouses and sometimes their dependents are eligible for retirement, disability and survivorship benefits.

The program has been updated and expanded over the years, to include more workers and provide added benefits. Medicare, the health care plan for people over 65, was added in 1966. In 1972, benefits were indexed to inflation, so that as the cost of living goes up, your Social Security payments increase too.

### BUILDING A RECORD

When you get a Social Security card, your account is open though it isn't activated until you begin working. Then, every year the amount you contribute is recorded. Because what you'll ultimately collect is based on what you pay in, it's important that the record is accurate.

The Social Security Administration sends you a Social Security earnings statement if you are 25 or older and haven't yet begun to collect payments. You should receive an updated copy each year, about three months before your birthday.

If you are younger than 25 and want to get a copy of your earnings statement, fill out an SSA form 7004 and mail it to the Social Security Administration. The forms are available at your local Social Security office, by calling 800-772-1213, or on the SSA website at www.ssa.gov.

If you discover your record is wrong— and it sometimes is, especially if you work more than one job—you can ask that it be corrected. You'll have to supply some evidence for your claim, such as the W-2 income-reporting forms that you file with your income tax. With that information, you should have no trouble correcting the problem. In fact, the SSA encourages people to check their earnings records carefully when they arrive, since recent errors are easier to fix than long-existing ones.

> **To get Social Security benefits, you must contribute to the system or be the spouse or dependent of someone who does.**

### PUTTING MONEY IN

Every year you work, you and your employer contribute equal amounts—in 2000 it's 7.65% of up to $76,200 and 1.45% of amounts over that—to Social Security as required by the Federal Insurance Contribution Act (FICA). Part of your capped contribution, 6.2%, goes to Social Security and the additional 1.45% goes to Medicare. The 1.45% you pay on salary over the cap—which increases each year—goes entirely to Medicare.

| 2000 salary | Your contribution |
|---|---|
| The first $76,200 | 7.65% ($5,829.30 maximum) |
| Amounts over $76,200 | 1.45% (no maximum) |

**Your Social Security Earnings**

| | Social Security | | | Medicare | | |
|---|---|---|---|---|---|---|
| Years | Maximum Taxable Earnings | Your Reported Earnings | Estimated Taxes You Paid | Maximum Taxable Earnings | Your Reported Earnings | Estimated Taxes You Paid |
| 1980 | 25,900 | $25,900 | $1,315 | 25,900 | 25,900 | 271 |
| 1981 | 29,700 | 29,700 | 1,588 | 29,700 | 29,700 | 386 |
| 1982 | 32,400 | 32,400 | 1,749 | 32,400 | 32,400 | 421 |
| 1983 | 35,700 | 35,700 | 1,927 | 35,700 | 35,700 | 464 |
| 1984 | 37,800 | 37,800 | 2,041 | 37,800 | 37,800 | 491 |
| 1985 | 39,600 | 39,600 | 2,257 | 39,600 | 39,600 | 534 |
| 1986 | 42,000 | 32,493 | 1,852 | 42,000 | 32,493 | 471 |
| 1987 | 43,800 | 43,800 | 2,496 | 43,800 | 43,800 | 635 |
| 1988 | 45,000 | 45,000 | 2,727 | 45,000 | 45,000 | 652 |
| 1989 | 48,000 | 14,670 | 2,101 | 48,000 | 14,670 | 502 |
| 1990 | 51,300 | 51,300 | 3,150 | 51,300 | 51,300 | 743 |
| 1991 | 53,400 | 53,400 | 3,310 | 125,000 | 57,657 | 836 |
| 1992 | 55,500 | 38,267 | 2,372 | 130,200 | 38,267 | 554 |
| 1993 | 57,600 | 25,000 | 1,550 | 135,000 | 25,000 | 362 |
| 1994 | 60,600 | Not Yet Recorded | | No Limit | Not Yet Recorded | |
| 1995 | 61,200 | No Limit | | No Limit | | |

Total estimated Social Security taxes paid $37,864.  Total estimated Medicare taxes paid $8,601.

### SOCIAL SECURITY FACTS

- 17% of the population (more than 42 million people) receive benefits
- The majority get retirement money
- 95% of the people over age 65 receive benefits
- Almost 70% of the people applying for retirement benefits each year are younger than 65
- Social Security paid over $379.3 billion in benefits in 1998

The maximum monthly Social Security benefit for a worker retiring at age 65 in January 2000 is $1,433. The average monthly benefit is $804.

# We've Got Your Number

Almost everybody is registered with Social Security. Your 9-digit number stays the same for life, even if you change your name.

**The first three digits** indicate the state where you applied for a card. The number changes as more cards are issued in that state.

**The second group of digits** doesn't have a particular meaning—though they are a related state code.

**The last four digits** are assigned in numerical order, for example 7091, 7092, 7093, and so on. One exception: Twins, triplets, or other multiple siblings don't get numbers in order.

## 074-82-0038

## GETTING MONEY OUT

People born before 1938 can collect full Social Security benefits when they turn 65. The qualifying age will increase gradually every year until it reaches 66 in 2009, and 67 in 2027.

You can collect a percentage—currently 80%—of your benefit if you retire at 62. But if you work beyond the full retirement age and keep on contributing, you increase your benefits.

When you die, your surviving spouse is entitled to your benefits unless he or she would collect more on his or her own work record. The exact amount your spouse will be eligible for depends on what you were collecting and how old he or she is.

## TAXING BENEFITS

If your total income for the year, including half your Social Security and your tax-exempt earnings, is greater than the level set by Congress—in 1999 it was $25,000 for single people and $32,000 for a married couple—you'll owe federal income tax on part of your Social Security benefits. The higher your total income, the greater percentage of your benefit is taxable, to a maximum of 85%.

About 20% of people getting Social Security benefits end up paying tax on part of what they receive. The Internal Revenue Service (IRS) provides a worksheet you can use to figure out exactly how much of your benefit you must include in your taxable income. If you pay estimated taxes, you'll have to be sure your installments cover what you'll owe.

## WORKING AFTER RETIREMENT

There's no law against working after you retire—but there are limits on what you can earn.

| Age | Limit you can earn without penalty | Impact on Social Security payment |
|---|---|---|
| 65 and over | No limit on earnings | None |
| 62–65 | $10,080 for 2000 | For every $2 you earn over the limit, your payment is reduced by $1 |

### for example

If you earn $11,580 in 2000 when you're age 63, your Social Security benefit will be reduced by $750.

|   | $ 11,580 | Earnings |
|---|---|---|
| − | $ 10,080 | Limit |
| = | $ 1,500 |  |
| ÷ | 2 | (You lose $1 for every $2 over the limit) |
| = | $ 750 | Reduction of benefit |

# Life Insurance

## Evaluating your life insurance needs is a key part of financial planning.

The simple answer to how much insurance you need is enough money to cover your dependents' immediate cash needs and living expenses.

If you support a family, keep a household running, have a mortgage, or expect the kids to go to college, insurance can fill the financial gap left by your death or disability. But if you don't have dependents, or they don't need your money to live on, your insurance needs may be very different.

In general, older people need less insurance because their financial obligations have been met—mortgages and college tuition are paid—and their investments are producing income. Experts disagree on how much coverage is enough. An old rule of thumb says that you need five to seven times (or even ten times) your annual salary. But a lot depends on your life style, number of dependents and other sources of income.

**FINANCIAL**

### ROUGHING OUT YOUR LIFE INSURANCE NEEDS

To estimate the amount of coverage you need to replace 75% of your take-home pay for the years you would have been working, multiply your salary by the factor at the intersection of your salary and your current age. In this example, it's $720,000.*

| Annual pay (before taxes) | Current age of person insured | | | | | | |
|---|---|---|---|---|---|---|---|
| | 25 | 30 | 35 | 40 | 45 | 50 | 55 |
| $30,000 | 14 | 13 | 12 | 10 | 9 | 7 | 5 |
| $40,000 | 13 | 12 | 11 | 10 | 9 | 7 | 5 |
| $60,000 | 12 | 12 | 11 | 9 | 8 | 6 | 5 |
| $80,000 | 12 | 11 | 10 | 9 | 8 | 6 | 4 |
| $100,000 | 11 | 10 | 9 | 8 | 7 | 5 | 4 |
| $150,000 | 10 | 10 | 9 | 8 | 7 | 5 | 4 |
| $200,000 | 9 | 9 | 8 | 7 | 6 | 5 | 5 |

*Doesn't take into account any income survivors can expect from Social Security, investments, or other sources. More or less coverage may be needed, depending on individual family circumstances.

Source: Principal Financial Group

## A FEW THINGS A FEE-ONLY INSURANCE ADVISER CAN DO

- Provide second opinions about policies you're planning to buy
- Tell you whether your existing insurer is financially sound
- Evaluate whether your existing policy or annuity is appropriate
- Help you select policies and choose options and riders
- Negotiate lower commissions from your insurance agent

## LIFE INSURANCE WORKCHART

You need enough life insurance to cover your dependents' living expenses. You can use this work-chart to estimate that amount, as the illustration below shows:

**1** Dependents annual living costs (including mortgage payments and other loans) **$ 65,000**

**2** Dependents sources of income
Salary $35,500
Investment income $3,500
Social Security, pensions and other $5,000 **– $ 44,000**

**3** Additional income needed (subtract 2 from 1) **= $ 21,000**

**4** Divide line 3 by the prevailing interest rate **÷ 7%**

**5** Face value of the policy you need **= $300,000**

To provide money for educational expenses, you can increase your coverage.

**SECURITY**

**UNDERWRITING** is the process insurance companies use to assess you as a risk and decide if they will sell you insurance. It's based on the information you provide in the application. If you don't tell the truth, your insurance may be cancelled, or the company may refuse to pay a claim.

## PAYING THE BILL

The cost of buying life insurance varies enormously, depending on the type you buy, the company you buy it from, and how long the company thinks you are likely to live.

Estimating the total cost can be tricky, since the **premium**, or amount you pay for some types of insurance, may increase over time. Further, two companies may charge very different amounts for the same coverage.

One way to do a search is to use a fee-only adviser, who can help you sift among the options and select the one that's best for you. Check to be sure the adviser is independent and won't earn a commission on any policy. As a rule, **group** life insurance provided through your employer is the least expensive.

## RISK VS. COST

The cost of insurance is largely determined by the risk you pose to the insurance company, as shown on an **actuarial table**. These tables project your life expectancy based on age, gender, health and life style.

If you're considered a high risk—for example, if you smoke, are overweight, or have a dangerous occupation or hobby—the company may charge you a higher premium than other people of the same age or gender, or refuse to insure you at all.

However, if you are a **preferred risk**—generally a nonsmoker whose health and life style make you likely to live longer—you may qualify for lower rates that significantly reduce your premium and save you money.

# Types of Life Insurance

You can buy life insurance that protects you for a limited period of time or stays in effect until you die.

All life insurance policies work on the same basic premise: You make payments—called **premiums**—to the insurance company, which promises to pay your beneficiaries a **death benefit** when you die.

But there are major differences between **term** and **cash value** policies. What you buy will depend on how much you can afford, how long you need the coverage, whether you want only protection or savings as well and how much effort you want to spend shopping for the best deal.

## TERM INSURANCE

The most straightforward and often least expensive type of coverage is **term insurance**. You can buy it one year at a time, or for a specific period—say five or ten years. If you die during the term, your beneficiaries collect. But if you're alive when the policy expires, the coverage ends and there's no payout.

With a **decreasing** term policy, the face amount diminishes each year. This gives you the most protection at the beginning and very little towards the end, when you may need less coverage anyway.

If you need life insurance for ten years or less, term insurance is almost always your best bet. Because initial premiums for term policies are lower than those for cash value policies—sometimes as much as ten times less—you may want to buy term and invest the difference, which often provides a better return and more control of your money.

But unlike cash value policies, term policies don't accumulate cash savings that you can get back or borrow against.

## TERM INSURANCE

**A**s long as you pay the premium, you're covered.

**I**f you die, your beneficiaries receive the death benefit.

**I**f you stop paying the premium, the policy ends and you get nothing back.

## RENEWABLE VS. LEVEL TERM

All term insurance isn't the same. **Annual renewable** policies can be renewed year after year, often with ever-higher premiums. With **level premium** policies, your payments are fixed for the entire term, say five or ten years. Though your initial premiums are higher, they don't rise during the term, which can mean substantial savings over time.

Consider a 45-year-old man who wants $250,000 of coverage for the next ten years. A company offers a renewable policy with premiums starting at $432 a year, projected to reach $920 in the tenth year. Or he could get a level premium policy for the same period, for $513 a year. Adding up the premiums for both policies, the level premium would be cheaper than the renewable policy by some $1,500.

According to The Wall Street Journal, fully half the cash value policies written are dropped within seven years. This means the coverage has been very expensive because high commissions and other fees have limited the amount of cash that could accumulate during that time.

## CAN YOU BORROW AGAINST YOUR INSURANCE POLICY?

Whether you can borrow depends on the type of policy you have. You can't borrow against a term policy. But with a cash value policy you can borrow against your cash reserve. If you don't repay, the amount of the loan is deducted from the benefit paid at your death. Loan rates on cash value policies are generally lower than prevailing market rates, but you risk leaving less for your dependents.

# CASH VALUE INSURANCE

**A**s long as you pay the premium, you're covered.

**I**f you die, your beneficiaries receive the death benefit.

**I**f you stop paying the premium, you get the cash surrender value.

## WHO SELLS INSURANCE?

If life insurance coverage is not available as part of your employee benefits, and you can't buy it through a group, you can contact an **insurance agent** or **broker**, visit your bank, speak with a financial planner or do online search.

An agent represents one insurance company, while a broker can offer policies provided by several different insurers. In most cases, you'll want to compare a number of policies to find the best one for you.

You can have any policies an agent proposes evaluated by a fee-only insurance consultant. You can find them listed in the yellow pages or on the Internet.

## CASH VALUE INSURANCE

In contrast to term policies, cash value policies—such as **whole life** and **universal life**—combine a death benefit with tax-deferred savings. Part of the premiums you pay forms a cash reserve, which accumulates tax-deferred. If you surrender the policy, you get the cash reserve back. When you die, your beneficiaries get the death benefit.

If you drop the policy, you get to keep some of the cash reserve—this is the **cash surrender value**—but you'll owe income tax on your gain if the cash surrender valve is greater than your net premiums. If you hold the policy until you die, however, your beneficiaries owe no income tax on the payment they receive.

## TYPES OF POLICIES

Despite the seemingly endless varieties, there are three basic types of cash value insurance:

**1 Whole life**, sometimes called **straight life**, is the most traditional. The premiums stay the same for the length of the policy. Once you've paid all the premiums, the policy remains in effect until you die. You accumulate a cash reserve, but you have no say over how the money is invested.

**2 Universal life** offers some flexibility. You can vary the amount of the premium by applying a portion of the accumulated savings to cover the cost. You can also increase or decrease the amount of the death benefit while the policy is in force. But you pay for this flexibility with higher fees and administrative costs.

Typically, there's a guaranteed rate of return on the savings portion for the first year, and a minimum, or floor, for the life of the policy.

**3 Variable life** is a form of cash value insurance designed for growth. You can choose how to allocate your cash value among the accounts the insurance company offers. The value of your policy at any point reflects how well your accounts are doing.

# Long-Term Care

Many people are concerned about long-term health care for themselves or their parents.

When you're doing financial planning, you have to think about some of the things you'd rather not consider, such as needing long-term health care. You may also be concerned about the costs of taking care of aging parents or disabled children.

Among the things that make planning for health care more complicated than accumulating tuition money or buying a home are that it's so unpredictable and so expensive. You don't know if you'll need care at all, or when, or for how long. And since health care costs have tended to escalate more quickly than most other expenses, it's difficult if not impossible to predict what you'll spend.

What's more, the role employer- and government-sponsored insurance might play in protecting your health-care needs is also difficult to predict.

But that doesn't mean you should throw up your hands. There are ways to plan for long-term care.

### MEDICARE

If you're eligible for Social Security, you're eligible for Medicare, the federal government-sponsored health insurance for people over 65. Remember though, that coverage is individual, so that younger husbands and wives need private insurance until they reach 65 as well.

## CHECK YOUR COVERAGE

You should start by finding out what kind of insurance coverage you currently have. In some cases, you may have the option of adding extra coverage for disability or catastrophic illness.

If your family depends on your income, or would have to hire someone to handle your responsibilities, **disability insurance** makes a lot of sense. It pays you a percentage of your salary during the period you are unable to work. Usually the most affordable plans are those available through your employer, union, or other organization. Commercial disability insurance—the type available directly from an insurer—tends to be expensive. You'll want to be sure that the amount you'd receive in benefits would justify the expense of the insurance.

**Catastrophic illness** insurance, which covers medical costs after you reach the maximum amount your regular health insur-ance will cover, may also be a good idea if you can get it reasonably through a group policy. Many regular health insur-ance plans do cap lifetime benefits. But before you act, be sure you understand the details of the policy. It's another case when an insurance adviser may be helpful (see page 107).

## LONG-TERM CARE INSURANCE

Long-term care insurance provides coverage for chronic illnesses and long-term disabilities that aren't covered by Medicare. Look for policies that pay for nursing-home care, care at home, and respite care, or help for the terminally ill and their families.

In most cases, people think about buying the coverage in their 50s, or 60s, when the premiums are still affordable. By then, they may be able to trim life insurance premiums, freeing up the money to pay for it.

If you're considering the coverage, you'll want to examine what various policies pay as well as what they cost. Make sure that your plan provides coverage for degenerative diseases such as Alzheimer's. Also check your plan's restrictive policies on payouts, prior conditions and other factors.

You'll also want to ask about inflation protection. While having it will probably add to the cost, the advantage of an inflation-indexed plan is that what you get at the point you begin to use the insurance will be more in line with the real costs. A $100 plan may cover a large part of the daily nursing home cost this year, but it will probably cover much less of the total bill ten years from now.

The most affordable coverage is generally available through group policies provided by your employer or some other association you belong to. You can get individual coverage from life insurance companies, too, though it may be expensive.

### THINGS TO CHECK FOR

If you're buying long-term care insurance, you'll want to ask these questions:

☑ What's the waiting period before payment begins?

☑ Does the plan cover degenerative diseases?

☑ Is there **inflation protection**?

☑ Is there a **waiver of premium**, which allows you to stop paying while you're using the benefits?

☑ Is there a **non-forfeiture clause**, so that you'll get partial coverage or your heirs will get money back even if you let the policy lapse?

☑ How often are policies revoked after they are issued?

### A DIFFERENT PLAN

Another choice you may be offered is a policy that promises to pay a specific amount under specific conditions, such as $100 per day while you are in the hospital. Though the coverage may seem cheap, the amount that's paid may be only a fraction of what you need. What's more, the plans are often loaded with conditions and exceptions.

# Estate Planning

Your estate contains the assets you have accumulated by the time of your death.

While much of the financial planning you do is designed to help you and your loved ones live the life you want, one aspect of it, called **estate planning**, deals with what happens to your assets after you die. There are many ways to ensure that they're transferred to the people you want to enjoy them, and that potential hassles are minimized or avoided.

The more you have, the more important it is to have a comprehensive plan using gifts, trusts and other strategies to disburse your assets. Otherwise, there could be huge tax bills. Even if your estate is modest, you don't want to run the risk of a court-appointed person

dividing up your property and potentially shortchanging people you care about. But that will happen if you don't plan.

Another aspect of estate planning is deciding who will take care of your minor children if you should die. If you don't leave specific instructions, the court will decide on a guardian.

FAMILY TRUST FUND

CHARITABLE TRUST

## SAVING YOUR HEIRS MONEY

There are a number of strategies you can use to save your heirs money after you die by reducing the size of your estate. This may seem like a strange approach if you've spent a lifetime building your assets. But there are real advantages.

### TAX-FREE GIFTS
Both you and your spouse can make annual tax-free gifts of up to $10,000 in cash or property to anyone you want. For example, by giving each of your three children a gift of $10,000 a year for seven years (for a total of $210,000), you could reduce an $800,000 estate to below $600,000.

### BYPASS TRUSTS
You can set up a bypass trust in your will to pass assets free of tax to your heirs after your surviving spouse's death. Because the trust exists independently, it isn't considered part of your spouse's estate even if he or she has had

access to income from the trust assets. For example, if your estate is worth $875,000, you could leave $200,000 to your spouse tax-free because of the unlimited marital deduction and put the rest in trust for the eventual use of your children or grandchildren.

### INSURANCE
If you avoid owning your own life insurance policy, the death benefit won't be added to your estate when you die. If it is in your name, it might mean risking estate taxes. Instead, you can assign ownership to someone else, have someone else buy a policy on your life, or set up a trust to own the policy.

### THE UNIFIED TAX CREDIT
Every person gets a federal unified tax credit, which can eliminate or reduce tax on gifts and assets that you give away during your lifetime or leave to your heirs. In 2000 and 2001, the credit is $220,550, which is the tax on $675,00. The maximum you can leave tax-free will rise to $700,000 in 2002 and 2003, to $850,000 in 2004, $950,000 in 2005, and then to $1 million in 2006.

The unified tax credit is cumulative and includes the taxes due on **taxable gifts** you've made throughout your life. For example, if you gave your daughter a house assessed at $250,000, the gift taxes would be about $70,000. At your death, the $70,000 would be subtracted from your tax credit, reducing the estate you could leave tax free. Nontaxable gifts of $10,000 or less per person per year don't count against this credit.

## GIVE IT OR WILL IT?

If you're deciding whether to give someone a gift equal to more than $10,000 while you're alive or leave the property in your will, there are some things to consider, including the tax consequences.

| | Outright gift | Inheritance |
|---|---|---|
| **Value for income tax purposes** | Value is what you paid for it originally. | Value is **stepped up**, or increased to what the property is worth at the time of inheritance. |
| **What taxes are due** | Potentially large capital gains tax on increased value will be due when property is sold. No inheritance tax due. Potential estate tax can't reduce size of gift. | Capital gains tax if property is sold probably less than if received as gift. Inheritance tax may be due. Potential that estate tax could reduce the size of the inheritance. |

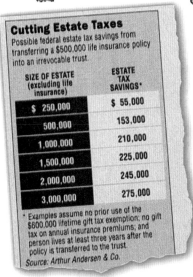

GIFTS TO ALMA MATER

DOLLAR GIFTS

GIFTS TO EMPLOYEES

### Cutting Estate Taxes

Possible federal estate tax savings from transferring a $500,000 life insurance policy into an irrevocable trust.

| SIZE OF ESTATE (excluding life insurance) | ESTATE TAX SAVINGS* |
|---|---|
| $ 250,000 | $ 55,000 |
| 500,000 | 153,000 |
| 1,000,000 | 210,000 |
| 1,500,000 | 225,000 |
| 2,000,000 | 245,000 |
| 3,000,000 | 275,000 |

\* Examples assume no prior use of the $600,000 lifetime gift tax exemption; no gift tax on annual insurance premiums; and person lives at least three years after the policy is transferred to the trust.

Source: Arthur Andersen & Co.

### USING UGMA

The Uniform Gifts to Minors Act (UGMA) and The Uniform Transfer to Minors Act (UTMA) are ways of giving minor children tax-free gifts of up to $10,000 a year. The advantage is simplicity: It's easy to set up an account with most financial institutions—no complicated legal documents are required. You, as the custodian, control the investment.

But remember, the gifts are irrevocable—you can't get the money back once it's given. And the child has the right to take control of the money at age 18 or age 21, depending on the laws of your state.

### WHAT'S IN YOUR ESTATE

Your estate includes all your assets, minus any debts or other financial obligations. Your assets include:

- Anything you own in your own name, including bank accounts, real estate, life insurance and investment assets, including retirement accounts
- Half of everything you own jointly with your husband or wife
- All of what you own jointly with anyone else, unless there's proof the other person paid
- Your share of any partnership or other business
- Property in revocable trusts and custodial accounts that you created and for which you are the trustee or custodian
- Any money you're owed

The liabilities that reduce your estate:

- Taxes you owe
- Outstanding debts
- The costs of settling the estate

When you die, the total value of your estate is computed to determine if your heirs will owe federal estate taxes and the amount of state inheritance tax that will be due.

# Making a Will

Two out of three Americans die *intestate*—without a will.

A will is a legal document that transfers what you own to your **beneficiaries** when you die. It also names the **executor** whom you want to carry out the terms of the will and a **guardian** for your minor children, if you have any.

Your signature and those of two witnesses make your will authentic. Witnesses don't have to know what the will says, but they must watch you sign it and you must watch them witness it. Hand-written wills—called **holographs**—are legal in about half the states, but most wills are typed and follow a standard format.

## CHANGING YOUR WILL

There are many reasons you might alter your will—the birth of a child, the death of a beneficiary, a new marriage or a divorce, increased personal wealth, or simply a change of mind.

Major revisions require a new will that clearly states it supercedes the old one. Minor changes are handled with a **codicil**, or written amendment, that you sign and date, and have witnessed. If you do change your will, you should be careful to destroy the old one, including any copies. If you don't, settling it will be delayed.

## LEAVING PEOPLE OUT

You can disinherit anybody except your spouse, and in some community property states you can even do that. If you want to disinherit some or all of your children, say so specifically because that makes your wishes harder to contest. Other people you can just omit. Or you might leave them $1. It makes your point.

## TIMING IS AN ISSUE

You can require that a beneficiary must survive you by a certain length of time—often 45 days—in order to inherit. This provision saves double taxes and court costs if the beneficiary should die shortly after you do, and it lets you determine who gets your property next.

Timing is also critical when a married couple dies at the same time. A **simultaneous death clause** in your will passes your property directly to your surviving heirs without delays.

# What's in a Will?

Your name and address.

A statement that it's your **will**. You should make a will as soon as you have any real assets or get married, and certainly by the time you have a child.

The names of the people and organizations—your **beneficiaries**—who will share in your estate. It's better to leave percentages of the estate rather than dollar amounts to the major (or primary) beneficiaries, since there's no way to tell precisely what your assets will be. You can leave specific amounts to charities and secondary inheritors.

An **executor** to oversee the disposition of your estate and **trustee(s)** to manage any trust(s) you establish. There should be a second person named for each position, in case the primary one is unable or unwilling to serve.

A **guardian** to take responsibility for your minor children and possibly a **trustee** to manage the children's assets in cooperation with the guardian.

**Designation of the funds or assets** that should be used to pay estate and inheritance taxes.

## IF YOU DON'T HAVE A WILL

Without a will, you die **intestate**. The law of your state then determines what happens to your estate and your minor children. This process, called administration, is governed by the probate court and is notoriously slow, often expensive and subject to some surprising state laws.

For example, in some states, if you remarried and have children only from your first marriage, your current spouse could get your entire estate and your children nothing. If you are unmarried and childless, your estate will be divided among relatives. Friends, partners and charities will not share.

## DO YOU REALLY NEED A LAWYER TO DRAFT A WILL?

The more complex your situation, or the more assets you have, the more it makes sense to consult a lawyer who specializes in wills and estates. Lawyers frequently charge by the hour, so you can save money by providing good records and making key decisions before your meeting.

Wills you prepare yourself using a standard format are valid if they have all the necessary information and are properly signed and witnessed. But requirements vary from state to state, so it's important to know the laws where you live. You might also consider having a lawyer review any will you write. Fill-in-the-blank wills, called statutory wills, restrict your options in leaving your property, so they have limited use.

BLUMBE
HER, NYC

A 184—Will with affidavit of subscribing witnesses, extra space. 4-89.

**I,** Charlotte Peck Gardner, residing in the County of Saratoga, State o

being of sound mind and memory, and considering the uncertainty of this life, do make,

and declare this to be my last **Will and Testament** as follows, hereby rev

other former Wills by me at any time made.

First, after my lawful debts are paid, I give all my tangible personal prope

to my husband, Ralph B. Gardner (hereafter called "my husband"), if he

me, or, if he does not survive me, to such of my children who survive

be divided as they agree, or, if they are unable to agree, to be divi

them in shares of as nearly equal value as possible by my executor, w

as to such division shall be final. If none of my husband or childre

me, I direct my executor to distribute my tangible personal property

my siblings who survive me, in shares of nearly equal value. My ex

judgment as to such division shall be final.

SECOND, I give $10,000 to the Library of Simpson College, my

to be used to expand their research collection in whatever manner

deem appropriate.

THIRD, I give my residuary estate, real and personal, inclu

gifts, to my husband, if he survives me. If my husband does no

I give my residuary estate to my issue, per stirpes, who surviv

however, that if either or both of my children shall not have

age of twenty seven (27) years at the time of my death, my re

estate shall not be distributed outright but shall instead be

distributed as provided in said Article SIXTH.

my trustee under Article SIXTH of this Will, to be held, adm

FOURTH, I appoint my husband to be executor of this W

eases to act for any reason, I appoi

e as executor. I appoint my husband

rustees of the estate created under A

Richard E. Williams, fails to quali

point my friend, Alice Boyd Walker,

my executor to pay from my residuar

and succession taxes, and any int

transfer, inheritance, and succession taxes, and any int

thereon, imposed by any state, federal, or at my execute

ro property passing under this Will.

A **living will** expresses your wishes about being kept alive if you're terminally ill or seriously injured. You can get a living will suited to the laws of your state by writing to Choice In Dying, 1035 30th Street, NW, Washington, DC 20007 or calling 800-989-WILL (9455).

# Trusts

Trusts shelter money for your heirs and provide for those who can't fend for themselves.

Trusts are legal entities—like corporations—that earn income, pay taxes, and distribute earnings. The trustee administers the trust, making investment decisions, paying taxes and distributing the income. You can give the trustee the authority to match the distributions to the specific needs of your heirs. For example, you might identify funds for paying tuition or buying property.

The trust can make regular distributions, or it can be set up as an **accumulation trust**, which retains and reinvests the income it earns for future distribution.

You can establish a trust for anyone you want to provide income for: your spouse, elderly parents, your children, or a close friend. For example, a trust might last for one parent's lifetime, until your children reach age 28, or until your grandchildren finish college.

## ADVANCE PLANNING

Trusts can be effective estate-planning tools in many different circumstances. They're certainly not only for the rich. But it is important to understand the different types of trusts available and how they can work for you before you visit your lawyer. Otherwise, you'll find yourself paying a substantial fee before the process of creating the trust ever begins.

You might use trusts to handle transfers that can be complicated if you use a will. For example, if you own property in a state where you don't live, you can streamline the probate process by putting the property into a living trust and passing it directly to your heirs.

If you want to leave money to people you're not sure can handle the responsi-

## HOW TRUSTS WORK

## The Donor

- Sets up the trust
- Names the beneficiaries
- Names the trustees
- Transfers property to the trust

## The Beneficiaries

- Receive the benefits of the trust according to its terms

bility, you can use a trust as well. Then the trustee can control how the assets are paid out. Or you can have a trustee control how assets are divided among a number of different beneficiaries, depending on their circumstances or whatever criteria you establish.

## TYPES OF TRUSTS

There are three major types of trusts:

**1** **Inter vivos** or **living trusts** are set up while you are alive. You can often serve as the trustee yourself, or you can name someone else. When you die, the trust's assets are distributed directly to your beneficiaries.

You can set up a living trust using a standard form, but there are potentially serious legal pitfalls. Poorly executed trusts can foil your best intentions for avoiding the hassle and costs of probate, and could end up costing you more money.

**2** **Testamentary trusts** are created by your will when you die and are funded by your estate. They are administered by trustees, whom you name in your will.

**3** **Pour-over trusts** combine aspects of both types: They are established while you are alive specifically to receive assets, like life insurance benefits, that are paid at your death. They can also receive assets specified in your will.

## CAN YOU CHANGE A TRUST?

A trust can be **irrevocable**—which means you can't make changes once it's set up—or **revocable**, meaning you can modify the terms over time. Their features are:

### Irrevocable Trusts

- You can't make any changes
- You lose control over the assets
- You cannot benefit from the assets
- Gifts are limited to $10,000 annually
- You may be able to avoid estate taxes

### Revocable Trusts

- You can modify them until you die
- You control assets and pay the taxes
- You can transfer assets in and out easily with no annual limits
- They will be taxed as part of your estate

## The Trust

- **Earns income**
- **Pays taxes**
- **Distributes benefits**

## The Trustees

- **Control the property in the trust**
- **Manage the trust's investments**
- **Oversee payouts**

## CRUMMEY POWERS

Using Crummey powers, you can take annual gift exclusions for money you contribute to create or fund a trust. It works if the beneficiary—even a minor child without a guardian—has the power to withdraw the gift within a fixed time period, often 30 to 60 days from when the gift was made.

The beneficiary must be notified of that right, and the money must be on hand to be withdrawn if the option is exercised. Including this option in a trust document is known as "using Crummey powers."

## NO TAX BENEFIT

The bulk of the earnings on trust property is taxed at the highest federal tax rate, eliminating any income tax savings that once came with establishing trusts.

## TRUSTS FOR SPECIAL PURPOSES

A **bypass trust**, also called an exemption-equivalent trust, pays your surviving spouse the income from the trust. But the trust itself is not part of his or her estate. When your spouse dies, the assets pass to your heirs. No estate taxes are due, even if the total accumulated value is more than the amount you can leave tax-free. That is, the estate's value can grow after you establish the trust, but it won't be taxed further.

A **Qualified Terminable Interest Property (QTIP) trust** leaves your estate to your spouse in trust, but lets you control its disposition after your spouse's death. Your spouse receives the trust income, but cannot use the principal or change the beneficiaries you have designated.

A **charitable remainder trust** benefits a specific charity—eventually. It has the double advantage of a lifetime income from the trust's investments for you (or your beneficiary) and tax deductions the year you contribute to the trust. At your (or your beneficiary's) death, the principal goes to the charity.

A **charitable lead trust** benefits a particular charity, which receives income generated by the assets in the trust for the term of the trust. When the term ends, your heirs get back what remains. You can value the gift at a reduced rate, based on IRS tables, and save on estate taxes because the benefit to your heirs is delayed.

A **life insurance trust** is set up while you are alive to own your life insurance policy. Your death benefit is paid to the trust, and so escapes estate taxes and probate.

A **blind trust** means you have no information about or influence on the decisions the trustee makes. Political figures use them to protect themselves from charges of conflicts of interest.

# Investing

When you invest, you're trying to increase your income and build the value of your assets.

It's never too soon to start thinking about **investing**. Investing means putting your money to work earning more money. Done wisely, it can help you meet your financial goals: buying a home, paying for a college education, enjoying a comfortable retirement, or whatever is important to you.

You don't have to be wealthy to be an investor. Investing even a small amount can produce considerable rewards over the long term, especially if you do it regularly. For example, $2,000 a year—only $38.46 a week—can add up to $244,692 in 30 years if it grows at an annual rate of 8%.

But investing means you have to make decisions about how much you want to invest and where to invest it. To choose wisely, you need to know what options you have and what risks you take when you invest in different ways.

## INVESTMENT BASICS

There are three basic investment categories: **stocks**, **bonds** and **cash**.

You can invest directly in any or all of the three, or indirectly, by buying mutual funds that pool your money with money from other people and then invest it. Stock mutual funds, for example, buy stocks, while money market funds make cash investments.

**Stocks are ownership shares investors buy in a corporation**

**Bonds are loans investors make to corporations and governments**

**Cash investments include money in bank accounts, Certificates of Deposit and U.S. Treasury bills**

## ENORMOUS OPPORTUNITIES

If you want to invest, you have a wealth of opportunities. In the U.S. alone there are thousands of stocks and mutual funds, and millions of corporate and government bonds to choose from. You can invest in markets around the world, in developed or emerging economies. You can work with one of the more than 5,000 brokerage firms, 9,000 banks, or tens of thousands of financial advisers in the U.S. You can invest directly with the issuer, whether corporation, investment company or government. And you can even invest online using your computer.

## CHOOSING THE BEST INVESTMENT

Selecting the best investments depends on your financial goals and general market conditions. For example, a good investment for a long-term retirement plan may not be a good investment for college savings. In each case, the right investment is a balance of three things: **liquidity**, **safety** and **return**.

### LIQUIDITY
### How accessible is your money?

If your investment money must be available to cover financial emergencies, you'll be concerned about **liquidity**, or how easily it can be converted to cash. Money market funds and savings accounts are very liquid as are investments with short maturity dates like CDs. But if you're investing for longer-term goals, liquidity is not an issue. What you're after in that case is growth, or building your assets. Certain stocks and stock mutual funds are considered growth investments.

### SAFETY
### What's the risk involved?

Investing means taking some risks. To many people, the biggest risk is losing money, so they look for investments they consider safe. Usually that means putting money into bank accounts and U.S. Treasurys. The opposite but equally important risk is that your investments will not provide enough growth or income to off-set the impact of inflation, the gradual increase in the cost of living. There are additional risks as well, including how the economy is doing. But the biggest risk is not investing at all.

### RETURN
### What can you expect to get back on your investment?

Safe investments often promise a specific, though limited, return. Those that involve more risk offer the opportunity to make—or lose—a lot of money.

### OTHER INVESTMENTS

You can find many other things to invest in, like gold, real estate, or futures and options, if you're looking for more variety or can afford to take added risks. But most experts agree that the basic three— stocks, bonds and cash—should be the core of any investment portfolio. High on the list of reasons for that advice are their easy-to-understand structure and the history of consistent performance that characterize these standard investments.

In addition, if you need to liquidate your assets quickly, you can sell these investments easily although you may not necessarily sell at a profit. That's not the case with collectibles or real estate.

### TAX-DEFERRED INVESTING

If you want your investments to grow even more quickly, you don't have to take more risks. What you can do is put money into tax-deferred investments, including Individual Retirement Accounts (IRAs) and salary reduction retirement plans like 401(k)s, Keoghs or SIMPLES (see page 101).

In most cases, there's a **cap**, or limit, on the amount you can invest tax-deferred each year. But many experts advise you to take the fullest advantage you can of this opportunity. You can always invest whatever additional money you can afford in taxable investments, on which there's no annual cap.

There is one drawback to tax-deferred investing. Generally you'll have to pay a penalty—as well as whatever tax is due—if you withdraw money from tax-deferred accounts before you reach age 59½. That's because the tax-deferral incentive is intended to get you to save for retirement.

If your concerns are the same as the majority of Americans, though, you're probably worried about having enough money when you retire. In that case, tax-deferred investing can be a ready-made solution. And there are situations when the withdrawal penalty is waived, including serious illness, paying college tuition or putting money down on a first-home purchase.

> *Securities*, by definition, are written proofs of ownership, like stock or bond certificates. But as electronic records replace paper, the term survives, even though it now refers to investments that are secured as computer files.

# Risk vs. Reward

Risk is the chance you take of making or losing money on your investment. The greater the risk, the more you stand to gain or lose.

Your range of investment choices—and their relative risk factors—is often described as a pyramid. Most experts recommend that you have a solid cash base (enough to cover three to six months of living expenses), the bulk of your portfolio in limited and moderate risk investments, and a small percentage of your total portfolio in the highest risk category.

**Low-risk investments**, like government bonds, guarantee that you'll get your money back, plus interest. **High-risk** investments, like stock in a new company, have no guarantees. But if the company succeeds, your investment could someday be worth lots of money.

There's no such thing as **zero risk**. There are always factors you can't control—like a recession, an oil embargo or high inflation.

**INVESTMENT STRATEGIES**

You can adapt your investment-picking approach from financial experts, or you can develop one on your own. Two things you will want to keep in mind, whatever method you use—the importance of **diversification**, or variety, in your portfolio, and the need for a **strategy**, or a plan, to guide your choices.

## High Risk
**FUTURES**
**SPECULATIVE STOCKS**
**HIGH-YIELD BONDS**

## Moderate Risk
**GROWTH STOCKS**
**LOW-RATED CORPORATE BONDS**
**INTERNATIONAL INVESTMENTS**

## Limited Risk
**BLUE CHIP STOCKS**
**HIGH-RATED CORPORATE BONDS**
**HIGH-RATED MUNICIPAL BONDS**
**BALANCED MUTUAL FUNDS**

## Low Risk
**TREASURY BONDS AND BILLS**
**MONEY MARKET FUNDS**
**BANK CDs**

Remember that the strength of the financial markets is never the result of how well—or poorly—a single investment does, but how a range of different ones perform over a period of time.

## INVESTMENT APPROACHES

The places you choose to put your money reflect the investment strategy you're using—whether you realize it or not. Most people adopt one of three approaches:

- **Conservative**
  Take only limited risk by concentrating on liquid, secure stock and high-rated, fixed-income investments

- **Moderate**
  Take risks by putting money into growth stocks, mutual funds and bonds

- **Speculative**
  Take major risks on investments with unpredictable results

## TAKING RISKS

If you take no chances, you run the risk of coming out short. The more you have in the safest investments like CDs, bank accounts, and Treasury bills, the smaller your chance of substantial reward. There's also the risk of outliving your assets because they won't keep up with inflation.

Similarly, the more you speculate, the greater the risk of losing your principal entirely. Often the more people understand about the principles of investing, the more apt they are to take the moderate approach, balancing their risks to get the kind of results they want.

That way, they can also afford to invest a small amount in speculative opportuni-

### WHAT YOU RISK

You take different risks with different types of investments. With corporate and municipal bonds, the risk is that the issuer will **default**, or not repay the principal. With stocks, the main risk is **loss of principal**, if the shares decline in value or the company goes bankrupt. With some derivative investments, though, you can lose even more than the amount you invest.

ties and keep some assets safe—and liquid—to meet immediate cash needs.

### OTHER RISKS

In addition, you need to take other kinds of risk into account, including volatility and the effect of changing market conditions.

**Volatility** means sudden swings in value—from high to low, or the reverse. The more volatile an investment is, the more profit you can make, since there can be a big spread between what you paid and what you sell it for. But you must also be prepared for the price to drop.

When stock or bond markets drop or interest earnings decline, many investors seek investments with the same yields they got in better times. They risk buying lower quality, often unfamiliar, investments that promise big returns. But the search for higher returns can result in higher losses as well.

Investors who sell when prices drop—as they do from time to time—risk not having the opportunity to benefit when prices go back up since they are no longer invested.

## RISK VS. RETURN: WHAT'S THE TRADE-OFF?

When it comes to investing, trying to weigh risk and reward can seem like throwing darts blindfolded. Investors don't know the actual returns that securities will deliver, or the ups and downs that will occur along the way.

Looking to the past can provide some clues. Over several decades, for instance, investors who put up with the stock market's gyrations earned returns far in excess of bonds and cash investments like Treasury bills.

| | AVERAGE ANNUAL RETURN* 1926–1998 | Best year | Worst year |
|---|---|---|---|
| **Small company stocks** | 12.4% | 142.9% (1933) | −58.0% (1937) |
| **Large company stocks** | 11.2% | 54.0% (1933) | −43.3% (1931) |
| **Long-term corporate bonds** | 5.8% | 42.6% (1982) | −8.1% (1969) |
| **Cash** (Treasury bills) | 3.8% | 14.7% (1981) | −0.02% (1938) |

* Price changes of securities plus dividends and interest income

Source: © Computed using data from *Stocks, Bonds, Bills & Inflation 1999 Yearbook™*, Ibbotson Associates, Chicago (annually updates work by Roger G. Ibbotson and Rex A. Sinquefield). Used with permission. All rights reserved.

# Figuring Your Return

## Return is what you get back in relation to the amount you invest.

**Return**, or what you get back on an investment you make, is one of the clearest ways to evaluate how your stock and mutual fund investments are doing in relation to each other and to the performance of investments in general. For example, if you start out with $1,000 and end up with $2,000, your return is $1,000 on that investment, or 100%. If a similar $1,000 investment grows to $1,500, your return is $500, or 50%.

But unless you held those investments for the same time period, you can't determine which has a stronger performance. What you need to compare your return on one investment with the return on another is the **annual return**, the average percentage that you've gained on each investment over a series of one-year periods.

For example, if you buy a share for $15 and sell it for $20, your profit is $5. If that happens within a year, your rate of return is an impressive 33% ($5÷$15=33.3%). If it takes five years, your return will be closer to 6%, since the profit is spread over a 5-year period.

| Sell at | Profit | Return |
|---------|--------|--------|
| Year 1 | $5 | 33% |
| Year 3 | $5 | 11% |
| Year 5 | $5 | 6.6% |

## MEASURING TOTAL RETURN

In addition to yield—which is generally the amount of income on your investment—total return also includes how much your investment gains, or loses, in value. For example, your total return on a stock is not just the dividends it pays, but how much you would gain or lose if you sold it.

$$\begin{aligned} & \textbf{Income} \\ +/- \quad & \textbf{Change in value} \\ \div \quad & \textbf{Investment costs} \\ \hline = \quad & \textbf{Total return} \end{aligned}$$

## GETTING A GOOD RETURN

There's no absolute standard that qualifies a specific figure as a good return. The average return on specific classes of investments—small company stocks, for example—over a specific historical period are a matter of record. And total return

figures for mutual fund performance are reported regularly. You can compare how well your investments are doing against those numbers, as a starting point.

Another factor to take into account when evaluating return is the current inflation rate. Investment experts agree that your return needs to be higher than the inflation rate if your investments are going to have real growth. But they don't always agree on how much more than inflation you should be aiming for.

### CAPITAL GAINS AND LOSSES

Investments, including real estate, which you hold for a period of time rather than buying and selling quickly are called **capital assets**. When you sell a capital asset at a higher price than you paid for it, the difference is a capital gain. If you sell at a lower price, you have a capital loss.

If you realize a capital gain after holding the investment for more than a year, it's a long-term gain. But if you realize the gain within a year or less, it's a short-term gain.

**The Wall Street Journal's MARKETS DIARY reports past and current activity in various financial markets.**

The **STOCKS** section shows the movement of the Dow Jones Industrial Average for the previous 18 months, and for the previous week. It also summarizes the activity of several major domestic and international indexes on the most recent trading day, as well as from the beginning of the current year, and during the previous 12 months.

The **BONDS** section shows the Lehman Brothers U.S. Treasury Bond (T-Bond) Index for the same periods and compares the price and yield of five different bond indexes for the previous two trading days and for the most recent 12 months.

The **INTEREST** section shows the interest rate charged on Federal funds, which is the money banks lend each other for short periods, often overnight. There's also a comparison of interest paid on U.S. Treasury bills, new CDs and other issues.

## FIGURING THE RETURN ON YOUR INVESTMENT IS NOT THAT SIMPLE

Figuring out the actual return on your investments can be difficult because:

- The amount of your investment changes. Most investment portfolios are active, with money moving in and out

- The method of computing return can vary. For example, performance can be **averaged** or **compounded**, which changes the rate of return dramatically, as the chart below from The Wall Street Journal shows

- The time you hold specific investments varies. **When** you buy or sell can have a dramatic effect on overall return

- The return on some investments—like limited partnerships or real estate investments—is difficult to pin down, partly because they're more difficult to liquidate easily. You have to evaluate them by different standards than you do stocks or bonds, including their tax advantages

## COMPOUND VS. AVERAGE RATE OF RETURN

Here are 6 sets of investment returns totaling 27% over 3 years. While the average annual return in each case is 9%, compound annual returns vary significantly.

| Investment | 1 | 2 | 3 | 4 | 5 | 6 |
|---|---|---|---|---|---|---|
| Year 1 | 9% | 5% | 0% | 0% | -1% | -5% |
| Year 2 | 9% | 10% | 7% | 0% | -1% | 8% |
| Year 3 | 9% | 12% | 20% | 27% | 29% | 40% |
| Average return | 9.00% | 9.00% | 9.00% | 9.00% | 9.00% | 9.00% |
| Compound return | 9.00% | 8.96% | 8.69% | 8.29% | 8.13% | 6.96% |

## USING BENCHMARKS

You can evaluate your portfolio's performance by comparing it to standard benchmarks, the indexes and averages that are widely reported in the financial press. In addition to the Dow Jones Industrial Average (DJIA), perhaps the best-known measure of stock market performance in the world, there are others that track specific categories of investments. The Standard & Poor's 500-stock index, for example, tracks 500 large company stocks, the Russell 2000 reports on small company stocks, and the Wilshire 5000 Equity Index includes all the stocks traded on the New York and American stock exchanges, plus actively traded Nasdaq stocks.

If you own bonds, you can identify an index that tracks the type you own: corporate, government or agency.

If your investments are in cash, you can follow the movement of interest rates on bills, CDs and similar investments.

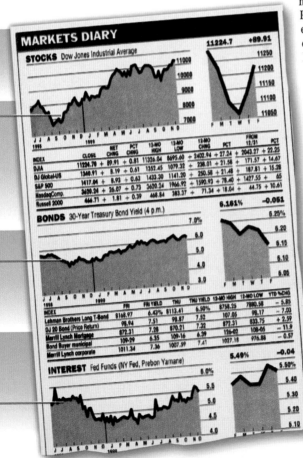

# Diversifying Your Portfolio

Even if you find risk exciting, you'll probably sleep better if you've got your investment nest eggs in different baskets.

Your best protection against risk is **diversification**—spreading your investments around instead of investing in only one thing. For example, you can balance cash investments like CDs and money market funds with stocks, bonds and stock or bond mutual funds. You can buy stocks of small **growth companies** while also investing in **blue chips**, or large, well-established companies. Usually when the return is down in one area, it's balanced by stronger performance in another.

You probably also want to evaluate your assets and re-align the investment mix from time to time. For example, if some stocks increase in value, they will make up a larger percentage of your portfolio. To keep the balance, you may want to de-crease your stock holdings and increase your bond or cash holdings.

## THE BENEFITS OF DIVERSIFICATION

Well-diversified portfolios—containing various mixes of stocks, bonds, mutual funds, cash equivalents like Treasury bills or money funds and sometimes other types of investments—can iron out a lot of the ups and downs in investing. And studies show that over lengthy periods, investors don't have to sacrifice much in the way of returns to get that reduced volatility. Finding the right portfolio mix depends on your assets, your age and your risk tolerance.

## WHAT A DIFFERENCE AN ALLOCATION MAKES

Asset allocation can make a real difference in portfolio performance over an extended period. Here's what a hypothetical $100,000 portfolio allocated three different ways and computed using the average return on each investment type—11.2% for stocks, 5.8% for bonds and 3.8% for cash—between 1926 and 1998 would yield in just one year. Actual annual returns could be quite different.

| 60% stocks 30% bonds 10% cash | OR | 30% stocks 60% bonds 10% cash | OR | 10% stocks 30% bonds 60% cash |
|---|---|---|---|---|
| **$8,840** earnings | | **$7,220** earnings | | **$5,140** earnings |

# Stocks, Bonds or Cash?

## What's the 'Right' Mix?

Recommendations from different asset-allocation services may vary, as shown by these suggestions from some major investment firms for four individual investors.

### THE BREADWINNER

Early-30s, nonearner spouse, two kids; "moderate" risk taker, with investment assets of $726,200 (41.6% cash, 6.8% fixed income, 51.6% growth).

| | FIRM A | FIRM B | FIRM C | FIRM D |
|---|---|---|---|---|
| CASH | 5.8% | 11.5% | 12.6% | 6 – 25% |
| FIXED INCOME | 32.5 | 39.7 | 25.0 | 19 – 37 |
| GROWTH | 61.7 | 48.8 | 62.4 | 61 – 84 |

### THE DINKS

Double income, no kids, late-20s, "moderate" risk takers with investment assets of $182,000 (11.5% cash, 66.5% fixed income, 22% growth).

| | FIRM A | FIRM B | FIRM C | FIRM D |
|---|---|---|---|---|
| CASH | 7.5% | 12.4% | 27.0% | 18 – 34% |
| FIXED INCOME | 33.0 | 47.2 | 25.4 | 33 – 53 |
| GROWTH | 59.5 | 40.4 | 47.6 | 25 – 41 |

### THE SINGLE PARENT

Late-30s, one child; "moderate to aggressive" risk taker; investment assets of $95,300 (10.8% cash, 20.7% fixed income, 68.5% growth).

| | FIRM A | FIRM B | FIRM C | FIRM D |
|---|---|---|---|---|
| CASH | 3.8% | 14.9% | 29.0% | 39 – 51% |
| FIXED INCOME | 29.9 | 36.4 | 37.4 | 24 – 40 |
| GROWTH | 66.3 | 48.7 | 33.6 | 18 – 31 |

### THE YOUNG ACHIEVER

Single, mid-20s; "aggressive" risk taker; investment assets of $14,000 (60.7% cash, 39.3% growth).

| | FIRM A | FIRM B | FIRM C | FIRM D |
|---|---|---|---|---|
| CASH | 2.7%* | 17.2% | 45.4% | 100% |
| FIXED INCOME | 10.9* | 26.4 | 23.0 | 0 |
| GROWTH | 86.4* | 56.4 | 31.6 | 0 |

*Broker would override allocation model to put this investor 45.5% in cash, 54.5% in growth.

*Chart adapted from one appearing in The Wall Street Journal.

## ASSET ALLOCATION

**Asset allocation** means dividing your portfolio among the three basic investment categories according to a particular formula. One typical allocation model, for example, would put 60% of your investment capital in stocks, 30% in bonds and the remaining 10% in cash.

No single portfolio is ideal for everyone. While a stock-heavy portfolio tends to grow faster, the value also fluctuates more. But you don't have to stick to a single model throughout your investing career.

Many experts suggest that young people put 80% or more of their investments in stock and stock mutual funds. People nearing retirement, on the other hand, might want more of their assets in income-producing investments such as U.S. Treasurys or high-rated corporate bonds.

# Investing in Stocks

Stocks are ownership shares in a corporation.

You can buy stock in more than 10,000 publicly traded companies, though chances are your portfolio will have only a tiny fraction of what's available.

When you buy stock in a corporation, you become one of its owners. If the company does well, you may receive part of its profits as dividends and see the price of your stock increase. But if the company fares badly, the value of your investment can drop, sometimes substantially.

A stock has no absolute value. At any given time, its value depends on whether the shareholders want to hold it or sell it, and on what other investors are willing to pay for it. If the stock is hot, and lots of people want shares, the value will go up. If a company is losing money or a particular industry is doing poorly, those stocks will probably drop in value. Some stocks are undervalued, which means they sell for less than analysts think they're worth, while others are overvalued.

Investors' attitudes are determined by several factors: whether or not they expect to make money with the stock, current stock market conditions and the overall state of the economy.

The caution that past performance is no guarantee of future profits is absolutely valid. Investing isn't about guarantees. It's about balancing risk with reasonable expectations of reward.

## MARKET CYCLES

The stock market goes through cycles, heading up for a time, and then correcting itself by reversing and heading down. A period of rising prices is known as a **bull market**—bulls being the market optimists who drive prices up. A **bear market** is a period when stock prices have dropped by 15% or more. Overall, the market has tended to rise more than fall. Between 1960 and 1999, there were only six bear markets.

## HOW DO INVESTORS MAKE MONEY?

**Investors buy stock to make money:**

**1** Through dividend payments while they own the stock

**2** By selling the stock for more than they paid

THE

11207

This certifies that

the record holder of

The Walt Disney Company

169169

## INVESTOR CONCERNS

Some people hesitate to invest in the stock market because they consider it too risky. Afraid of choosing the wrong stock or being battered in a crash, they prefer to stick with investments they consider safe.

The problem with that approach, experts agree, is that by skipping stocks, investors are missing out on the most reliable source of long-term gains. While you could lose money in single year or on a single stock, investors who have held a portfolio of stocks through any 15-year period since 1926 have always come out ahead.

Usually, the greater danger is not sticking with stocks. Investors who sell their shares when the market drops, rather than riding out the downturn, are more likely to lose money than people who leave their portfolios alone, or those who buy additional shares when prices are depressed.

## TAX ISSUES

The **dividends** you earn on stocks and any **capital gain**, or profit, you have when you sell are taxable in the year you execute the trade unless you bought the stock as part of an IRA or qualified retirement plan (see pages 98-101).

Your dividends are taxed as regular income, but long-term capital gains are taxed at a maximum federal rate of 20% if you're in the 28% tax bracket or higher, and at 10% if you're in the 15% bracket. Further, if you're in the 15% bracket and realize a capital gain on an investment you've held five years or more, your gain is taxed at just 8%. (After 2005, a similar 2% reduction in the capital gains tax will be available to taxpayers in the higher brackets.)

LT DISNEY COMPANY

INCORPORATED UNDER THE LAWS OF THE STATE OF DELAWARE

CERTIFICATE IS TRANSFERABLE IN THE CITY OF BURBANK OR NEW YORK

NE INVESTOR

NON-ASSESSABLE SHARES OF THE COMMON STOCK OF

Dated: MAY 22, 1992

COMMON
PAR VALUE $0.025
SEE REVERSE FOR CERTAIN DEFINITIONS
CUSIP 255555 55 5

When some investors choose a stock, they keep it through thick and thin, a strategy known as buy and hold. Other investors buy and sell frequently, which means they select stocks they think are going to increase rapidly in value. When the price goes up a certain percent—15% to 20% is often typical—they sell and buy something else. Both approaches work, though you generally have to decide which one you're going to use.

## STOCK OPPORTUNITIES

You can select stocks on your own, with the help of your financial adviser or as part of an investment club. There are more than 36,000 clubs around the country, and the number keeps growing.

Most clubs are formed by friends or associates with similar investment goals. By pooling their money—usually a fixed amount each month—and sharing responsibility for researching various companies and industries to find smart investments, the group is able to achieve greater diversification than most investors can manage on their own.

Some groups work with a financial adviser or invite people with different investment expertise to speak at their meetings. Others pride themselves on their ability to choose wisely among themselves. And as an added plus, some investors use their colleagues' research to make individual investments in addition to those made through the group.

You can get information about how to establish an investment club and a description of the guidelines that most clubs follow from the National Association of Investors Corporation (NAIC). You can call them at 877-275-6242 or visit them on the Internet at www.better-investing.org.

# The World of Stocks

Understanding the wide variety of stocks you can purchase is one key to successful investing.

When you're choosing stocks from among the thousands that are available in the U.S. and around the world, you can narrow the field in lots of ways. Some people buy shares in the company they work for. Other investors concentrate on companies they know, either because they're local firms or because they provide products and services the investors use. Still others make some investments in large, well-established companies, for instance, and others in companies that are just emerging as leaders in a new field.

## INCOME VS. GROWTH

Stocks with histories of paying consistent dividends are known as **income stocks**. Investors often buy them for the current income that regular dividends provide. Companies like General Electric and Pfizer have paid dividends for more than 50 consecutive years.

**Growth stocks** are shares in companies that reinvest much of their profits to expand and strengthen the business. Although they typically pay few if any dividends, investors buy these stocks because they expect the price to go up as the company grows.

As an added appeal, you don't owe income tax on earnings the company reinvests. If you hold the stock for more than a year before you sell, any profit is taxed at the capital gains rate.

## PENNY VS. BLUE CHIP

Stocks in the largest, long-established and consistently profitable companies are known as blue chips, after the most valuable poker chips. It's not an official designation, though, and the list does change from time to time.

Often more expensive than stock in lesser-known or smaller companies, **blue chips** usually offer investors stable and predictable income and steady if slow growth in value.

**Penny stocks** are at the other end of the scale. They generally sell for $5 or less a share, which makes them more attractive than higher priced stocks. Some penny stocks have increased substantially in value. But you have to recognize that many of the companies may never be profitable, or may fold entirely.

**Value stocks** are also less expensive, for one of a variety of reasons. Often the company has had financial difficulties, their potential for growth has been underestimated or they're part of an industry out of favor with investors.

## WHAT IS A STOCK SPLIT?

If a company thinks the price of its stock is too high to attract investors, it can split the stock—that is, give stockholders more shares and revalue the stock at a lower price.

If the stock is split two for one, the price is cut in half and the number of shares is doubled. Initially, the total value of your stock is the same—like getting two nickels for a dime. But if the price climbs back toward its presplit price, the value increases. For example, if you had 100 shares of a stock selling for $80 a share that was split two for one, you'd have 200 shares valued at $40 a share.

Stocks can split three for one, three for two, ten for one, or any other combination. There can even be a **reverse split**, where you exchange more shares for fewer. Then each new share is worth more than an old one. Reverse splits can make a stock attractive to many institutional investors who often do not buy stocks priced under $5 per share.

## DEFENSIVE VS. CYCLICAL

Defensive stocks in industries like utilities, drugs, health care and food are often more resilient in recessions and stock market slides—at least theoretically—because product demand continues. Many investors include them in their portfolios as a hedge against sharp losses in other stocks.

Cyclical stocks, on the other hand, may flourish in good times and suffer when the economy dips. Airlines, for example, lose money when business and pleasure travel are cut back. If you buy cyclical stocks as the economy rebounds, the cycle may work in your favor.

## COMMON VS. PREFERRED

Some companies offer different classes of stock to appeal to different types of investors. If you have **common stock**, you share directly in the success or failure of the business. If it has large profits, your return increases. If it has a bad year, so does your investment.

With **preferred stock**, the dividends are fixed and are paid before dividends on common stock. You may even get some of your investment back even if the company goes out of business. The downside is that your dividends usually stay the same even if company profits jump.

## SMALL COMPANIES VS. LARGE COMPANIES

Another choice is between large and small companies. A company's size is determined by its **market capitalization**, or the number of outstanding shares multiplied by the current price of one share.

Large company stocks may pay dividends, although many provide growth as well. They're often more resilient in tough times because they

have more assets. But they tend to be more expensive than other stocks.

Small company stocks are usually bought as growth stocks, but sometimes stocks in profitable small companies provide income as well. Small companies have fewer resources to fall back on in tough economic times, so declining profitability can hurt the value of your investment.

## EXCHANGE LISTING REQUIREMENTS

Each of the major U.S. exchanges sets its own listing requirements. Any corporation that wants to be traded on a specific exchange must meet its criteria.

| Exchange | | Minimum number of shares issued* | Minimum market value* |
|---|---|---|---|
| NYSE | New York Stock Exchange | 1.1 million shares | $100 million |
| NASDAQ | Nasdaq Stock Market | 1.1 million shares | $8 million |
| NASDAQ | Nasdaq Small-Cap Market | 1 million shares | $5 million |
| AMEX | American Stock Exchange | 500,000 shares | $3 million |

*As of December, 1999

# Tracking Your Investments

Keeping tabs on your investment paper trail gives you up-to-date information on your portfolio's performance.

Keeping track of your account statements gives you a valuable snapshot of your financial position and a sense of how you're doing in meeting your goals. A brokerage statement gives you a record of all the security trades you made during the most recent account period. You will also find a summary of income produced by each security, including any dividends, interest and capital gains.

If you own mutual funds, the fund company will also send regular statements summarizing deposits and withdrawals, distributions and capital gains. In addition, you'll receive a year-end summary of your brokerage and mutual fund accounts and a Form-1099, which you should keep with your income tax records.

### PHONE AND ONLINE INQUIRIES

Most brokerage houses have phone inquiry systems that allow you to get information about your balance and the daily performance of particular funds using your account number and a password or identification number. Almost all firms also make account information accessible on a password-protected section of their websites. Using the Internet is the way for you to get the most up-to-date information.

## A typical monthly or quarterly statement includes two basic sections.

### PORTFOLIO SUMMARY

Typically, a brokerage statement breaks down your investments by categories such as stocks, bonds and mutual funds. You may get a separate statement for your IRA.

The bottom line tells you the current market value of the cash and securities in your account. Comparing the summary from month to month can give you an idea of how volatile your holdings are and the kind of return you're getting. Month-to-month and even

## CONFIRMATION STATEMENT

The confirmation statement you get from your broker after you buy or sell a security spells out the details of a trade. The type of transaction, the exchange where the trade was made and the terms and conditions are explained on the back. You should keep all transaction confirmations as part of your tax records.

The base amount of your purchase is figured by multiplying the number of shares by the market price.

Securities Company, Inc.

MEMBER

**SIPC**

SECURITIES INVESTOR
PROTECTION CORPORATION

| B - YOU BOUGHT<br>S - YOU SOLD | | DESCRIPTION | PRICE |
|---|---|---|---|
| B | 200 | SYNTEX CORPORATION      E | 45.0000 |

Most investors buy stocks in multiples of 100, or **round lots**. If they aren't round lots, they're called **odd lots**. With odd lots, the commission may be higher.

Most brokerages are covered by the Securities Investor Protection Corporation (SIPC), which insures your account up to $500,000 if the brokerage firm goes bankrupt. (You're not insured against market losses.)

The price per share reports the price you paid. You can buy or sell at the current market price, or you can authorize a trade when the price hits a certain amount.

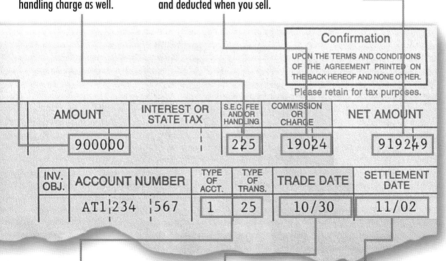

**Client Statement**
September 1 - September 29

Ref: 00000923 00002448

Your Financial Consultant
HARRY BEDFORD

Account number 167-90807-17 004

I9600490807167
NORRIS A SENNETH
117 DIVER ROAD
GRANDVIEW NY 10960-4903

### Account value

| | |
| --- | --- |
| Cash balance | $ 23.00 |
| Money funds | 423.28 |
| Accrued money fund dividends | .82 |
| Stocks | 64,649.65 |
| Net value this period | $ 65,096.75 |
| Net value last period | $ 62,716.35 |

### Earnings summary

| | This period | This year Taxable | Non-taxable |
| --- | --- | --- | --- |
| Dividends | $ 78.00 | $ 678.61 | $ 0.00 |
| Money funds earnings | 1.41 | 101.20 | 0.00 |
| Total | $ 79.41 | $ 779.81 | $ 0.00 |

### Cash and money funds balance

| | This period |
| --- | --- |
| Opening balance | $ 366.87 |
| Dividends credited | 78.00 |
| Money funds earnings reinvested | 1.41 |
| Closing balance | $ 446.28 |

### Portfolio details

This section shows the holdings in your account. It reflects values as of the close of business on 09/27/96.

| | Description | No. of shares | Market value | Accrued dividends | Annualized Dividend Yield | Comment |
| --- | --- | --- | --- | --- | --- | --- |
| Money funds | | | | | | |
| | SB MONEY FUNDS CASH PORT CL A | 423.28 | $ 423.28 | $ .82 | 4.58% | |
| | | | $ 423.28 | $ .82 | | |
| Total value of money funds | | | | | | |

year-to-year fluctuations are typical, because they reflect movement in the markets as well as what's happening in your account.

One signal that it's time to reevaluate your holdings is a declining or sluggish return when the market in general is booming.

## ACCOUNT ACTIVITY

The account activity section shows additions and subtractions from your accounts, including sales and purchases, cash deposits and withdrawals. It also includes information about reinvested dividends and income or capital gains distributions.

The Securities and Exchange Commission (SEC) imposes a fee on most transactions. Some brokerages impose a modest handling charge as well.

You pay brokers' commissions every time you buy or sell stock. The charges are added to the amount you pay when you buy, and deducted when you sell.

The net amount includes the cost of the security plus commissions and fees.

### Confirmation

UPON THE TERMS AND CONDITIONS OF THE AGREEMENT PRINTED ON THE BACK HEREOF AND NONE OTHER.

Please retain for tax purposes.

| AMOUNT | INTEREST OR STATE TAX | S.E.C. FEE AND/OR HANDLING | COMMISSION OR CHARGE | NET AMOUNT |
| --- | --- | --- | --- | --- |
| 900000 | | 225 | 19024 | 919249 |

| INV. OBJ. | ACCOUNT NUMBER | TYPE OF ACCT. | TYPE OF TRANS. | TRADE DATE | SETTLEMENT DATE |
| --- | --- | --- | --- | --- | --- |
| | AT1 234 567 | 1 | 25 | 10/30 | 11/02 |

These numbers, explained on the back, confirm whether you made a cash trade, bought on margin, sold short or any one of several other transactions.

The trade date is the day of the transaction—usually either the day you authorize a trade or the day the security reaches the price you specify to buy or sell it.

The settlement date is the deadline for paying your bill or getting your proceeds. Investors must settle their security transactions within three business days.

# Tricks of the Trade

## Though it's tough to beat the market consistently, knowing some of the tricks of the trade can help even the odds.

Experienced investors sometimes buy stocks on margin or sell stocks short, two techniques that can boost profits though they may also result in losses. The profits occur when you anticipate correctly what a stock will cost in the future, and the losses result from getting the direction wrong or having to wait a long time for the anticipated change to occur. Like other leveraged investments, for which you borrow part of the cost, you must repay the loan regardless of how the deal turns out.

## HOW BUYING ON MARGIN WORKS

| | Stock Value $10 | Stock Value $15 | Stock Value $7.50 |
|---|---|---|---|
| **You open a margin account—$5,000 of your money and $5,000 of your broker's money** **You purchase 1,000 shares at $10 each** | | **You profit if stock price rises** | **You lose if stock price drops** |
| **The value of your investment** | **Your break-even point** **$5,000** | **$10,000** | **Margin call** **$2,500** |
| **Your broker's investment** | **$5,000** | **$5,000** | **$5,000** |

### BUYING ON MARGIN

**Buying on margin** means borrowing money from your broker to finance part of a stock purchase. You use a **margin account**, in which you deposit cash or securities to fund your share of the purchase. Under current rules, you can borrow up to half the cost of any transaction. You pay interest on the loan, but usually at less than market rates.

The advantage of **leverage**, or using a little of your own money to purchase something of greater value, is that the return on your investment is magnified.

For example, suppose you buy $10,000 worth of stock with $5,000 of your own money and $5,000 from your broker, and it increases in value to $15,000. When you sell and repay the loan (plus interest) you've made almost $5,000 on a $5,000 investment—or 100% profit.

Without the margin loans, you'd have to lay out the whole cost yourself. If you didn't have the cash, you might have to buy less, which would mean you'd make less profit.

The disadvantage of margin buying is that if your investment loses money, you absorb the total loss but must still pay back the loan.

### WHAT'S A MARGIN CALL?

Brokers protect themselves against losses by requiring you to deposit extra money in your margin account if the value of your investment falls below a specified percentage of its original value. If you won't—or can't—meet the **margin call**, you must sell and take the loss.

### BUYING RIGHTS

Companies sometimes offer their stockholders the opportunity to buy more shares below market price during a limited time period. These written offers, called rights, are actively traded in many stock markets around the world.

## PROFESSIONAL ANALYSIS

Professional stock analysts use different methods to evaluate a stock's prospects and decide which ones they will advise investors to buy or sell.

**Fundamental analysis** concentrates on the economic health—the balance sheet and income statements—of individual companies, and on their management and their position in the industry, in order to forecast a stock's future performance.

**Technical analysis** uses past performance to predict how individual companies, industries, or the market as a whole will do in the future. These analysts use charts or computer programs to identify and project price trends, usually in the short term.

However, there are skeptics who discount the importance of any analysis, arguing that a randomly chosen portfolio would do as well.

## HOW SELLING SHORT WORKS

You borrow 100 shares at $10 per share from your broker

You sell the 100 shares at the $10 price, getting $1,000

You profit if stock price drops

You lose if stock price rises

| | Stock Value $10 | Stock Value $7.50 | Stock Value $12.50 |
|---|---|---|---|
| **Shares you owe your broker** | 100 Shares | 100 Shares | 100 Shares |
| **Your cost to pay back the shares** | | $750 | $1,250 |
| **Your profit—or loss** | | $250 Profit | $250 Loss |

## SELLING SHORT

**Selling short** is selling a stock before you buy it because you think the price is going down. To sell short, you use a **margin account**, and borrow stock you don't own from your broker. Ideally, when the price drops, you **cover your short position** by buying the stock for less than you sold it for. You give the stock to your broker to replace the shares you borrowed and pocket your profit.

For example, if you sell short 100 shares at $10 a share, the price drops and you buy 100 shares two weeks later for $7.50 a share, you make $2.50 profit per share (minus the interest and commission you owe your broker). That's approximately a 33% return.

The risk is that the price of the stock might go up instead of down. Then you may have to cover your short position by paying more for the stock than you sold it for, so you could potentially lose more than the amount you invested.

## WHAT ARE WARRANTS?

When you buy a **warrant**, you pay a small price now for the right to buy a certain number of shares at a fixed price during a specified period. For example, you might pay $1 a share for the right to buy the stock at $8 within five years. If you **exercise**, or use, your warrant when the selling price is $12, you'll be $3 ahead ($12 − ($8 + $1) = $3).

If the price of the stock is below the **exercise price** when the warrant expires, the warrant is worthless. But before it expires, the warrant can increase in value if the stock price rises. Because a warrant has a long life span, it is less risky than an option, which rarely lasts longer than nine months (see page 151).

**Warrants** are sold by companies that plan to issue stock, or by those that want to raise cash by selling stocks they hold in reserve. Once a warrant is offered, it has a life of its own, and can be bought and sold as well as exercised.

# Taking Stock of Your Investments

To invest intelligently, and to track how well you're doing, you have to understand the language of stocks.

Stock tables, like the one reporting activity on the New York Stock Exchange (NYSE) that's shown here from The Wall Street Journal, provide a daily summary of what has happened in the market they track. The phrase **composite transactions** means the chart includes trading on the regional exchanges in addition to New York.

**Company names** are abbreviated, listed alphabetically, and followed by their trading symbol. Most symbols are related to the name of the company, like BIR for Birmingham Steel. Preferred stocks are indicated by a **pf** following the stock name and warrants with a **wt**.

An **S** in the first column shows the company stock has split within the last year—as Calpine has.

**COMPOSITE TRANSACTIONS**

| | 52 Weeks | | Stock | Sym | Yld Div % | PE | Vol 100s | Hi | Lo | Close | Net Chg | | 52 Wee Hi L |
|---|---|---|---|---|---|---|---|---|---|---|---|---|---|
| | Hi | Lo | | | | | | | | | | | |
| | 27¹¹/₁₆ | 19½ | BethStl pfB | | 2.50 10.5 | ... | 5 | 23⅞ | 23¾ | 23¾ + | ⅛ | | 35 |
| | 8³/₁₆ | 3½ | BeverlyEnt | BEV | ... | dd | 4838 | 4⁵/₁₆ | 4¹/₁₆ | 4¼ + | ¼ | S | 71¹⁵/₁₆ |
| s | 24⁵⁷/₆₄ | 11¾♠ | BrdlyWest | BDY | .06 | .4 26 | 4124 | 16½ | 14½ | 15¾ + | 1⅛ | | 35⅞ |
| s | 45 | 17⅝ | Biomatrx | BXM | | 22 | 516 | 19⁹/₁₆ | 19 | 19½ | ... | | 28¼ |
| | 94⅝ | 32⅜ | Biovail | BVF | g | ... 44 | 5699 | 92¹⁵/₁₆ | 86¾ | 92¹⁵/₁₆ + | 5¹⁵/₁₆ | | 26⅜ |
| n | 57⅜ | 23 | Biovail wt | | | ... ... | 294 | 55 | 49½ | 54⅝ + | 4½ | | 26¹¹/₁₆ |
| | 9¹/₁₆ | 3¼ | BirmghamStl | BIR | | ... 10 | 500 | 5 | 4⅞ | 5 | ... | | 25 |
| | 64⅝ | 41 | BlackDeck | BDK | .48 1.0 | 16 | 3809 | 49⅝ | 49 | 49⁷/₁₆ | ... | | 13⅜ |
| | 25⅝ | 20⁵/₁₆ | BlackHills | BKH | 1.04 4 6 | 19 | 314 | 22⅞ | 22¹/₁₆ | 22¹³/₁₆ + | ³/₁₆ | | ⅜ |
| | 9¹⁵/₁₆ | 8⅞ | BlkrkAdv | BAT | .60 6.6 | ... | 21 | 9¹/₁₆ | 9¹/₁₆ | 9¹/₁₆ | | | 53¹⁵/₁₆ |
| | 16 | | | | | | | | | | | | |

**Highest and lowest prices** of each stock are shown for the last 52 weeks. Stocks reaching a new high or low for the year are marked with an arrow in the lefthand margin. The range between the prices is a measure of the stock's **volatility**. The more volatile a stock is, the more you can make or lose within a relatively short investment period. The percentage of change is more significant than the dollar amount: a $5 change from $5 to $10 shows more volatility than a $5 change from $30 to $35, a 17% change.

**Percent yield** tells you the percentage of a stock's price paid as a dividend. Here, the yield on Black and Decker is 1.0%, which means the annual dividend payments are equal to 1.0% of the price.

Yield provides only a partial picture. Sometimes the yield can look very attractive—say 10%—because price of the stock has fallen but management hasn't adjusted the dividend downward. And some companies choose not to pay a dividend, preferring to reinvest profits in new products or factories, which may result in higher profits later. If there's no dividend, yield cannot be calculated and the column is marked with an ellipsis (...).

**Price/Earnings ratio (PE)** shows the relationship between a stock's price and the company's earnings for the past four quarters. It's figured by dividing the current price per share by the earnings per share.

There is no ideal P/E ratio. A stock with a low P/E ratio—say 10—may seem like a bargain. But the company could have problems that will hurt future earnings.

Meanwhile, a stock with a high P/E—say 50 or more—seems overpriced. But it could be growing so fast that its future earnings will be much higher, justifying the price.

While P/E ratios can help you evaluate a stock, P/E is not the only factor to consider.

## LOOK AT THE COMPANIES, TOO

You can get other information about companies that issue stock from financial advisers or brokers, the media, and prospectuses and annual reports.

**Earnings per share** is one measure of the company's health. Investors see improved earnings per share as a sign of increasing profitability.

**The book value** of a company is like your own net worth statement—the difference between assets and liabilities. If a company has more assets than it thinks or says it has, the book value may be unrealistically low and the stock may be a bargain. But if the book value is low because the company has too much debt, its profitability may suffer.

**Return on equity** is computed by dividing the earnings per share by the company's book value. Returns over 10% are generally considered healthy, and over 15% outstanding.

**The payout ratio** shows the percentage of net earnings being paid as dividends. It can range from zero at companies that pay no dividends to more than 100%, but any payout over 70% should be regarded with suspicion.

## CALCULATING VOLATILITY— THE BETA FACTOR

Some analysts measure the volatility of a given stock's price by comparing its price changes to the average price changes of a control group of stocks. This is called the stock's **beta**. If the average is 1, a stock with a beta of 1.8 is more volatile than the market as a whole, and a stock with a beta of .8 is less volatile. On that basis, analysts predict the first stock would rise 18% if the market went up 10%, for example, and fall 18% if the market fell 10%.

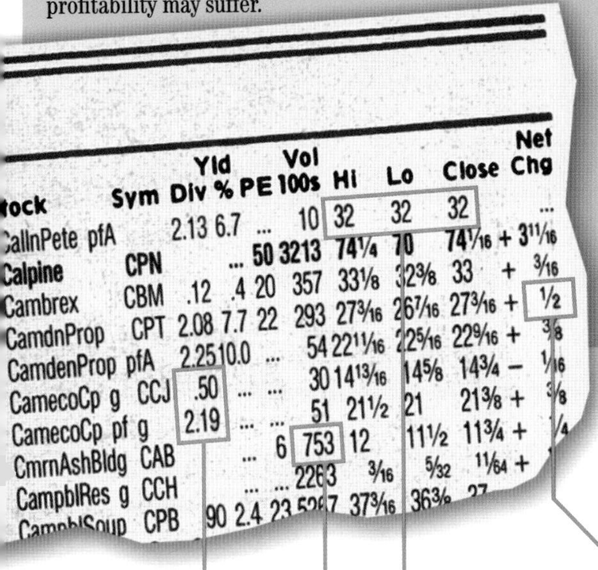

| Stock | Sym | Yld Div % | PE | Vol 100s | Hi | Lo | Close | Net Chg |
|---|---|---|---|---|---|---|---|---|
| CalInPete pfA | | 2.13 6.7 | ... | 10 | 32 | 32 | 32 | ... |
| Calpine | CPN | ... | 50 | 3213 | 74¼ | 70 | 74¹⁄₁₆ | + 3¹¹⁄₁₆ |
| Cambrex | CBM | .12 .4 | 20 | 357 | 33⅛ | 32⅜ | 33 | + ³⁄₁₆ |
| CamdnProp | CPT | 2.08 7.7 | 22 | 293 | 27³⁄₁₆ | 26⁷⁄₁₆ | 27³⁄₁₆ | + ½ |
| CamdenProp pfA | | 2.25 10.0 | ... | 54 | 22¹¹⁄₁₆ | 22⁵⁄₁₆ | 22⁹⁄₁₆ | + ⅜ |
| CamecoCp g | CCJ | .50 | ... | 30 | 14¹³⁄₁₆ | 14⅝ | 14¾ | − ¹⁄₁₆ |
| CamecoCp pf g | | 2.19 | ... | 51 | 21½ | 21 | 21⅜ | + ⅜ |
| CmrnAshBldg | CAB | ... | 6 | 753 | 12 | 11½ | 11¾ | + ¼ |
| CampblRes g | CCH | ... | | 2263 | ³⁄₁₆ | ⁵⁄₃₂ | ¹¹⁄₆₄ | − ¹⁄₆₄ |
| CampblSoup | CPB | .90 2.4 | 23 | 52967 | 37³⁄₁₆ | 36⅜ | 27 | |

**Cash dividend per share** is an estimate of the anticipated yearly dividend per share in dollars and cents. Notice that the prices of stocks that pay dividends tend to be less volatile than the prices of stocks with no dividend. Cameco's yearly dividend is estimated at 50 cents per share. If you owned 100 shares, you'd receive $50 in dividend payments, probably in quarterly payments of $12.50. Preferred stocks tend to pay higher dividends.

**High, low, and close** tell you a stock's highest, lowest, and closing price for the previous day. Usually the daily differences are small even if the 52-week spread is large.

**Sales in hundreds** refers to the volume of shares traded the previous day. Unless a Z appears before the number in this column, multiply by 100 to get the number of shares. (A Z indicates the actual number traded.) An unusually large volume, indicated by underlining, usually means buyers and sellers are reacting to some new information.

**Net change** compares the closing price given here with the closing price of the day before. A minus (−) indicates a lower price, and a plus (+) means it's higher. Here, Camden Properties closed at 27³⁄₁₆, up ½ point from the day before. Stocks that show a price change of 5% or more are in **boldface**, as Calpine is.

---

**The prices are quoted in this chart in dollars and fractions, from ¹⁄₁₆ to ¹⁵⁄₁₆ of a dollar. Each fraction equals a number of cents.**

| | | | | | | | | | |
|---|---|---|---|---|---|---|---|---|---|
| | | | | | | | | | ¹⁵⁄₁₆ 93¾¢ |
| | | | | | | | | ⁷⁄₈ 87½¢ | |
| | | | | | | | ¹³⁄₁₆ 81¼¢ | | |
| | | | | | | ¾ 75¢ | | | |
| | | | | | ¹¹⁄₁₆ 68¾¢ | | | | |
| | | | | ⅝ 62½¢ | | | | | |
| | | | ⁹⁄₁₆ 56¼¢ | | | | | | |
| | | ½ 50¢ | | | | | | | |
| | ⁷⁄₁₆ 43¾¢ | | | | | | | | |
| ⅜ 37½¢ | | | | | | | | | |
| ⁵⁄₁₆ 31¼¢ | | | | | | | | | |
| ¼ 25¢ | | | | | | | | | |
| ³⁄₁₆ 18¾¢ | | | | | | | | | |
| ⅛ 12½¢ | | | | | | | | | |
| ¹⁄₁₆ 6¼¢ | | | | | | | | | |

**By mid-2000, prices will be quoted in decimals.**

# Investing in Bonds

**Bonds attract more investors because they usually pay regular interest income and pledge to repay the amount of the bond.**

Bonds are loans you make to corporations or governments. Unlike buying stocks (also called **equity** securities), which make you a part-owner in a company, buying bonds (or **debt** securities) makes you a creditor.

Bonds are called fixed-income securities because they pay a specified amount of interest on a regular basis. However, one of their limitations for individual investors is their cost. Few sell for less than $1,000, and it's often hard to buy just one. Investing in a bond mutual fund may be an alternative, though these funds do not pay a fixed rate of interest or promise return of principal.

## TYPES OF BONDS

| Type | Description | Features |
|---|---|---|
| **Corporate Bonds** | Bonds are the major source of corporate borrowing. **Debentures** are backed by the general credit of the corporation. **Asset-backed bonds** are backed by specific corporate assets like property or equipment. | • Sold through brokers<br>• Fully taxable<br>• Top-rated bonds nearly free of risk of default but not as safe as federal bonds<br>• Higher yield than government bonds |
| **Municipal Bonds** | Millions of bonds have been issued by state and local governments. **General obligation** bonds are backed by the full faith and credit of the issuer, and **revenue bonds** by the earnings of the particular project being financed. | • Sold through brokers<br>• Pay lower interest rates than comparably rated corporate bonds and U.S. Treasurys<br>• Tax-exempt interest<br>• Not as safe as federal bonds |
| **U.S. Treasury Notes and Bonds** | Intermediate (2–10 years) and long-term (10–30 years) government bonds are a major source of government funding. | • Bought through brokers or directly through Treasury Direct<br>• Highest credit quality<br>• Inflation-indexed bonds offer income protection<br>• Sold in $1,000 units |
| **U.S. Treasury Bills** | Largest components of the money market, where short-term (13 to 52 weeks) securities are bought and sold. Investors use T-bills for part of their cash reserve or as an interim holding place. Interest is the difference between the discounted buying price and the amount paid at maturity. | • Bought through broker or directly through Treasury Direct<br>• Treasury Direct allows reinvestment for up to two years without a new application<br>• Maximum safety, but lower return<br>• Sold in $1,000 units |
| **Agency Bonds** | Federal, state and local agencies sell bonds. The best known are federally guaranteed mortgage-backed bonds sold by the Government National Mortgage Association (GNMA). | • Bought directly through banks, or from brokers<br>• Marginally higher risk and higher interest than Treasury bonds<br>• Prices vary widely from $1,000 to $25,000 and up |

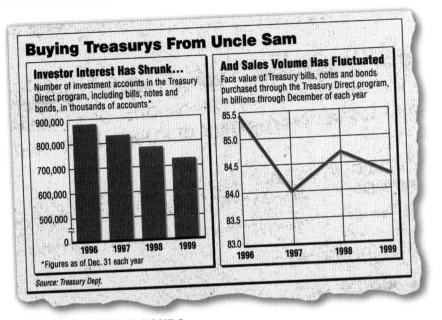

**Buying Treasurys From Uncle Sam**

**Investor Interest Has Shrunk...**
Number of investment accounts in the Treasury Direct program, including bills, notes and bonds, in thousands of accounts*

*Figures as of Dec. 31 each year

**And Sales Volume Has Fluctuated**
Face value of Treasury bills, notes and bonds purchased through the Treasury Direct program, in billions through December of each year

Source: Treasury Dept.

## INVESTMENT-GRADE BONDS

High-quality, or **investment-grade**, bonds are considered safe investments because you're virtually certain of getting regular interest payments plus the face, or **par**, value of the bond when it matures.

**Treasury bonds notes**, and **bills** are considered as good as gold. They are backed by the "full faith and credit" of the government, which means it has the power to tax its citizens to pay its debts. Corporate and municipal bonds are evaluated by independent rating services—the best known are Standard & Poor's and Moody's—which measure the financial stability of the issuer and assign a rating—from AAA (or Aaa) to D. Any bond rated Baa or higher by Moody's, or BBB or higher by Standard & Poor's, is considered investment quality. Usually, the higher a bond's rating, the lower the interest it must pay to attract buyers.

## AVOIDING COMMISSIONS ON TREASURY BONDS

The cheapest way to buy and sell U.S. Treasurys—bonds, notes and bills—is without commission through the federal system called **Treasury Direct**. You can set up an account and buy, sell, or reinvest by mail, phone, on the Internet at www.treasurydirect.gov. The system will deposit your interest and principal electronically in your bank account, but you must send a check for new purchases.

> The **long bond** is the 30-year Treasury bond. The going interest rate at Treasury auctions and the price of long-term bonds in the secondary market are used as benchmarks of investor attitudes toward the economy.

## SAVINGS BONDS: TRIED, TRUE AND BETTER TOO

You can buy U.S. Savings Bonds—up to $15,000 a year—from banks, through payroll deductions or on the Internet at www.savingsbonds.gov.

- They're inexpensive—you can invest as little as $25—and get a guaranteed rate of interest if you hold them until they mature, or five years.

- There's no commission, and no state or local tax on the interest. Plus, you don't owe federal taxes until you redeem the bond. You may be able to avoid taxes entirely if you use the bonds to pay for your child's education.

## WHAT ARE JUNK BONDS?

Investors willing to take risks for high yields buy corporate or municipal bonds with low ratings—or no ratings at all—commonly known as junk bonds.

## INFLATION PROTECTION

One risk of buying most bonds is that the income you earn is fixed for the term of the loan. But if you buy inflation-indexed U.S. Treasury bonds, the interest you earn will be increased to keep pace with inflation. That lets you maintain the buying power provided by the fixed-income portion of your investment portfolio.

**137**

# The Value of Bonds

Some of the factors to consider in evaluating bonds as potential investments: the purchase price, the interest rate and the yield.

If you buy a bond at face value, or **par**, when it is issued and hold it until it matures, you'll earn interest at the stated, or **coupon**, rate. For example, if you buy a 20-year $1,000 bond paying 8%, you'll earn $80 a year for 20 years. The **yield**, or your return on investment, will also be 8%. And you get your $1,000 back.

You can also buy and sell bonds through a broker after their date of issue. This is known as the **secondary**, or resale, market. There the price fluctuates, with a bond sometimes selling at more than par value, at a **premium price**, and sometimes below, at a **discount**.

Changes in price are directly tied to the interest rate of the bond. If its rate is higher than the rate being paid on similar bonds, buyers are willing to pay more to get the higher interest. But if its rate is lower, the bond will sell for less to attract buyers, as the example to the right shows. However, as the price goes up, the yield, or what you earn on your investment, goes down. When the price goes down, the yield goes up.

## UNDERSTANDING BOND PRICES

Corporate bond prices are quoted in increments of **points** and seven **fractions** of a point, with a par of $1,000 as the base. The value of each point is $10, and of each fraction, $1.25, as the chart shows:

| | |
|---|---|
| ⅛ = **$1.25** | ⅝ = **$6.25** |
| ¼ = **$2.50** | ¾ = **$7.50** |
| ⅜ = **$3.75** | ⅞ = **$8.75** |
| ½ = **$5.00** | 1 = **$10** |

So a bond quoted at 86½ would be selling for $865, and one quoted at 100⅜ would be selling for $1,003.75.

Treasury bonds, in contrast, are measured in 32nds rather than in 100ths of a point. Each 1/32 equals 31.25 cents, and the fractional amount is dropped when stating a price. For example, if a bond is quoted at 100.2 or 100 + 2/32, the price translates to $1,000.62.

## FIGURING CURRENT YIELD ON BONDS

If you pay premium price for a bond, you still earn the same interest that was paid when the bond was issued at par. But since you paid more, the **current yield**—or the return on your investments—is less.

**Using a par value 8¾ bond selling for $1,040 as an example:**

$$\frac{\$87.50 \text{ Interest}}{\$1,040 \text{ Current market price}} = 8.4\% \text{ Current yield}$$

## HOW YIELD CHANGES

| Yield from a $1,000 bond with an interest rate of 8% | Interest payment | Yield |
|---|---|---|
| If you buy it at par value of $1,000: | $80.00 | 8% |
| If you buy it at a discount price of $800: | $80.00 | 10% |
| If you buy it at a premium price of $1,200: | $80.00 | 6⅔% |

## WHAT IS YIELD TO MATURITY?

The way to evaluate your return on a secondary market bond is its **yield to maturity**. This calculation is based on the interest payments you'll receive until the time it matures and what you pay for the bond (above or below its par value). Your broker can tell you a bond's yield to maturity or you can use mathematical tables sold in bookstores to figure it out.

**To avoid losing any interest, you should redeem mature U.S. savings bonds right after the quarterly interest is credited. Banks where you cash in the bonds can tell you when those payments are made.**

# NEW YORK EXCHANGE BONDS

| Bonds | Cur Yld. | Vol. | Close | Net Chg. |
|---|---|---|---|---|
| BurNo 3.20s45 | 7.6 | 10 | 41⅞ | |
| CamdPr 7.33s01 | cv | 20 | 110 | + 5 |
| Caterplnc 6s07 | 6.6 | 35 | 91½ | − 1¾ |
| Caterplnc 9¾s19 | 9.5 | 10 | 102¼ | − 1¾ |
| ChaseM 6½s05 | 6.8 | 25 | 96⅛ | + 1 |
| ChaseM 6¾s08 | 7.1 | 15 | 95¼ | |
| CPoV 7¼s12 | 7.8 | 7 | 93½ | ... |
| ChespKe 9⅛s06 | 10.3 | 15 | 89 | − 3½ |
| ChiqBr 10s09 | 13.2 | 110 | 75⅞ | + 1½ |
| ClrkOil 9½s04 | 13.7 | 176 | 69½ | − 2⅛ |
| CoeurDA 7¼s05 | cv | 20 | 55 | + 1½ |
| Consec 8⅛s03 | 8.1 | 34 | 100½ | − ¾ |
| Convrse 7s04 | cv | 185 | 25 | − 1⅛ |
| Deere 8½s22 | 8.1 | 10 | 104½ | − ⅜ |
| DelcoR 8⅝s07 | 9.5 | 20 | 91 | − ½ |
| Dole 7s03 | 7.4 | 5 | 94⅛ | − 1 |
| DukeEn 7s00 | 7.0 | 5 | 100 | + ⅛ |
| DukeEn 6⅞s23 | 7.8 | 3 | 88 | |
| DukeEn 7⅞s24 | 7.9 | 5 | 99⅝ | + 1 |
| DukeEn 6¾s25 | 7.9 | 57 | 85⅞ | + ⅞ |
| DukeEn 7⅛s25 | 7.8 | 35 | 96 | + ¼ |
| DukeEn 7s33 | 7.8 | 65 | 90⅛ | + 3 |
| Florsh 12¾s02 | 13.7 | 5 | 93 | + 1⅛ |
| Fortune 8⅝s21 | 8.5 | 25 | 102 | + 2⅝ |
| FourSeas zr29 | ... | 50 | 30 | + 5½ |
| GECap 7½s35 | 7.7 | 10 | 97 | + ½ |

| Bonds | Cur Yld. | Vol. | Close | Net Chg. |
|---|---|---|---|---|
| NETelTel 6⅞s23 | 7.9 | 62 | 87⅜ | + ⅝ |
| NJBTl 7⅜s12 | 7.7 | 10 | 95⅞ | − ⅛ |
| NYTel 5⅞s03 | 6.1 | 20 | 95¾ | |
| NYTel 7¼s24 | 7.9 | 10 | 92 | + 1½ |
| NYTel 6s07 | 6.6 | 12 | 91¼ | − ½ |
| Noram 6s12 | cv | 13 | 88 | + 1 |
| OcciP 10⅛s01 | 9.8 | 10 | 103⅝ | |
| OcciP 10⅛s09 | 8.8 | 10 | 115⅜ | + 1⅞ |
| OreStl 11s03 | 10.7 | 20 | 103 | + ¼ |
| OutbM 7s02 | cv | 1 | 79 | + 3 |
| ParkElc 5½s06 | cv | 10 | 85½ | − 1¼ |
| PepBoys zr11 | ... | 100 | 53 | − ½ |
| PhilPt 9.18s21 | 8.9 | 10 | 103¼ | + ¼ |
| PhilPt 8.49s23 | 8.5 | 8 | 100 | + 1 |
| PhilPt 7.92s23 | 8.1 | 5 | 97½ | |
| Polaroid 11½s06 | 11.9 | 45 | 97 | + ⅛ |
| PotEl 5s02 | cv | 17 | 94 | |
| PrmHsp 9¼s06 | 9.7 | 25 | 95½ | − 2½ |
| PSEG 9⅛s05 | 8.7 | 30 | 105 | + 2 |
| PSVEG 7s24 | 7.9 | 434 | 89⅛ | |
| Quanx 6.88s07 | cv | 45 | 100 | + 1½ |
| Rallys 9⅞s00 | 10.2 | 10 | 97 | − ½ |
| RalsP 8⅛s23 | 8.2 | 2 | 99¼ | |
| RelGrp 9s00 | 9.5 | 160 | 94½ | + ½ |
| RelGrp 9¾s03 | 11.7 | 45 | 83¼ | |

In this example from The Wall Street Journal, the current yield on a Duke Energy 6¾ bond is up to 7.9%, or almost a full percentage point *greater* than the coupon rate. But its price is down to 85⅞, or $858.75.

In contrast, the bond issued by PSEG at 9⅛ has a current yield of 8.7%—or almost half a percentage point *lower* than the coupon rate. That's because the current closing price is 105, or $1,050, which is more than par.

## BUYING T-BILLS

New U.S. Treasury bills are sold weekly through an auction process. Institutional investors, like pension funds, submit written bids indicating how much they are willing to pay for the issue and how many bills they want. One fund might offer $980 for a $1,000 bill, for example, and another, $970. Individual investors can submit non-competitive bids through Treasury Direct at the same time. They send a check for the total value of their bid: Three bills would be $3,000.

The government fills the large orders at the highest prices it can get, and then fills individual orders at the average sale price. For example, if the cut-off price is $970, all bidders at that price and higher get bills.

The difference between the check you submitted and the cost of the bills you buy is refunded directly to your checking account. When the bills mature, the par value of $1,000 per bill is deposited in your account unless you reinvest.

# TREASURY BONDS, NOTES & BILLS

## GOVT. BONDS & NOTES

| Rate | Maturity Mo/Yr | Bid | Asked | Chg. | Ask Yld. |
|---|---|---|---|---|---|
| 10¾ | May 03 | 112:18 | 112:22 | + 5 | 6.46 |
| 5½ | May 03n | 97:07 | 97:09 | + 5 | 6.40 |
| 5⅜ | Jun 03n | 96:27 | 96:29 | + 5 | 6.38 |
| 5¼ | Aug 03n | 96:08 | 96:10 | + 5 | 6.41 |
| 5¾ | Aug 03n | 97:26 | 97:28 | + 5 | 6.42 |
| 11⅛ | Aug 03 | 114:15 | 114:19 | + 6 | 6.51 |
| 4¼ | Nov 03n | 92:22 | 92:24 | + 5 | 6.41 |
| 11⅞ | Nov 03 | 117:25 | 117:29 | + 6 | 6.53 |
| 4¾ | Feb 04n | 94:03 | 94:05 | + 5 | 6.39 |
| 5⅞ | Feb 04n | 98:03 | 98:05 | + 5 | 6.43 |
| 5¼ | May 04n | 95:17 | 95:19 | + 5 | 6.48 |
| 7¼ | May 04n | 102:26 | 102:28 | + 5 | 6.54 |

## U.S. TREASURY STRIPS

| Rate | Maturity Mo/Yr | | Bid | Asked | Chg. | Ask Yld. |
|---|---|---|---|---|---|---|
| Nov 04 | | bp | 72:30 | 73:01 | + 5 | 6.60 |
| Nov 04 | | np | 73:10 | 73:14 | + 5 | 6.48 |
| Feb 05 | | ci | 71:24 | 71:28 | + 6 | 6.51 |
| Feb 05 | | np | 72:01 | 72:04 | + 6 | 6.60 |
| May 05 | | ci | 70:19 | 70:22 | + 6 | 6.61 |
| May 05 | | bp | 70:17 | 70:21 | + 6 | 6.50 |
| May 05 | | np | 70:30 | 71:01 | + 6 | 6.62 |
| Aug 05 | | ci | 69:12 | 69:15 | + 6 | 6.64 |
| Aug 05 | | bp | 69:09 | 69:13 | + 6 | 6.52 |
| Aug 05 | | np | 68:11 | 68:15 | + 6 | 6.59 |
| Nov 05 | | ci | 68:23 | 68:26 | + 7 | 6.50 |
| Feb 06 | | ci | 67:00 | 67:04 | | |

# Special Types of Bonds

There's something for everybody in the bond market.
The trick is figuring out the best choices for you.

You can choose different types of bonds to fit your financial needs, whether you're investing for college, looking for tax-free income, or want to limit risk. That's why it's important to have a sense of how the various types work.

## ZERO-COUPON BONDS

Zero-coupons bonds are sold at deep discount, or a fraction of their par value, by corporations and governments. Investors don't collect interest. Instead the value of the bond increases to its full value when it matures. In this way, zero-coupons are like old Series E Savings Bonds that you bought for $37.50 and could cash in for $50 after seven years.

Some zero-coupon bonds are created when a brokerage firm or government strips, or divides, the coupons from a bond and sells the two separately.

### ZERO-COUPONS HAVE SOME DRAWBACKS

**1** You must pay taxes on the interest that **accrues**, or builds up, each year even though you don't receive it. This doesn't apply if your zero-coupons are in a tax-deferred retirement account or you buy tax-exempt municipal zero-coupons.

**2** The prices are extremely volatile, so you may lose money if you don't hold them to maturity.

**3** Rising interest rates may leave you stuck with a low-paying investment.

## MUNICIPAL BONDS

Municipal bonds—known as **munis**—are sold by states, cities and other local governments. Interest is exempt from federal tax. It's also exempt from state or city tax for people who buy munis of the state or city they live in. In a high-tax area, like New York City, **triple tax-free** munis appeal to high-income investors.

If a government's bond rating drops, it may have to raise the interest rate it offers to attract investors the next time it issues bonds. That can create a Catch-22: Investors can earn higher interest—but their taxes pay for it.

### MINI-MUNIS

Mini-munis, sometimes called baby bonds, cost much less—often between $500 and $1,000—and are designed for investors who want the benefits of tax-exempt munis but not the price tag of conventional ones.

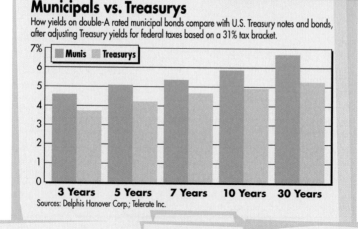

### Municipals vs. Treasurys

How yields on double-A rated municipal bonds compare with U.S. Treasury notes and bonds, after adjusting Treasury yields for federal taxes based on a 31% tax bracket.

Legend: ■ Munis  ■ Treasurys

(Chart showing yields at 3 Years, 5 Years, 7 Years, 10 Years, 30 Years, scale 0 to 7%)

Sources: Delphis Hanover Corp.; Telerate Inc.

## MORTGAGE-BACKED BONDS

**Mortgage-backed bonds** are backed by a pool of mortgage loans. They're sold by government agencies and private corporations to brokers who resell to investors.

With mortgage-backed bonds, each payment you get typically includes both principal and interest. When interest rates go down and people refinance their mortgages, mortgage-backed bonds can be paid off more quickly than you expect. **Collateralized mortgage obligations (CMOs)** are more complex versions of mortgage-backed bonds, and you may find that evaluating their risks and rewards can be complicated.

## CONVERTIBLE BONDS

**Convertible bonds** offer you the option of acquiring stock instead of getting your cash back. The terms of the exchange—generally a certain number of shares for each $1,000 bond—are spelled out in the initial offering. However, you don't have to exercise the option.

Convertibles appeal to investors who think the corporation is growing and that the price of its stock is going up. The question is whether the potential for buying stock is worth the lower interest.

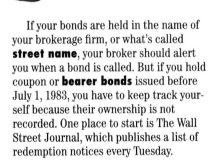

## CALLABLE BONDS

Some bonds are issued with a **call provision**, which means they can be paid off before their due date. Information about the first date on which a bond can be called should be included in the offering.

Issuers will sometimes call bonds when interest rates drop, so they can reduce their debt. Investors, however, can lose expected income if their bonds are called and they have to reinvest their money at a lower rate.

If your bonds are held in the name of your brokerage firm, or what's called **street name**, your broker should alert you when a bond is called. But if you hold coupon or **bearer bonds** issued before July 1, 1983, you have to keep track yourself because their ownership is not recorded. One place to start is The Wall Street Journal, which publishes a list of redemption notices every Tuesday.

### WHAT'S AN INSURED BOND?

Some municipal bonds have their principal and interest payments guaranteed by an insurance company. In exchange for that security, the bonds pay a lower rate of interest and the insurance company collects a fee from the issuer. One catch: If the insurer has financial problems, it could jeopardize both the payments and the rating of the bond.

### WHAT ABOUT BOND FUNDS?

You can also buy bond mutual funds. Most funds invest in specific types—like intermediate-term municipals, long-term corporates, or bonds of a particular state.

But investing in bond funds isn't the same thing as buying a bond. When you buy a bond fund, you're buying a share of the fund, not the bonds that the fund owns. And bond fund managers don't usually buy and hold bonds until they mature. Rather, they trade them, sometimes frequently, in an effort to provide both yield and capital gains. When interest rates move higher, the value of the bonds the fund holds can drop and trades can produce capital losses. So the price you get when you redeem your shares may be more or less than you paid.

# It's a Fund-Filled World

If you're looking for simplicity and variety, mutual funds may be the solution you're seeking.

Mutual funds simplify what many investors, maybe you included, find most complicated: Figuring out what to buy and when to sell to meet particular goals or objectives. Because each fund is designed to meet a specific goal, your decisions are limited to choosing the funds you'll invest in and tracking how well they're doing in meeting your expectations.

## FAMILIES OF FUNDS

Most mutual fund companies offer several different funds (known as a family), and let you move money back and forth among them. Individual funds within a family have different investment goals and strategies, reflecting the different interests of investors. One caution: Profit or loss from exchanges among funds must be reported to the IRS just as if you redeemed or sold the shares outright. Many investors own funds in several different families, choosing those with the best performance records or with the investment goals best suited to their needs.

| TYPE OF FUND | OBJECTIVE AND RISK |
| --- | --- |
| **Aggressive-growth funds** invest in new companies and industries and those that are in financial trouble or out-of-favor. They are sometimes called capital appreciation funds. | • Above-average increase in price, with little current income<br>• Volatile and speculative |
| **Growth funds** invest in well-established companies whose earnings are expected to increase. **Small-company growth funds** specialize in smaller companies. | • Strong price increases, with little current income<br>• Can be volatile |
| **Growth and income funds** and **equity-income funds** invest in companies that consistently pay good dividends and also have strong growth potential. | • Combination of current income and long-term price increases<br>• Less volatile |
| **Income funds** invest in income-producing securities such as dividend-paying stocks, bonds or a combination of the two. | • Current income<br>• Less volatile |
| **Balanced funds** invest in a mix of bonds, preferred stock and common stock. | • Current income and some growth<br>• Less volatile |
| **International funds** invest in overseas markets. **Global funds** invest in both international and U.S. markets. | • Profit from strong markets abroad<br>• Risk that currency fluctuations offset price gains |
| **Bond funds** invest in government, corporate or tax-exempt bonds with different maturities. | • Current income<br>• Moderate risk |
| **High-yield funds** invest primarily in lower-rated corporate bonds (junk bonds). **Tax-free high-yield funds** invest in lower-rated municipal bonds. | • Very high current income<br>• High risk |
| **Money market funds** buy short-term government and corporate debt. Many offer check-writing privileges. | • Income based on current interest rates<br>• Nearly total safety |

## NEARLY INFINITE VARIETY

There are more than 7,500 mutual funds available to U.S. investors and about five times that many available around the world—a reflection of the demand for the kind of investment opportunities they offer. The appeal, for many people, is that funds offer simplicity as well as performance. By doing the research, making the buy and sell decisions, handling the paperwork and providing regular updates on performance, funds take the hassle out of investing.

Equally important, the relatively small amounts of money required to open and add to an account mean that you can put your money to work quicker and build your portfolio faster.

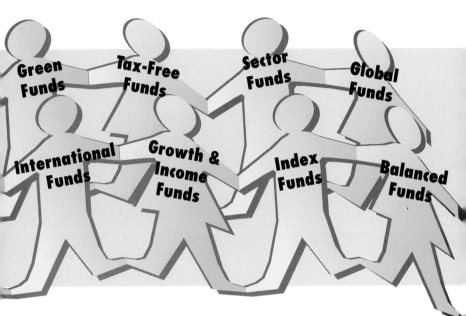

Green Funds

Tax-Free Funds

Sector Funds

Global Funds

International Funds

Growth & Income Funds

Index Funds

Balanced Funds

## FUNDS WITH SPECIAL OBJECTIVES

**Index funds** buy stocks in the companies included in a specific market average, or **index**, like Standard & Poor's 500-  stock index of large companies. Each fund mirrors the movements of the market it tracks. Fees tend to be low because little management is required.

**Tax-free funds** invest in municipal bonds with tax-exempt interest. They pay less than corporate and agency bonds, but offer  tax savings to investors who live in high-tax states and buy funds investing in those states.

**Green funds**, also known as conscience funds, attract investors with strong political or social commitments who want to invest in companies whose poli-  cies they agree with. A green fund might avoid certain companies, like tobacco producers, and target others, like those with strong environmental records.

**Sector funds** focus on particular industries like health care, technology or energy. Each fund buys stocks in one field, so the risk level is greater—but so is the potential for gain.

**Precious-metal funds** trade mostly in mining stocks, with possibly a small portion of their assets in gold bullion. They're usually bought as a hedge against turmoil in the financial markets.

**Unit Investment Trusts (UIT)** put money into corporate bonds with fixed yields, agency bonds 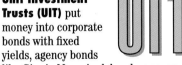 like Ginnie Maes, junk bonds, or even stocks. The investments are constant for the life of the trust, but there's no guaranteed return. And since their performance is not tracked by any index, it's difficult to assess how well they do.

# Investing in Mutual Funds

Mutual funds offer investors the benefits of economy, diversification, and the expertise of a professional manager.

When you put money into a mutual fund, it's pooled with other investors' money and used to make investments that the fund's manager has identified as likely to produce the results the fund wants. Skilled managers can mean a fund performs better than funds with similar objectives and sometimes better than the stock or bond markets as a whole. But it's the rare manager that beats the market year in and year out, which is one reason index funds are so popular.

Because a fund makes many investments, rather than just a few, you get the advantage of **diversification** as well. This means that even if some of the investments are performing less well than the manager expects, others are apt to be doing better. A typical stock fund, for example, might own shares in more than 100 companies. And you can get added diversification by buying several different funds, with different objectives.

## MUTUAL FUND COMPANY

**Investors buy shares in the fund**

## THE INVESTORS

**The fund pays distributions to the investors**

### PROFESSIONAL FUND MANAGER

### How Do Mutual Funds Work?
Professional managers direct the funds, continually buying and selling. Investors are regularly credited with profits, or loss, in proportion to the number of shares they own. Profits are either paid out as distributions or reinvested in the fund.

For most funds you'll have to make an initial investment of $500 to $3,000. Once your account is open, you can make additional purchases whenever you like, usually for as little as $25 to $100.

## OPEN-END VS. CLOSED-END FUNDS

In an **open-end fund**, the more you—and other investors—put in, the larger the fund grows. You can invest directly, by mail, or through your stockbroker or financial adviser.

**Closed-end funds** are traded on the major exchanges. There is a fixed number of shares available because the fund raises its money all at once. Shares often trade at a discount from their original selling price, but sometimes cost more if they're hot. Most funds that invest in a single country—like a Mexico fund—are closed-ended.

## THE ADVANTAGES OF MUTUAL FUNDS

- Convenience of buying and selling
- Diversity in investments
- Professional management
- Automatic reinvestments
- Distribution options
- Telephone redemptions and transfers

## INVESTING OVERSEAS

Many investors use mutual funds to expand their portfolios to include world-wide markets. Most experts agree that international investing is smart, both as a hedge against slow times at home and to take advantage of strong economies abroad. But investing overseas can be complicated, for reasons ranging from currency values to taxation policies. Funds handle these difficulties for you, making the process easier.

## WHEN SHOULD YOU INVEST?

Almost anytime, but not just before a stock fund makes its annual capital gains and income distributions, usually in December. If you invest then, you'll pay more per share, and owe tax on the distribution. Then the price will drop.

## WHAT TO LOOK FOR

### Performance

How much the fund returns, whether the returns are consistent, and how they stack up against the returns of comparable funds. Be wary of any fund whose high returns are based on one or two stellar years and eight or nine dull ones.

### Risk

How likely you are to earn money or lose it. Risk isn't bad if you're investing for the long term and you can tolerate some setbacks without selling in panic if the fund drops in value.

### Costs

If you pay high commissions or fees, less of the money you put into your account is actually producing investment income. For example, if you pay a 5% commission on each $1,000 you put in, only $950 of it is actually invested.

The fund invests the money in a range of securities

## THE INVESTMENTS

Successful investment adds value to the fund

## LOAD VS. NO-LOAD FUNDS

If you buy a mutual fund through a broker, it will probably be a **load** fund, which means you pay a commission, typically between 2% and 5%. With a **front-end load** you pay when you make a purchase and sometimes on your dividend reinvestments as well. With a **back-end load** you pay when you redeem, or sell, your shares. With **level-load** funds, you pay a percentage of assets each year.

**No-load funds**, which you buy directly from the mutual fund company, have no commissions but some funds may charge fees to cover sales and marketing costs.

## DOLLAR COST AVERAGING

Dollar cost averaging means investing a fixed dollar amount every month, no matter what's happening in the financial markets. That way, the price you pay evens out over time, and you'll never pay only the highest or lowest price.

For example, if the price per share varies over a year from $10.65 to $8.45, you will have bought some high and some low. In the long run you may come out better than by trying to pinpoint the moment the price hits bottom or tops out. Dollar cost averaging doesn't mean, though, that you can't lose money, or that you can't make more if you invest large amounts at the beginning of a market rise.

# Anatomy of a Prospectus

By law, mutual funds have to provide detailed information before they accept your money. Dissecting the prospectus uncovers the workings of a fund.

Mutual fund companies provide a **prospectus** for each fund they offer. It includes a statement of objectives, a description of how the fund operates, often a summary of its investments and information about its management. **Annual** and/or **quarterly reports** give details about past performance as well as the fund's investments. Companies will also supply a **Statement of Additional Information (SAI)**, which has detailed financial information, if you ask for it.

## WHAT DOES A SHARE COST?

The dollar value of one share of a fund's stock is its **net asset value (NAV)**. It's figured by adding up the value of all the fund's holdings and dividing by the number of shares. If you buy a no-load fund, you pay the NAV when you buy shares.

Load funds charge you more than the net asset value to buy because commissions are figured in, but they may pay straight net asset value when you sell.

While you can't usually buy a fractional share of stock, you can buy fractional shares of mutual funds. For example, if you invest a round sum like $500 in a fund with a NAV of $18, you'll buy about 27.77 shares.

## FUND MANAGEMENT

The person who manages the fund makes the decisions that determine how well a fund does. Find out if the manager responsible for the fund's success is still on the job and if the fund's management is achieving its objectives. If not, it may pay to look further—like finding out where the manager has gone.

You should also evaluate the manager's investment style: Some styles do well at certain times—like buying undervalued small stocks—but do poorly at other times. Check for a long-term success rate.

## HOW THE FUND IS INVESTED

Make sure that you understand what the fund is buying and that you are comfortable with it. The prospectus provides a detailed accounting.

## FEES CAN AFFECT YOUR YIELD

Though mutual funds—especially no-loads—are the least expensive way to invest, you may still pay some or all of the following fees:

**Annual management fees**. They typically range from .25% to 1.5% of your investment and vary from company to company. They are stated in the prospectus, so you can check before you buy.

**Fees (called 12b-1 fees)**. They cover marketing and advertising costs and sometimes sales commissions. About half of all funds levy this charge, which can seriously erode your earnings, especially if the charge is high.

**Exit fees** for leaving the fund, **redemption fees** for withdrawing funds before a certain time has elapsed, and **deferred sales charges**. You can choose funds that don't charge them, or you can wait out the minimum investment period, which varies by fund. Then these fees may disappear.

## REGULAR INVESTMENTS

Automatic investment plans, also called **contractual plans**, let you contribute regularly, either through automatic transfers or direct deposit. The advantage is steady growth in your investment principal, so opportunity for more growth.

## DISTRIBUTIONS

Distributions are what you earn, and they can be paid in different ways. You can request regular checks, have the money deposited in another account, have it reinvested in the same fund, or you can choose a combination of payout and reinvestment. Taxable earnings are reported to the IRS even if they are reinvested.

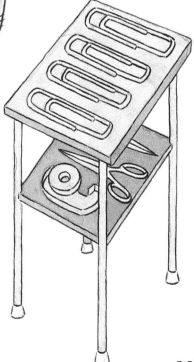

# Tracking Mutual Fund Performance

## Mutual funds get lots of coverage, so their performance can be easy to track.

Financial publications regularly review and rank mutual fund companies and their individual funds, rating their one-year, five-year, and ten-year performances. The Wall Street Journal publishes mutual fund quotations every day, providing more detailed information monthly, quarterly, and annually. It also lists the best performers in a selected category every day in the Mutual Fund Scorecard, based on information provided by Lipper, Inc., and prints Lipper's Mutual Fund Indexes.

These indexes report the performance of more than two dozen categories of mutual funds over the previous week and since Dec. 31. You can evaluate individual fund performances by comparing them with the appropriate index.

### SELLING A FUND?

Most people close out a fund because they need the money or want to change their investment strategy. However, there are certain sell signals that may make getting out of a fund the right move:

- More than three consecutive years of poor performance, especially if other similar funds are doing well

- A radical change in investment style

- A fund that grows too large or too fast

### LONG-TERM INVESTMENTS

Most experts stress the advantages of treating mutual funds as long-term investments, especially those that concentrate on growth. While the value of a fund usually changes very little in the short term, growth funds in particular can produce strong returns and increased value over an extended period.

| | Annual Exp As % | NAV $ 12/31 | Performance One Year |
|---|---|---|---|
| Exit | | | |
| 4548 | | | |
| 10 | 0.60 | 9.51 | −1.2-C |
| | 0.47 | 10.59 | −0.9-B |
| | 1.50 | 15.28 | 57.3-B |
| | 1.25 | 19.41 | 140.2-A |
| | | 7.64 | 2.3-B |
| | 0.35 | | 129.5-A |
| | | | 28.3-B |

The same long-term approach is valid for funds whose investment style emphasizes value, buying securities whose prices are currently low but are expected to rise. They usually need some breathing space to meet their potential.

That doesn't mean you should consider yourself stuck with a fund once you've chosen it, or if your own investment objectives have changed. But it does mean riding out possible downturns in performance, especially when what's happening in the fund reflects what's happening in the markets as a whole, or in the particular segments of the market in which the fund invests.

## Calculating Gains or Losses on Mutual Fund Shares

To figure the taxable gain or loss on mutual fund shares you sell, you have to determine your purchase cost, using one of three methods.

The best choice is often the **specific identification** method, in which you specify exactly which shares you are selling. If you make a profit, you can minimize your tax bill if you are able to show that you're selling the shares that cost you the most to buy. The IRS can be tough: You should be able to show that you told your broker or your fund exactly which shares to sell. The IRS also wants written confirmation of which shares were sold, though many funds don't do this.

If you can't identify which shares you sold, the IRS says to assume that you sold those shares you acquired first. The big disadvantage of this **first-in**, **first-out** approach is that the shares you bought first usually had the lowest cost, so selling them results in the highest tax. On the other hand, if the value of your fund plunged, this approach would give you the biggest **capital loss**.

An alternative for some investors is the **average cost**, or **average basis** method, which requires calculating the average per-share price for all your shares in the fund. Once you've used this method, you always use it for that fund's shares.

The mutual fund company's **name** comes first, with its funds listed in alphabetical order. Fremont Funds, for example, sponsors ten individual funds. The details of each fund's investment performance are reported separately.

**NAV** stands for **net asset value**, or the dollar value of one share of the fund's stock. To compare purchase costs, check the NAV of similar funds—growth stock funds offered by different companies, for example—rather than the NAVs of different types of funds sponsored by the same company.

**Risk** is assigned with a letter grade, **A** being the least risky and **E** being the most.

**Performance** is the percentage gain (+) or loss (−) on a fund, assuming that all distributions have been reinvested. The impact of load is not included. The total return appears for one-, three- and five-year periods. Here, Fremont's Global fund has a one-year return of 22.4% and annualized returns of 14% over three years and 15% over five years. It's risk rating is A for the one-year period, and C for the others.

# MUTUAL FUNDS

## QUARTERLY REVIEW

| Annualized Five Years† | Fund Name | Objective | Max. Sales Charge | | Annual Exp As % | NAV $ 12/31 | Performance & Rank †Annualized | | |
|---|---|---|---|---|---|---|---|---|---|
| | | | Initial | Exit | | | One Year | Three Years† | Five Years† |
| | **FREMONT FUNDS** | ☎ 800-548-4539 | | | | | | | |
| 8.7-A | Bond | IB | NO | NO | 0.60 | 9.51 | −1.2-C | 6.0-A | 8.7-A |
| 6.1-A | CA Intmdt | IM | NO | NO | 0.47 | 10.59 | −0.9-B | 3.9-B | 6.1-A |
| 13.9-D | Emerging Markets | EM | NO | NO | 1.50 | 10.75 | 90.5-A | 9.1-B | NS |
| NS | Global | MP | NO | NO | 0.85 | 15.30 | 22.4-A | 14.0-C | 15.0-C |
| NS | Growth | LV | NO | NO | 0.82 | 15.95 | 17.2-B | 20.5-C | 24.0-C |
| 42.1-A | Intl Growth | IL | NO | NO | 1.50 | 15.28 | 57.3-B | 16.5-C | 13.9-D |
| 19.7-E | Instl US Micro-Cap | SG | NO | NO | 1.25 | 19.41 | 140.2-A | NS | NS |
| 19.8-B | Real Estate Sec | SE | NO | NO | 1.09 | 7.64 | 2.3-B | NS | NS |
| 19.7-E | US Micro Cap | SG | NO | NO | 1.94 | 39.35 | 129.5-A | 36.2-A | 42.1-A |
| 19.8-B | US Small Cap | SG | NO | NO | 1.50 | 24.15 | 125.2-A | NS | NS |
| | **FUNDMANAGER TRUST** | ☎ 800-344-9033 | | | | | | | |

The **investment objective**, expressed as a two-letter code, indicates the types of investments the fund makes. The Wall Street Journal uses several different categories of stock funds, taxable bond funds, municipal bond funds and a stock/bond blend. The MP for Fremont's Global indicates such a blend.

**Maximum sales charge** is the commission you pay to buy or sell a fund. No means it's a no-load fund. The **expense ratio** is the amount, as a percentage of your total investment, that you pay annually in operating expenses. Generally, the fees are higher for funds that require more research. Fremont's expense ratio, for example, is higher—at 1.94%—for its micro-cap fund than for its others.

Suppose you bought 1,000 shares of a mutual fund at $10 each in January, of year 1. Then, through automatic reinvestment of dividends, you received another 50 shares that July valued at $10 a share; 50 more shares in December, valued at $11 a share; 50 shares in July of year 2 also valued at $11 a share; and 50 shares in December of year 2 valued at $12 a share. Then you sold 100 shares late in December of year 2 at $12 a share, for a total of $1,200.

| **SPECIFIC ID** | **FIRST-IN, FIRST-OUT** | **AVERAGE-COST** |
|---|---|---|
| Sale proceeds $1,200 | Sale proceeds $1,200 | Sale proceeds $1,200 |
| Highest-cost shares: − $1,150 | Cost of first 100 shares: − $1,000 | Average cost − $1,017 |
| Short-term* gain: $50 | Long-term gain: $200 | Long-term gain: $183 |
| Based on 50 shares at $11 in July of year 2 and 50 shares at $12 in December of year 2. | Based on 100 shares at $10 a share purchased in January of year 1. | Based on dividing total purchase price of $12,200 by 1,200 shares for an average price of $10.17 a share. |

*The shares sold were held for less than one year.

# Futures and Options

If you're willing to deal with constantly changing prices, you might consider futures and options.

Futures contracts and options are derivative investments. That means their price at any given time depends on the changing value of their underlying investment. You can buy futures contracts on agricultural or financial products, natural resources, interest rates and currency values. You can buy options on stocks, stock and bond indexes, interest rates, currency values and futures contracts. And you can buy to hedge or to speculate.

# Futures are obligations to buy or sell

**A futures contract is a deal you make now to buy or sell a commodity in the future.**

When you buy or sell a futures contract, you're making a deal now to buy or sell a product in the future. But product prices, and therefore contract prices, can change dramatically during the life of the contract as a result of changes in supply and demand as well as other market pressures.

The futures market benefits **hedgers**, who produce or use commodities or who own large investment portfolios, because they want to avoid risk by locking in a price. For example, a baking company might buy a futures contract to buy wheat at a set price so that a potential crop failure won't increase their production costs.

**Speculators**, on the other hand, aren't interested in the commodity, but buy and sell futures contracts because they're willing to take risks that prices will rise or fall in the direction they predict. They can make—or lose—large amounts of money because they **leverage** their purchase, which means investing a small amount—often 10%—to purchase a futures contract worth much more. For example, a speculator might buy a wheat contract worth $17,500 for $1,750.

**OFFSETTING CONTRACTS**
While some futures contracts result in commodities changing hands, most contracts are **offset** when the investor buys an opposing contract. That is, someone with a contract to buy offsets it by buying a contract to sell the same product.

One of the reasons that futures trading can be so hectic is that profit or loss can depend on very small prices differences, which must be acted on quickly. And if prices drop sharply, it can be difficult to act quickly enough to prevent big losses.

**WHERE YOU TRADE**
You can trade futures contracts on commodities exchanges, futures and options exchanges, certain stock markets and over the counter. While some individual investors participate in the market, they're often more likely to get involved by buying mutual funds that trade derivatives. Most futures transactions, especially trading in financial futures like currency values and interest rates, are carried out by institutional investors, such as pension funds or mutual funds.

## WHAT OPTIONS COST

The **premium**, or nonrefundable price of an option, depends on a number of factors:

- The type of investment the option is on
- The difference between the underlying investment's price and the strike price, or what it would cost to exercise the option
- The current state of the financial markets and what's expected
- The time remaining until expiration

## ZERO-SUM MARKETS

Commodity futures markets are zero-sum markets. That means for every dollar an investor makes, another investor loses a dollar (or a little more). But that doesn't mean half the investors make money in commodities trading. Statistics show that between 75% and 90% of individual, non-institutional traders lose money in the futures markets every year. Institutional traders do better.

# Options may be a right or an obligation to buy or sell

**If you buy options, you may choose to buy or sell. If you sell them, you may have to buy or sell.**

A buy option gives you the right—for a fee—to decide whether or not you want to buy or sell an underlying investment, such as shares of a stock, a futures contract or various financial products, at an agreed-upon price, called the **strike price**, before a specific **expiration date**. You lose only the **premium**, or the price of the option, if you don't **exercise**, or act on, the option. But you may be able to buy at a good price, hedge potential losses, or offset your cost.

A sell option means you must go through with a trade if the investor you sold the option to decides to exercise it. The most common, and least risky, sell options for individual investors are **covered stock options**, which means you own the underlying stock and have it available to sell. In addition, you collect a premium when you sell the option.

## OFFSETTING TRADES

Like futures contracts, options can be sold for a profit before the expiration date or neutralized with an offsetting order. Unlike most futures contracts, though, options are frequently exercised when the underlying item reaches the strike price. That's because part of the appeal of options—stock options in particular—is that they can be converted to actual investments, often at an attractive price.

## WHAT KINDS OF OPTIONS ARE THERE?

All options fall into two broad categories: puts and calls. You can buy or sell them.

|  | Calls | Puts |
|---|---|---|
| **BUY** *(go long)* | The right to buy the underlying investment at a fixed price until the expiration date | The right to sell the underlying investment at a fixed price until the expiration date |
| **SELL** *(go short)* | Known as writing a call, it's selling the right to buy the investment from you until the expiration date | Known as writing a put, it's selling the right to sell the investment to you until the expiration date |

# Investing in Real Estate

You may buy property to stake a claim, but real estate is also a good way to diversify your portfolio.

Investing in real estate can range from owning your home to a partnership in a huge construction project, from buying an empty wooded lot to owning a castle in Spain.

If you **leverage**, or borrow money to pay for your investment, selling at a profit can mean a healthy return. But leverage also magnifies your losses if prices go down.

A primary appeal of real estate investing has been that prices have often increased dramatically over time, though a primary drawback is that it's sometimes hard to sell, especially at the price you want.

### VACATION AND RETIREMENT PROPERTY

Second homes appeal to investors who buy them either as an investment or primarily for their own use but welcome the extra income that renting can provide. Complex rules limit their usefulness as tax shelters, and overbuilding has cut resale value in some areas.

## Real Estate Investing

### THE PLUSES

- Provides a hedge against inflation
- Permits tax deductions in some cases
- Produces big profits in some markets

### AND THE MINUSES

- Can be difficult to get your investment back
- May be overpriced in some markets and undervalued in others
- Subject to zoning laws, environmental issues

## REAL ESTATE INVESTMENT TRUSTS

REITs are funds that trade like stocks and work like mutual funds. Your investment is pooled with other people's, and the trust invests it.

For many people REITs are attractive real estate investments because the trust makes the investment decisions, it's easy to trade the shares and the yields can be high.

REIT share prices fluctuate in response to market conditions, the size of the dividend the trust pays and changes in real estate values. Long-term profitability depends on the under-lying value of the properties and the quality of the management.

**Equity** REITs buy properties that produce income or have growth potential. Some buy only certain types of property, while others diversify. In general, well-established equity REITs have been better investments than **mortgage** REITs, which invest in real estate loans, start-up offerings, or **blind** REITs that don't list the properties they own or intend to buy.

## MORE THAN JUST RETURN

It can be harder to figure the return on a real estate investment—especially if the property is also your home—than on other investments you make. Part of your investment cost pays for a place for you to live. You get tax breaks on your mortgage interest and your local taxes. And you won't owe capital gains tax on up to $500,000 profit when you sell ($250,000 if you're single), if you've lived there long enough.

## EMPTY LAND

Called unimproved or raw property, empty land is usually the most speculative and the least liquid real estate investment. If you pay high taxes or have big carrying costs, it's hard to make money.

## LIMITED PARTNERSHIPS

Limited partnerships invest in income-producing properties, often of a particular type like shopping malls or low-income housing, or in a specific geographic area.

The appeal is that several **limited partners** pooling their money can invest in larger properties with the potential for greater profits. The limited partners have no management responsibility and no liability beyond their investment.

**Private limited partnerships** are restricted to high-asset investors and established for a set period of time, often seven to twelve years. Most have large fees, are difficult—maybe impossible—to get out of and provide no assurance of return on investment. And they no longer serve as tax-shelters.

## RENTAL PROPERTY

Rentals are traditional real estate investments. The key to making money is to charge at least enough to cover the mortgage, insurance, taxes and repairs.

### Among the advantages of rental property:

- You can deduct all your repair and improvement expenses up to the amount of rent you collect. You may also be able to deduct losses on your investment against your regular income

- Buying rental property to fix up and sell can produce a big profit if the market is right, but frustrations and big losses if it's not

### But there are also potential disadvantages:

- If rents drop or space stays empty, you could end up subsidizing instead of profiting by your investment

- Owning rental property makes you a landlord, which is an investment of time and energy

# Paying Taxes

Taxes pay the bills of the government that collects them.

When you pay your federal income taxes, you're funding the cost of keeping the U.S. government operating. The right to collect those taxes, as well as the right to pass tax laws, set tax rates and authorize how the funds are spent belongs to the Congress, according to the 16th Amendment to the Constitution.

The U.S. tax system is **progressive**, which means that people who have more income pay tax at a higher rate than people who earn less. A system that taxes everyone at the same rate—the way a sales tax does—is known as a **flat** or **regressive** tax. Advocates of progressive taxes stress their fairness, because they impose a greater percentage of the burden on people who have higher incomes. Advocates of a flat tax stress its simplicity and its elimination of the kind of tax breaks that can favor the well-to-do.

### THE TREASURY AND THE IRS

The U.S. Treasury Department administers the tax law and sets collection policies. The Internal Revenue Service (IRS), which is part of the Treasury, collects taxes, primarily through withholding, or having the money taken out of your salary or other income as it is paid.

Other IRS functions include providing tax forms and tables to simplify the process of figuring what you owe, interpreting the tax laws that Congress passes and determining how those laws apply to individual (and corporate) tax payers.

## HIGHLIGHTS IN THE HISTORY OF INCOME TAX

### 1862

The first income taxes were imposed by the U.S. government to pay for the Civil War. Collected between 1863 and 1871, they were repealed in 1872.

### 1894

A 2% income tax on personal income over $4,000 was enacted. It was rejected as unconstitutional by the U.S. Supreme Court in 1895.

### 1909

A constitutional amendment was proposed to permit a personal income tax. It was ratified by the required 36 states in 1913 and became law. Taxes have been collected ever since.

## CHANGING LAWS

Though the basic U.S. tax structure is fairly stable, tax laws change all the time. Some years the changes are minor. But other times there are major changes in the code, imposing new restrictions, allowing new deductions or requiring different tax-planning decisions or strategies.

An area of tax law that continues to evolve is the one that covers salary reduction retirement plans and Individual Retirement Accounts (IRAs). As more workers fund their own retirement plans, new rules evolve to govern how much can be contributed, when it must be taken out and what taxes and penalties will apply.

**The IRS typically receives more than 125 million individual income tax returns every year. Most taxpayers receive refunds, typically a little more than $1,000.**

## OTHER TYPES OF TAXES

Most people pay taxes in addition to federal income taxes. All but seven states impose **state income taxes**—the exceptions are Alaska, Florida, Nevada, South Dakota, Texas, Washington and Wyoming. New Hampshire and Tennessee tax only unearned income, or what you collect in interest and dividends.

All but five states and many local governments charge **sales taxes** on the value of goods and services sold in the state, and most have some sort of **property tax**, on either real estate or personal property, or both. The taxes pay for local services, often including public schools.

Federal and state governments charge **excise taxes** on the manufacture, sale and consumption of certain products, such as tobacco, sometimes setting aside the revenues for special projects. **Luxury taxes** are taxes on expensive items, such as cars priced over $38,000.

**Gift and estate taxes** are imposed by federal and state governments on property that's passed from one owner to another, if it reaches a certain value. Federal law allows individuals to make tax-free gifts of up to $10,000 per recipient each year and give gifts or leave an estate valued at up to $650,000 without incurring estate taxes in 2000 and 2001. That amount will increase to $1 million in 2006.

## ROUND NUMBERS

The Internal Revenue Service collected
**$879,480,000,000**
from individual taxpayers during the year ending Sept. 30, 1999, but calculates that billions more were owed but not paid.

## 1943

**Withholding was introduced in 1943 to provide a steady stream of income to fund the costs of waging World War II.**

## 1952

**The IRS was reorganized to end the system of appointing its agents through political patronage, making it instead a career service.**

## 1987

**The first online tax returns were filed.**

# The Tax Brackets

Under the U.S. income-tax structure, the more you earn, the higher the rate at which you pay.

Under the progressive U.S. tax system, income is divided into specific ranges or **brackets**, each with a separate tax rate. The part of your income that falls into each bracket is taxed at the rate for that bracket. In 2000, there were five brackets and rates.

**15%** For the lowest bracket

**28%** For the next bracket

**31%** For the next bracket

**36%** For the next bracket

**39.6%** For the top bracket

In fact, people in the upper tax brackets pay even more, because they lose some or all of the tax advantages, such as deductions for dependents, that other taxpayers get.

**THE RATE YOU PAY**
The rate, or rates, at which you pay tax depends on your income and your filing status, which is linked to whether or not you're married and how your family is set up. Filing status is a key reason that people with essentially the same income pay different amounts of tax.

Your **marginal** tax rate is the rate at which your last dollar of income is taxed—or the highest rate at which you pay.

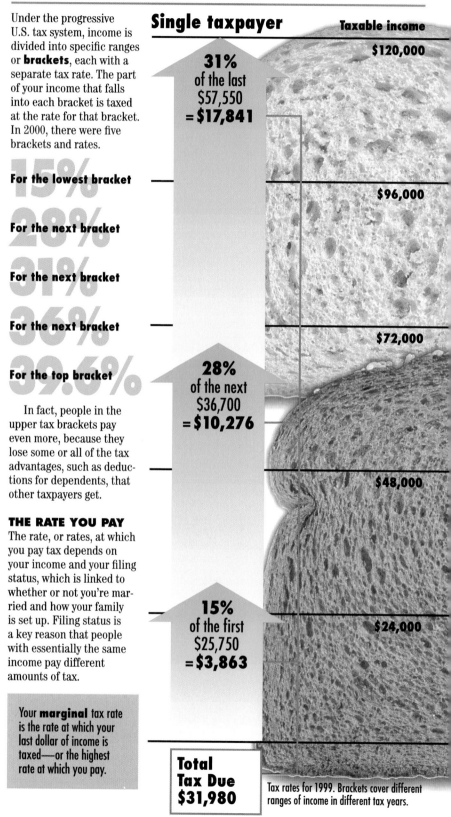

**Single taxpayer**

**Taxable income**

$120,000

**31%** of the last $57,550 = **$17,841**

$96,000

$72,000

**28%** of the next $36,700 = **$10,276**

$48,000

**15%** of the first $25,750 = **$3,863**

$24,000

**Total Tax Due $31,980**

Tax rates for 1999. Brackets cover different ranges of income in different tax years.

As a taxpayer, you fit into one of several categories of filing status, including:

- Single
- Married filing jointly
- Married filing separately
- Head of household

## Married filing jointly

**31%**
of the last
$15,950
= **$4,945**

**28%**
of the next
$61,000
= **$17,080**

**15%**
of the first
$43,050
= **$6,458**

Total
Tax Due
**$28,483**

The filing status you claim must reflect your actual situation as the IRS defines it. Some options can save you money—like filing as head of household instead of single, provided that you qualify. Others almost always cost more—like filing separately instead of jointly if you're married.

For example, a hypothetical single taxpayer with a taxable income of $120,000 paid $31,980 in taxes for 1999, crossing three tax brackets. The taxpayer was in the 31% bracket, the highest rate at which part of the income was taxed.

But, in another hypothetical case, a married couple with $120,000 in taxable income who filed a joint return paid only $28,483 in taxes. The lower rates apply to larger brackets of income, though they're also in the 31% bracket.

The average American household worked from Jan. 1 through May 11, 1999, just to pay all federal, state and local taxes for that year, according to the Tax Foundation, a Washington-based research group. In April 1986, it took until April 30.

**ALTERNATIVE MINIMUM TAX**
The alternative minimum tax (AMT) applies to people who have lots of tax-sheltered income. The AMT doesn't affect huge numbers of people, although the numbers are rising rapidly. It can catch you if you don't do tax planning. It's also complex to calculate, so you'll probably need a tax professional if you get stuck paying it.

People paying at today's top rate of 39.6% might feel better knowing that it hit 94% during World War II.

**COMPLEX RETURNS**
Complexity depends more on where your money comes from, and what expenses you have, than on how much you earn. If you have a good salary but no other income, your situation is usually much simpler than that of someone who makes less money but gets it from several different sources.

# The Reporting System

The IRS provides four forms for figuring what you owe: the 1040EZ, the 1040A, the 1040 and the 1040PC.

When you file your tax return, you use the 1040 form that best suits your filing status, your income and the deductions or credits you can claim.

You mail your return—and any payment that's due—to the IRS processing center that serves the region where you live. If you don't get a preprinted envelope with your return, you can find the address in the Forms and Instructions booklet. The return must be postmarked by midnight, April 15. When the 15th falls on a Saturday or Sunday, you don't have to mail your return until the following Monday.

## ELECTRONIC FILING

You can file your tax return electronically using an approved online service, your personal computer, or the telephone. Filing electronically offers several advantages, including speed and accuracy. Your return arrives more quickly and can be processed more speedily, with fewer mistakes. If you're due a refund and file electronically, you typically receive the money more quickly as well.

There's another advantage to filing electronically, in addition to speed and accuracy. You may be able to simplify your life a bit by filing an electronic state tax return at the same time you file your 1040.

## CHOOSING THE RIGHT FORM

You can actually report your tax liability using any format you like—as long as you cover all of the required information. See Publication 1167 to find the form you should use.

### 1040EZ

If your financial affairs are simple, the 1040 EZ—only 12 questions long—can make short work of tax preparation. But you must be single or married filing jointly to file it, with taxable income of less than $50,000. Other rules apply.

### 1040A

You can use the expanded 1040A, an intermediate form, to report income from several different sources, subtract IRA deductions and take child-care credits. You *can't* use it, though, to itemize deductions or report taxable income of more than $50,000.

**The IRS estimates it should take you about 4 hours and 33 minutes to fill out the 1040, plus 40 minutes to copy, assemble and send it to the IRS—after you've spent 5 hours and 40 minutes getting your records together and learning what you need to know about tax laws.**

## TELEFILING

You can file a paperless 1040EZ by telephone using TeleFile if you receive a TeleFile tax package in the mail. You'll get the tax package automatically if you qualify, but you can't order it, or file by phone without it. In 1998, the IRS received about six million TeleFile returns.

## FINDING THE FORMS

If you filed a return last year, the IRS will send you a current version in January. Or, they'll send you a simpler one if that's all you need.

The forms you get in the mail come with a preprinted address label the IRS asks you to use when you file. The rumor that the label is coded, and could make you vulnerable to audit, is emphatically denied by the IRS.

All the standard forms are available in local post offices, banks, libraries and regional IRS offices. You can get the other forms and schedules you need by calling 800-829-3676 or visiting www.irs.gov.

## MAKING MISTAKES

If you make a mistake, you can file an **amended tax return** on Form 1040X. It's used to report things you left out or figured wrong, or to get a refund. Some refund claims must be made within three years from the date the original return was filed or two years from the date the tax was actually paid.

## FILING LATE

You can get an automatic filing extension by sending in Form 4868, "Application for Automatic Extension of Time to File U.S. Individual Income Tax Return," by April 15. That gives you until August 15. If you're still not ready, you may be able to get another extension until October 15 by filing Form 2688, as long you have an excuse acceptable to the IRS, such as illness or missing records.

The catch? You still have to pay the full amount of the tax you owe by April 15 or face penalties and interest.

## 1040

Nearly 70% of all taxpayers use Form 1040 and file several of the more than 70 additional forms, schedules and attachments to explain their sources of income and the benefits they claim. The IRS says about 70% of all returns take the standard deduction. The rest itemize.

## 1040PC

With IRS-approved tax preparation software, you can print your tax return, plus information from the additional forms and schedules you need to support it, in a three-column format. The IRS estimates you'll need only two pages, not the usual 11, to file.

**159**

# Completing a Return

When you're ready to file, you add up your income and figure out what you owe.

The tax form you use will walk you through the calculations you have to make to get to the bottom line, or the tax you owe. Each form comes with its own set of instructions, explaining line by line what to do. There are also a number of workcharts to help you make detailed calculations or resolve whether you're eligible for certain credits, deductions or exemptions.

The instructions also refer you to IRS publications that provide more information, and to the supplemental forms that you may need to file as backup.

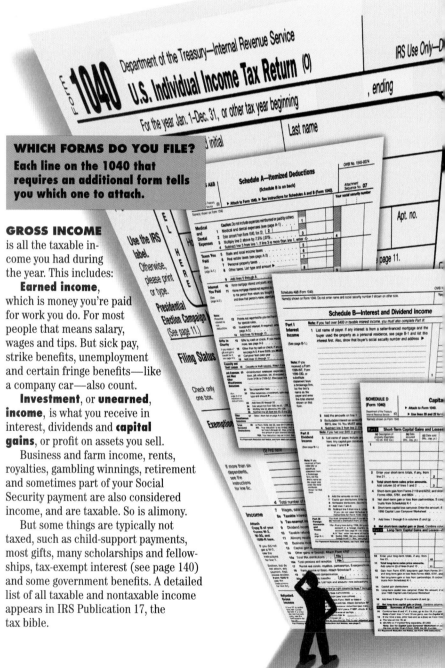

**WHICH FORMS DO YOU FILE?**
**Each line on the 1040 that requires an additional form tells you which one to attach.**

**GROSS INCOME** is all the taxable income you had during the year. This includes:

**Earned income**, which is money you're paid for work you do. For most people that means salary, wages and tips. But sick pay, strike benefits, unemployment and certain fringe benefits—like a company car—also count.

**Investment**, or **unearned**, **income**, is what you receive in interest, dividends and **capital gains**, or profit on assets you sell.

Business and farm income, rents, royalties, gambling winnings, retirement and sometimes part of your Social Security payment are also considered income, and are taxable. So is alimony.

But some things are typically not taxed, such as child-support payments, most gifts, many scholarships and fellowships, tax-exempt interest (see page 140) and some government benefits. A detailed list of all taxable and nontaxable income appears in IRS Publication 17, the tax bible.

# FROM GROSS INCOME TO TAX OWED

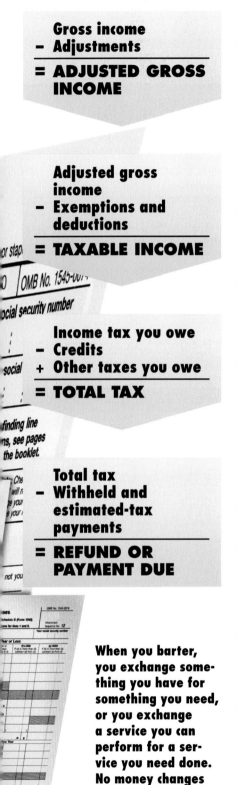

Gross income
− Adjustments
---
= **ADJUSTED GROSS INCOME**

Adjusted gross income
− Exemptions and deductions
---
= **TAXABLE INCOME**

Income tax you owe
− Credits
+ Other taxes you owe
---
= **TOTAL TAX**

Total tax
− Withheld and estimated-tax payments
---
= **REFUND OR PAYMENT DUE**

**When you barter, you exchange something you have for something you need, or you exchange a service you can perform for a service you need done. No money changes hands. But legally you must report the value of what you got as income.**

**Adjustments** are amounts you can subtract directly from your gross income for certain retirement investments, alimony you pay and a number of self-employment expenses.

**Adjusted Gross Income (AGI)** is your income minus adjustments. If your AGI is more than a certain amount set by Congress, you can't deduct your IRA contribution, and the amount of exemptions and total itemized deductions may be limited.

**Exemptions** reduce your income by letting you subtract a fixed amount of money for yourself, your spouse and each of your dependents. Exemptions are **indexed**, or keyed to the rate of inflation, and may change every year. Exemptions are reduced for many taxpayers once they hit certain income levels and are eliminated entirely for others.

**Deductions** are amounts you can subtract for certain kinds of personal expenses. Most taxpayers can use the standard deduction, a fixed dollar amount set for each year. Or, if the deductions you're eligible to take total more than the standard amount allowed, you can **itemize**, or list, your deductions and subtract that amount.

**Taxable income** is the amount on which you owe tax. You look up the tax using the tax tables (for amounts up to $100,000) or figure what you owe using the tax rate schedules (for amounts over $100,000). Both are provided in the tax package.

**Credits** are subtracted from the tax you owe. Child-care credit and credit for the elderly and disabled let you subtract money you paid other people to care for your dependents, up to a set limit.

**Taxes already paid**, like withholding and estimated payments, are actually pre-payments (see page 162–163). You must prepay most of what you owe.

**Refund** or **tax payment due** is determined by what you've paid against what you owe in total income taxes. If you've paid more than you owe, you get a refund. If you haven't paid enough, you must pay the outstanding balance due.

# Withholding— Prepaying as You Go

## When you file your tax return on April 15, you're really settling your tax bill with the IRS.

Most people prepay—and often over-pay—the tax they owe through payroll **withholding** and **estimated payments**.

If you earn a salary, taxes are ordinarily deducted or **withheld** from each pay-check. By year's end, you will have paid all or most of your federal, state and local income tax for that year.

In addition, you can expect to have money withheld from any tips you earn, as well as from sick pay, pensions and annu-ities. Even gambling winnings—like lotteries, sweepstakes and bets that pay over $1,000—are subject to withholding.

You may also have to pay **backup withholding** on your interest and divi-dends if you refuse to provide taxpayer identification, give it incorrectly, or have a history of underreporting your invest-ment income.

### WHAT'S A W-4 FOR?

To determine how much your employer should withhold from each paycheck, you must complete an IRS Form W-4.

The form provides worksheets to help you figure the number of withholding allowances to claim. It may help to have your previous year's tax return handy, especially your itemized deductions (Schedule A) and your interest and divi-dend income (Schedule B), so you can estimate your current situation.

## Form W-4

**Want More Money In Your Paycheck?**
If you expect to be able to take the earned income credit for 1999 and a child lives with you, you may be able to have part of the credit added to your take-home pay. For details, get Form W-5 from your employer.

**Purpose.** Complete Form W-4 so that your employer can withhold the correct amount of Federal income tax from your pay. Because your tax situation may change, you may want ... holding each year.

and includes unearned income (e.g., interest and dividends) and (2) another person can claim you as a dependent on their tax return.

**Basic Instructions.** If you are not exempt, complete the Personal Allowances Worksheet. Additional worksheets are on page 2 so you can adjust your withholding allowances based on itemized deductions, adjustments to income, or two-earner/two-job situations. Complete all the worksheets that apply to your situation. The worksheets will help you figure the number of withholding allowances you are entitled to claim. However, you may claim fewer allowances than this.

**Head of Household.** Generally, you may claim head of household filing status on your tax ... only if you are unmarried and pay more ... of the costs of keeping up a home ... and your dependent(s) or other ... individuals.

... ge Income. If you have a large amount ... age income, such as interest or ... ds, you should consider making ... ed tax payments using Form 1040-ES.

Otherwise, you may fin... additional tax at the en...
**Two Earners/Two Job**
spouse or more than c...
number of allowances ...
on all jobs using work...
W-4. This total should ...
jobs. Your withholding ...
accurate when all allo...
the W-4 filed for the ...
zero allowances are ...

**Check Your Withhol**
takes effect, use Pu...
Correct for 1996?, t...
amount you are hav...
your estimated total...
especially if you us...
Worksheet and you...
(Single) or $200,00...
919, call 1-800-82...
telephone director...
number for further ...

**Sign This Form.** F...
valid unless you s...

**Personal Allowances Worksheet**

...ou as a dependent . . . . . . . .
...one job; or
...ne job, and your spouse does not work; or
... or your spouse's wages (or the total of both) are $1,000 or
...se to enter -0- if you are married and have either a wo...
...ving too little tax withheld) . . . . . .
...spouse or yourself) you will claim on your tax return .
...on your tax return (see conditions under **Head of Hous**...
...or dependent care expenses for which you plan to clai...
... amount may be different from the number of exemptions you claim ...
...claim adjustments to income and want to reduce your ...
...et on page 2.
...ve more than one job and your combined earnings fro...
... a working spouse or more than one job, and the combin...
...ner/Two-Job Worksheet on page 2 If you want to avoid ...

ner/Two-Job Worksheet on page 2

### IN ADDITION TO YOUR SALARY, THE AMOUNT WITHHELD WILL DEPEND ON THREE THINGS:

**1** Whether you choose the higher **single rate** or the lower **married rate**.

**2** The number of allowances you claim. The greater the number, the less your employer will withhold. (However, if you take more than 10 allowances, your employer will send a copy of your W-4 to the IRS.)

**3** Any additional amounts you want to withhold.

For further information, get IRS Publication 919, "Is My Withholding Correct?"

worksheets that apply. $50,000, see the Two-Ea...ner/Two-Job Worksheet
• If **neither** of the above situations applies, **stop here** and enter the number from line ...

Cut here and give the certificate to your employer. Keep the top portion for you...

**Employee's Withholding Allowance Certifica**

Form **W-4**
Department of the Treasury
Internal Revenue Service
▶ For Privacy Act and Paperwork Reduction Act Notice, see reverse

1 Type or print your first name and middle initial | Last name

3 ☐ Single ☐ Married ☐
Note: If married, but legally separated, or ...

Home address (number and street or rural route)

4 If your last name differs from ... here and call 1-800-772-121...

...wn, state, and ZIP code | ...ksheets on page 2 ...

# WHAT AFFECTS WITHHOLDING?

There's no simple equation for figuring the right amount to withhold.

**Things that mean you should withhold more:**

- Having more than one job
- Both spouses working
- High income, which restricts or eliminates some deductions
- Large investment earnings that are not tax-exempt or tax-deferred

**Things that mean you should withhold less:**

- Home ownership—which generally increases itemized deductions for mortgage interest and real estate taxes
- A large number of dependents
- High state and local income taxes
- Large tax credits—child-care expenses, for example

**Some people use withholding as a forced savings plan, purposely withholding more than they'll owe in taxes. But there are better ways to save, since you earn no interest on the money you prepay and you have to wait for the government to refund it.**

## ESTIMATED TAXES

If your withholding doesn't cover what you owe, or if you have no taxes withheld—because you're self-employed, unemployed or live on unearned income—you have to pay estimated taxes.

IRS Form 1040-ES can help you project your tax. It also provides a payment voucher. You can make a lump-sum payment at the beginning of the tax year or pay estimated amounts quarterly.

If your income is constant, paying estimated taxes is relatively simple. But if your situation changes or your earnings are sporadic, meeting IRS requirements can be complex. You may owe a penalty if you underpay a quarterly amount, even if you get a refund back at the end of the year. That's why experts counsel that it's usually smart to get professional advice.

### Making a Mistake on Estimated Taxes Can Be Costly

Penalties are relatively small for taxpayers whose estimated-tax payments are off by a few thousand dollars. But bigger mistakes get costly, as do mistakes repeated over several quarters.

| Amount of Tax Deficiency | Maximum penalty if deficiency paid with next estimated-tax installment | Penalty for deficiency in second quarter if unpaid until April 15 | Penalty for deficiency in second quarter that is repeated in third and fourth quarters and unpaid until April 15 |
|---|---|---|---|
| $ 5,000 | $150 | $ 374 | $ 745 |
| 10,000 | 300 | 748 | 1,490 |
| 15,000 | 450 | 1,122 | 2,235 |
| 20,000 | 600 | 1,496 | 2,980 |
| 25,000 | 750 | 1,870 | 3,725 |

Figures are based on a 9% penalty rate. There are no penalties for first-quarter deficiencies since taxpayers can rely on the previous year's tax bill for that payment. *Source: KPMG Peat Marwick*

**You can charge your income tax payment to your American Express, Discover or MasterCard account. If you don't pay the bill in full when it arrives, you'll owe interest but no IRS penalty.**

## CHANGING YOUR WITHHOLDING

If you change jobs, take a second job, expect a lot of outside income, or get married or divorced, you should fill out a new W-4 to recalculate the right amount of withholding.

# Tax Planning Is a Must

Short of breaking the law by not filing—and ending up like Al Capone—there isn't much you can do to avoid taxes altogether. But you can take advantage of several strategies to reduce what you owe.

Tax-deferred and tax-exempt investments, year-end tax planning and taking full advantage of the tax laws can all save you money on April 15.

**Tax-exempt** means no tax is due, now or ever. Earnings in a Roth IRA, for example, are tax-exempt. So is interest paid on municipal bonds sold by state or local governments. If you don't live in the state or city where the bond is issued, you typically won't owe federal taxes on the interest you earn, but you may owe taxes in your own state.

**Tax-deferred** means you don't owe tax on your earnings now, usually because you don't have use of the money. Tax-deferred investments include money in 401(k), 403(b) and other qualified retirement plans, as well as IRAs and certain annuities. But you'll owe the tax later, when you withdraw the money. In theory your rate will be lower, so you'll owe less.

You can also defer taxes on investments that appreciate in value, as long as you hold on to them. For example, if you buy a stock for $5 a share and it goes up to $50 a share, you don't owe any tax on your paper profit—until you sell.

### SELLING SECURITIES

You can avoid taxes on some or all of your capital gains by selling securities on which you are losing money—especially if you think they're not worth holding on to. Losses may be valuable to offset your gains, or in some cases ordinary income as well.

### HOME EQUITY LOANS

Since interest on many home equity loans is deductible—while interest on consumer loans and credit cards is not—it may pay to arrange a home equity loan if you need to borrow money. The danger is owing more than you can repay comfortably (see page 77).

### BORROWING FOR INVESTMENT

If you borrow money to make an investment, you can usually deduct the interest you pay on the loan. This and mortgage interest are the only deductible interest. IRS Publication 550 spells out the rules.

## PAYING EXPENSES WITH PRETAX DOLLARS

Many employers offer **flexible-spending plans** that let you exclude a fixed dollar amount from your salary to pay certain medical and dependent-care expenses.

Under these plans, you pay the expenses and are then reimbursed from your flexible-spending account. Since this money is not included in your salary for tax purposes—

hence the term **pretax dollars**—you pay less tax. As a rule, the higher your tax bracket and the more you contribute to the plan, the greater your savings will be.

For example, if you contribute $2,100 to a flexible-spending plan, you may reduce your tax bill by several hundred dollars.

**Compare two wage earners, each earning $75,000 a year, and claiming tax deductions of $15,000. Both file a joint return. The first wage earner covers $2,100 in medical expenses under a flexible-spending plan, while the second one does not.**

*Tax rates for 1999.

| | Wage earner using flexible spending | Wage earner paying expenses |
|---|---|---|
| Salary | $75,000 | $75,000 |
| Flexible spending | − 2,100 | 0 |
| Reportable income | 72,900 | 75,000 |
| Tax deductions | 15,000 | 15,000 |
| Taxable income | 57,900 | 60,000 |
| **Tax** | **$12,872** | **$13,460** |

The wage earner using the flexible-spending plan **saves $588** in taxes.

### SHIFTING INCOME TO CHILDREN

If your children are over 14, their tax rate is determined by their individual incomes. If the rate is less than yours, you can shift money or investments to them and save tax on the earnings, or on the sale of property that has increased in value.

Children under 14 owe tax at their parents' tax rate after their first $1,400 of unearned income, but at their own rate before reaching that amount. Since they'd need a substantial investment to earn more than $1,400 annually, it may pay to shelter some investments this way. However, there are some drawbacks to this strategy (see page 93).

### SHIFTING INCOME AND DEDUCTIONS

Sometimes you have the option of postponing income to next year, pushing it forward, or **accelerating** it, into the current year, or bunching deductions so that your miscellaneous expenses exceed 2% of your adjusted gross income in alternate years. By planning those moves ahead of time, you can often save on your tax bill. But you should get tax advice when you use these strategies.

### PLANNING NOW TO AVOID TAXES LATER

By planning ahead, you can also reduce the amount of tax the government will collect from your estate when you die. The surest ways are giving away your assets or setting up one or more trust funds for your heirs (see pages 116-117).

### GIVING TO CHARITY

If you make a contribution of stocks or other securities that have **appreciated**, or increased in value, you get the same deduction as you would for giving cash, but you avoid the capital gains tax. As this chart from The Wall Street Journal shows, you come out ahead, as long as you've held the stock more than a year.

**A Better Way to Give**

A hypothetical couple pledged $5,000 to a college and have decided to sell $5,000 in stock for which they paid $1,000 years ago. But they will reap a big tax advantage if they simply give the shares to the college instead.

| | GIVE THE CASH, SELL THE SHARES | GIVE THE SHARES |
|---|---|---|
| Value charity receives | $5,000 | $5,000 |
| Tax savings from charitable deduction | 1,500 | 1,500 |
| Capital gains tax due | 1,200 | 0 |

NOTE: Assumes combined federal and state tax rate of 30%. Donors not subject to alternative minimum tax.

# January Reading: The W-2

## In addition to your wages or salary, Form W-2 shows the amount of tax your employer withheld.

You should receive a copy of Form W-2 from your employer by January 31. If the information—such as your name or Social Security number—is not correct, make the corrections on your W-2 and notify your employer. If any dollar amounts are wrong, ask your employer for a Form W-2c, showing the corrected amounts.

Though W-2 forms vary in appearance, boxes with the same numbers always contain the same kind of information, as mandated by the IRS. For example, federal withholding always appears in Box 2. Some customized W-2s may also omit boxes, such as those dealing with tips, when they don't apply.

**Boxes lettered *a* through *e* provide information about you and your employer. Be sure it's all right.**

**Box 1** reports your salary or wages for the year, your tips and any other income your employer paid you. It doesn't include any pretax contributions to a salary reduction plan (see page 100) or flexible-spending account (see page 165).

**Box 2** shows the federal income tax withheld.

**Boxes 3–4** cover your Social Security and Medicare wages and the amounts withheld. Box 3 reports the wages on which Social Security tax was withheld, up to the annual maximum that's taxed. Box 4 reports the amount of tax withheld. If you have more than one job, your total Social Security withholding may be more than you're liable for. In that case, you can get back the excess amount you paid when you file your tax return.

**Box 5** reports your Medicare wages and tips.

**Box 6** reports the amount withheld for Medicare. There's no cap on what's withheld.

**Box 7** covers tips covered by Social Security withholding and **Box 8** is for allocated tips.

**Box 9** reports any earned-income credit paid in advance, and **Box 10** any dependent-care benefits you received.

| a Control number | | | |
|---|---|---|---|
| 001032 C923 | 22222 | Void | |

b Employer's identification number
13-3066000010

c Employer's name, address, and ZIP code
Any Co.
1185 6th Avenue
New York, NY 10036

d Employee's social security number
123-45-6789

e Employee's name (first, middle initial, last)
John M. Employee

123 West 45th Street
New York, NY 10036

f Employee's address and ZIP code

| 16 State | Employer's state I.D. No. | 17 State wages, tips, e |
|---|---|---|
| NY | 123456789 | 16,043.50 |

Form **W-2** Wage and Tax Statement

Copy A For Social Security Administration

## FILING YOUR W-2 FORM

**Copy A** Goes to Social Security Administration

**Copy B** File with your federal return

**Copy C** Retain for your own records

**Copy D** Stays with your employer

**Copy 1** File with your state return

**Copy 2** File with your local return

## OTHER PEOPLE'S TAXES

Because countries tax their citizens in different ways, making meaningful comparisons can be difficult. One approach is to measure taxes as a percentage of gross domestic product, the measure of goods and services produced within the country. From that perspective, U.S. citizens pay less than their counterparts in other developed countries. But they also get less in benefits.

| Country | % of GDP paid as tax |
|---|---|
| France | 44.1% |
| Germany | 39.3% |
| Canada | 36.1% |
| Britain | 34.1% |
| Japan | 27.8% |
| U.S. | 27.6% |

**Box 11** covers any contributions you made to nonqualified retirement accounts. You owe tax on these earnings, and they're included in the amount in Box 1.

**Box 12** reports the total value of any extra benefits you got as part of your compensation, like a company car. The amount is included in the total in Box 1.

**Box 14**, labeled *other*, shows deductions for state disability insurance if your state has such a plan. If it doesn't, the box will be empty.

**Box 15** may provide details about you, including whether you're included in a pension plan, are a household worker or will receive deferred compensation.

**Boxes 16–21** report state income tax information, and local tax information, if it applies.

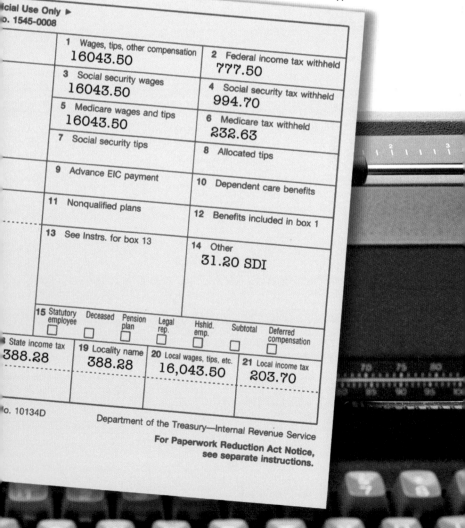

# Keeping Records

## To figure your taxes, you need records that show what you earned and what you spent.

Your employer, the sources that pay you interest and the companies that pay you dividends provide details of your earnings to you and to the IRS. You should receive your copies by January 31.

Most of the 1099 forms you get don't have to be filed with your return, but you should keep them with your records. You must submit any 1099-Rs, though. They show retirement income.

### TYPICAL TAX RECORDS

| Form | What it reports |
|------|-----------------|
| 1099-R | Retirement income or distributions |
| 1099-DIV | Dividend earnings |
| 1099-INT | Interest income |
| 1099-G | Tuition payments |
| 1099-MISC | Miscellaneous earnings |
| 1065/Schedule K-1 | Partnership gains or losses |

If your broker holds your securities for you—which is known as holding securities in **street name**—you'll get a Consolidated or Substitute 1099.

Year-end statements that report your annual earnings are also important to keep. If you earn tax-exempt interest, you may not get a 1099 INT, even though you must report the interest to the IRS.

### KEEPING YOUR OWN RECORDS

You must keep your own records of earnings from other sources, like rental income, freelance work or royalties. You must also keep records of your expenses if you plan to itemize deductions or plan to claim any exclusions or credits.

Experts advise you to take all of the deductions you're eligible for, as long as you have the records to substantiate your claims. If you're worried that the IRS might question something, you can include an explanation when you file your return.

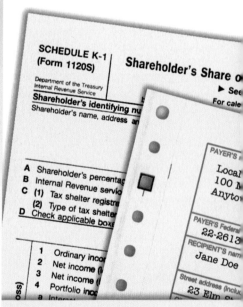

## HOW LONG SHOULD YOU KEEP YOUR RECORDS?

The IRS usually has three years—called a **period of limitations**—to audit your return, so you should keep all the relevant records at least that long. But it's important to keep some records longer:

| Type of record | How long to keep it |
| --- | --- |
| Most records of income and expense | At least three years, seven if possible |
| Investment other than real estate | Until you sell |
| Real estate (initial cost, improvements, costs of selling) | Until seven years after you sell |
| Tax returns | At least six years, ideally forever |

If you've underreported your income by 25% or more, the IRS has six years to audit your return. And if you don't file, or you file a false return, they have forever.

## VERIFYING EXPENSES

Hold on to the evidence that you spent money for specific things. Your records should include who was paid, when, the type of expense and the business purpose.

Receipts and cancelled checks are usually good records. The IRS recommends that you keep all expense receipts, no matter the amount.

Credit card charge slips sometimes provide a place on the back to record details of an expense. Or you can write on the back anyway, and keep the slip with your other records.

Regular entries in an appointment book or expense log, noting costs and other details of a meeting or purchase are also valid records.

There are special record-keeping requirements for tips, business use of your car, travel and entertainment, and non-cash charitable contributions. For details see Publication 17, or Publication 526, "Record Keeping and How to Report."

## SEND NO ORIGINALS

If you're providing backup documentation of your expenses or deductions, never send your originals to the IRS. Instead send photocopies. Papers can get lost or misplaced, and in any case, it's unlikely you'll ever see them again. That could pose a real problem if you need the information in the future.

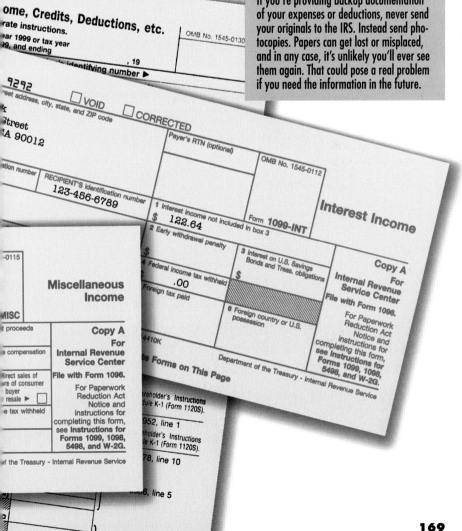

# Tax Help

Whether people are buffaloed by the process, think they're missing out on ways to save money or are terrified of an audit, they turn to tax preparers in droves.

## Almost half of all taxpayers use accountant, and most of the from various tax guides, or helpful friends and relatives

## PROFESSIONAL PREPARERS

Preparers can find ways to save you money—legally—by taking advantage of all of the tax strategies that are part of the tax code. Legitimate preparers fall into four categories. In addition, a number of volunteer groups provide help.

| Preparer | Comments |
|---|---|
| Tax preparation services | ● Prepare 15% of all returns<br>● Usually modest cost<br>● Prepare uncomplicated returns of middle-income people<br>● Can go with you to audits, but can't represent you |
| Enrolled agents | ● Accredited by IRS, with continuing education requirements<br>● Certified by Treasury department<br>● Can represent you before the IRS in an audit or appeal<br>● Fees from $100–$300 |
| Certified Public Accountants | ● Clients are typically professionals, corporate executives or people with complex investments or financial situations<br>● Often maintain year-round relationships with clients for tax planning<br>● Can represent you in IRS proceedings<br>● Charge by the hour, with total fees in the $500–$2,500 range<br>● Not all CPAs are tax specialists |
| Tax attorneys | ● Provide advice rather than tax preparation<br>● Familiar with details of tax law and tax rulings<br>● Experts in interpretation and litigation<br>● Can represent you before the IRS and in court<br>● Hourly fees range from $150–$500, with total charges running thousands of dollars |

## TAXING QUESTIONS

| What to find out before turning your return over to a paid preparer: | ● Is doing tax returns a regular part of your business?<br>● What kind of training do you have as a preparer?<br>● Are you available to answer questions throughout the year?<br>● Are you experienced with tax situations like mine?<br>● Are you conservative or aggressive in interpreting tax laws and regulations?<br>● How much help will you provide if I am audited?<br>● How much will preparing my return cost? |
|---|---|

Using IRS advice to figure your taxes protects you against investigation and claims for more tax—if you've got advice in writing. But if you ask your questions over the phone, you have no absolute assurance that you won't be held responsible if the advice was incorrect.

# a professional preparer or others depend on assistance computer programs in filing their returns.

## HELP FROM THE IRS

The IRS provides several kinds of taxpayer assistance—though not necessarily with a view to saving you money.

There are more than 120 free IRS publications on specific tax subjects, including the comprehensive Publication 17, "Your Federal Income Tax." You can order them by phone by calling 800-829-3676, on the Web at www.irs.gov, receive them by fax by calling 703-368-9694, or by mail from three regional forms distribution centers.

Toll-free telephone assistance is also available at 800-829-1040, but it's often hard to get through and the information is not always accurate by the IRS's own admission.

**Tele-Tax**, a prerecorded information service, lets you call a toll-free number 24 hours a day, seven days a week, for information on about 140 topics—including a directory of the topics available. The IRS "Guide to Free Tax Services" provides a list of topics and the code numbers you need to access them. The basic telephone number is 800-829-4477, though large cities have individual numbers.

You can also get help if you walk into most IRS offices, where assisters will help you prepare your return. And if you need special help because you're blind, hearing-impaired or aren't fluent in English, you can get assistance at a number of IRS offices. The hearing-impaired TTY/TDD phone number is 800-829-4059.

## IRS CD-ROM

Local libraries often have an IRS CD-ROM with step-by-step instructions for filling out all three tax forms, plus Schedules A and B.

You can buy a copy by calling 877-233-6767 or order it on the Internet at www.irs.gov/cdorders. There are also a number of tax-assistance programs for the elderly, people with special needs, and non-English-speaking people.

## TAX GUIDES

If you do your taxes yourself, you can find thousands of pages of instruction and advice at your local bookstore, library, or on the Internet. J. K. Lasser, Ernst & Young, H & R Block and others publish step-by-step guides to filling out tax forms. They're updated annually, with tax-saving tips and tricks of the trade. The hard-core information is the same as the IRS's, but in the better books the format is friendlier and the information more helpful. Almost all of these financial companies also have websites with helpful tax-related information and services.

## COMPUTER PROGRAMS

Software programs for figuring taxes are increasingly popular. They are also relatively inexpensive (usually less than $40), and they can help reduce both stress and math errors. But they may not be entirely satisfactory for people with highly complex tax questions or unusual financial situations. Those people probably need professional advice.

# The Dreaded Audit

When the IRS questions the details of your tax return, they can make you produce your records and explain how you figured your tax. In most cases, you end up owing them money.

## WHAT'S AN AUDIT?

An audit is an IRS examination of your tax return and the records that back it up. The IRS wants to know if you've reported correctly—usually because the agency thinks you owe more tax. IRS computers flag most of the returns that are audited using a complex Discriminant Function (DIF) System based on taxpayer norms. For example, the program allows a certain—but secret—level of deductions related to your income. Not surprisingly, there are lots of educated guesses about what's safe.

## TYPES OF AUDITS

A **correspondence** audit is done by mail and is usually the easiest to deal with—though you may still end up owing money. The IRS asks you to send specific records to back up your return. One key bit of advice: Send copies and hold on to the originals. An **office** audit is held in an IRS office with a tax auditor. You are told which areas are being examined and the materials you should bring with you. A **field** audit is done by an IRS revenue agent, usually in your home or office. It can also be at your tax professional's office if that person can practice before the IRS. Your whole return is open to examination, as well as the supporting documentation.

## AUTOMATED ADJUSTMENTS

Adjustments are technically not audits, but notices, called CP-2000s, that you owe additional tax. You do have the right to appeal—in writing within 60 days—if you disagree. The IRS can, and often does, make mistakes in matching the millions of pieces of information the agency gets each year.

## TAXPAYERS COMPLIANCE MEASUREMENT PROGRAM (TCMP)

TCMP is the IRS's way of establishing norms. From time to time it has subjected thousands of randomly chosen taxpayers to an ultra-intensive examination of their returns. The results helped the IRS update the formula it uses in deciding which taxpayers to audit. However, the TCMP audits can be very burdensome to taxpayers, and none has been conducted in recent years.

Perhaps in response to Congress's 1998 IRS Reform and Restructuring Act, the number of IRS audits has been reduced to about one in 300.

## THE APPEALS PROCESS

You have the right to ask for a review of any audit findings you don't agree with. You appeal first to the examiner's supervisor and then to the IRS Appeals Office. Publication 5, "Appeal Rights and Preparation of Protests for Unagreed Cases," outlines the process you have to follow. You can represent yourself or have a tax professional represent you. Most appeals are settled at this level, often through a compromise.

## WHAT'S THE TAXPAYER BILL OF RIGHTS?

IRS Publication 1, "Your Rights as a Taxpayer," is often referred to as a bill of rights because it spells out the rules that the IRS must follow in questioning your return.

Congress requires the IRS to ensure that taxpayers know their rights in any tax investigation, and also imposes some limits on the agency. For example, it's illegal to use the amount of extra tax an auditor collects as part of the evaluation process for promotion.

As a taxpayer, you have rights in any appeal or other dispute with the IRS. They include your rights to:

- Produce only the documents the IRS asks for
- Ask for explanations
- Have representation in IRS hearings
- End an interview in order to consult a tax professional or take additional time to prepare
- Record interviews
- Propose installment payments
- Appeal audit findings and tax liens

## TAX COURT

You can take your tax case to court, either before or after you pay the additional tax the IRS demands. But most litigation is expensive and slow. If the claim being contested is less than $10,000, you can argue your case yourself in Tax Court under "small claims simplified procedures." But you can't appeal the decision. If your case involves more than $10,000, it's heard by the Tax Court, a federal district court, or the Claims Court—depending on whether you pay the disputed amount before bringing your case. You can represent yourself, but probably need professional help. The court of last resort—if your case goes on that long—is the U.S. Supreme Court.

**Revenue agents have a legal right to see your place of business but may not insist on entering your home unless you use it for business or ask them in.**

# INDEX

# INDEX